Secret Science Behind Miracles
by Max Freedom Long

AND

Thought Vibration
by William W. Atkinson

by

Max Freedom Long & William W. Atkinson

ClassicBooksAmerica

Published by Classic Books America
Copyright © 2009 by Classic Books America
Cover Copyright © 2009 by CBA, all rights reserved.

All rights reserved. Without limiting the rights under copyright reserved above. No part of this book may be reproduced, stored in or introduced into a retrieval system, or transmitted, in any form, or by any means (electronic, mechanical, photocopying, recording, or otherwise), without prior written consent from the publisher, except brief quotes used in reviews.

First Printing 2009
Printed in the United States of America.
10 9 8 7 6 5 4 3 2 1

If this is a work of fiction, it is not meant to depict, portray or represent any particular real persons. All the characters, incidents and dialogues are the products of the author's imagination and are not to be construed as real. Any references or similarities to actual events, entities, real people, living or dead, or to real locales are intended to give the novel a sense of reality. Any similarity in other names, characters, entities, places and incidents is entirely coincidental.

Classic Books America
New York, New York

Table of Contents

Home—Dr. Hereward Carrington. Storing vital force. Vital force in healing—laying on of hands. Mesmer and "animal magnetism." Vital force in hypnotism.

Page 54.

Chapter 4 The Two Souls of Man and the Proofs That There Are Two Instead of One

Christian concept of one spirit in man. Huna concept of two spirits, conscious and subconscious, dwelling in the body, called unihipili and uhane. Functions and abilities of unihipili and uhane. Case 8. Vital force in kahuna "Death Prayer" as related to two spirits in man. Cases to show fear plays no part in "Death Prayer." Vital force (mana) has three strengths.

Page 67.

Chapter 5 The Kahuna System and the Three "Souls" or Spirits of Man, Each Using Its Own Voltage of Vital Force. These Spirits in Union and in Separation

Importance of concept of third spirit of man (aumakua). In religion, God a triplicity, in Huna, man a triplicity. Kinds of ghosts listed according to kahuna lore. Case 9. Multiple personality. Case 10. Gen. Lee's mother. Case 11. Two girls in one body. "Realization" is super logical. Schizophrenia and insanity. Separation of conscious and subconscious.

Page 81.

Chapter 6 Taking The Measure of the Third Element in Magic, That of the Invisible Substance Through Which Consciousness Acts by Means of Force

Three invisible ghost bodies of man. Hawaiian term kino aka, shadowy body (also halo). Greek and Egyptian concepts. The "True Light," secret psychology of Huna, especially regarding superconscious. Indian lore of pranic energy. Shadowy body threads adhere. Flow of vital force on threads. Thoughts have shadowy bodies. Thought forms. Telepathy.

Page 88.

Chapter 7 Psychometry, Crystal Gazing, Visions of the Past, Visions of the Future, Etc., Explained by the Ancient Lore of the

inside," hinders. Low self impressed by tangible things. Case 21. Proof through apports.

Page 180

lous healing. Healings at shrines. Ectoplasm. High Self may bring healing if not directly asked.

Page 238.

Chapter 21 How The Kahunas Controlled Winds, Weather and the Sharks by Magic

Apprenticeship of High Self as guardian over lower creation. Case 30. White man controls winds. Case 31. Control of sharks and turtles. Kahuna training of children. "Introduction" or thread-connecting between kahunas and High Selves presiding over lower forms of life.

Page 243.

Chapter 22 The Practical Use of the Magic of the Miracle

Helps for individuals working alone. Group work. Central organization for reports needed. Effect of Huna on world social structures.

BOOK II:

CHAPTER I

THE DISCOVERY THAT MAY CHANGE THE WORLD

This report deals with the discovery of an ancient and secret system of workable magic, which, if we can learn to use it as did the native magicians of Polynesia and North Africa, bids fair to change the world ... provided the atom bomb does not make all further changes impossible.

As a young man I was a Baptist. I attended the Catholic Church often with a boyhood friend. Later on I studied Christian Science briefly, took a long look into Theosophy, and ended by making a survey of all religions whose literatures were available to me.

With this background, and having majored in Psychology at school, I arrived in Hawaii in 1917 and took a job teaching because the position would place me near the volcano, Kilauea, which was very active at the time and which I proposed to visit as often as possible.

After a three days' voyage in a small steamer out of Honolulu, I at last reached my school. It was one of three rooms and stood in a lonely valley between a great sugar plantation and a vast ranch manned by Hawaiians and owned by a white man who had lived most of his life in Hawaii.

The two teachers under me were both Hawaiian, and it was only natural that I soon began to know more about their simple Hawaiian friends. From the first I began to hear guarded references to native magicians, the kahunas, or "Keepers of the Secret."

My curiosity became aroused and I began to ask questions. To my surprise I found that questions were not welcomed. Behind native life there seemed to lie a realm of secret and private activities which were no business of a curious outsider. Furthermore, I learned that the kahunas had been outlawed since early days when the Christian missionaries became the ruling element in the Islands, and that all activities of the kahunas and their clients were strictly sub rosa, at least in so far as a white man was concerned.

Rebuffs only whetted my appetite for this strange fare which tasted largely of black superstition, but was constantly spiced to tongue-burning proportions by what appeared to be eye-witness accounts of both the impossible and the preposterous. Ghosts walked scandalously, and they were not confined to the ghosts of deceased

Hawaiians. The lesser gods walked as well, and Pele, goddess of the volcanoes, was suspected repeatedly of visiting the natives both by day and by night in the disguise of a strange old woman never seen before in those parts, and given to asking for tobacco—which she got instantly and without question.

Then there were the accounts of healing through the use of magic, of magical killings of people guilty of hurting their fellows, and, strangest of all to me, the use of magic to investigate the future of individuals and, if it was not good, change it for the better. This last practice had a Hawaiian name, but was described to me as "Make luck business."

I had come up through a hard school and was inclined to look with a suspicious eye on anything that savored of superstition. This attitude was reinforced when I received from the Honolulu Library the loan of several books which told what there was to tell about the kahunas. From all accounts—and these had been written almost entirely by the missionaries who had arrived in Hawaii less than a century earlier—the kahunas were a set of evil scoundrels who preyed on the superstitions of the natives. Before the arrival of the missionaries in 1820, there had been great stone platforms throughout the eight islands, with grotesque wooden idols and stone altars where even human sacrifices were made. There were idols peculiar to each temple and locality. The chiefs had their own personal idols very often, as the famous conqueror of all the Islands, Kamehameha I, had his hideous war god with staring eyes and shark's teeth.

Near my school, in a district where I was later to teach, there had stood an extra large temple from which each year the priests set forth in procession, carrying the gods for a vacation trip through the countryside and collecting tribute.

One of the outstanding features of the idol worship was the amazing set of taboos imposed by the kahunas. Almost nothing at all could be done without the lifting of a taboo and the permission of the priests. As the priests had been backed by the chiefs, the commoners had a difficult time of it. In fact, so great had the imposition of the priests become that, the year before the arrival of the missionaries, the head kahuna of them all, Hewahewa by name, asked the old queen and the young reigning prince for permission to destroy the idols, break the taboos to the last one, and forbid the kahunas their practices. The permission was granted, and all kahunas of good will joined in burning the gods which they had always known were only wood and feathers.

The books provided fascinating reading. The high priest, Hewahewa, had evidently been a man of parts. He had possessed psychic powers and had been able to look into the future to the extent that he could advise Kamehameha I wisely through a campaign that lasted years and ended with the conquering of all other chiefs and the uniting of the Islands under one rule.

Hewahewa was an excellent example of the type of Hawaiians of the upper class who possessed a most surprising ability to absorb new ideas and react to them. This class amazed the world by stepping out of a grass skirt into all the vestments of civilization in less than a generation.

Hewahewa seems to have spent hardly five years in making his personal transition from native customs and ways of thought to those of the white men of the day. But he made one bad mistake in the process. When conservative old Kamehameha died, Hewahewa set to work to look into the future, and what he saw intrigued him greatly. He saw white men and their wives arriving in Hawaii to tell the Hawaiians of their God. He saw the spot on a certain beach on one of the eight islands where they would land to meet the royalty.

To a high priest this was most important. Evidently he made inquiries of the white seamen then in the Islands and was told that the white priests worshiped Jesus, who had taught them to perform miracles, even to raising the dead, and that Jesus had risen from the dead after three days. Undoubtedly the account was properly embroidered for the benefit of the Hawaiian.

Convinced that the white men had superior ways, guns, ships and machines, Hewahewa took it for granted that they had a superior form of magic. Realizing the contamination that had overtaken temple Kahunaism in the Islands, he promptly decided to clear the stage against the arrival of the white kahunas. He acted at once, and the temples were all in ruins when, on an October day in 1820, at the very spot on the very beach which Hewahewa had pointed out to his friends and the royal family, the missionaries from New England came ashore.

Hewahewa met them on the beach and recited to them a fine rhyming prayer of welcome which he had composed in their honor. In the prayer he mentioned a sufficient part of the native magic—

in veiled terms—to show that he was a magician of no mean powers, and then went on to welcome the new priests and their "gods from far high places."

Official visits with royalty finished, and the missionaries assigned to various islands with permission to begin their work, Hewahewa elected to go with the group assigned to Honolulu. He had already found himself in rather a tight box, however, because, as it soon developed, the white kahunas possessed no magic at all. They were as helpless as the wooden gods which had been burned. The blind and sick and halt had been brought before them and had been taken away, still blind, still sick and still halt. Something was amiss. The kahunas had been able to do much better than that, idols or no idols.

It developed that the white kahunas needed temples. Hopefully, Hewahewa and his men set to work to help build a temple. It was a fine large one made of cut stone and it took a long time to complete. But, when it was at last done and dedicated, the missionaries still could not heal, to say nothing of raising the dead as they had been supposed to do.

Hewahewa had fed the missionaries and befriended them endlessly. His name appeared frequently in their letters and journals. But, soon after the church at Waiohinu was finished, his name was erased from the pages of the missionary reports. He had been urged to join the church and become a convert. He had refused, and, we can only suppose, went back to the use of such magic as he knew, and ordered his fellow kahunas back to their healing practices.

A few years later, what with Christianity, hymn-singing and reading and writing being accepted by the chiefs in their rapid stride into civilized states, the missionaries outlawed the kahunas.

They remained outlawed, but as no Hawaiian police officer or magistrate in his right mind dared arrest a kahuna known to have genuine power, the use of magic continued merrily—behind the backs of the whites, so to speak. Meantime, schools were established and the Hawaiians slid with incredible speed from savagery into civilization, going to church on a Sunday, singing and praying as loudly as the next, and on Monday going to the deacon, who might be a kahuna on week days, to be healed or to have their future changed if they had found themselves in the midst of a run of bad luck.

In isolated districts the kahunas practiced their arts openly. At the volcano several of them continued to make the ritual offerings to Pele, and acted as guides for tourists on the side, often astounding them with a certain magical feat of which I shall tell in detail very soon.

To continue my story, I read the books, decided with their authors that the kahunas possessed no genuine magic, and settled back fairly well satisfied that all the whispered tales I might hear were figments of imagination.

The next week I was introduced to a young Hawaiian who had been to school and who had thought to show his superior knowledge by defying the local native superstition that one might not enter a certain tumbled temple enclosure and defile it. His demonstration took an unexpected turn and he found his legs useless under him. His friends carried him home after he had crawled from the enclosure, and, after the plantation doctor had failed to help him, he had gone to a kahuna and had been restored by him. I did not believe the tale, but still I had no way of knowing.

I asked some of the older white men of the neighborhood what they thought of the kahunas, and they invariably advised me to keep my nose out of their affairs. I asked well educated Hawaiians and got no advice at all. They simply were not talking. They either laughed off my questions or ignored them.

This state of affairs prevailed for me all that year and the next and the next. I moved to a different school each year, each time finding myself in isolated corners where native life ran a strong undercurrent, and in my third year found myself in a brisk little coffee-growing community with ranchers and native fishermen in the hills and along the beaches.

Very quickly I learned that the delightful elderly lady with whom I boarded at a rambling cottage hotel, was a minister, and that she preached each Sunday to the largest congregation of Hawaiians in those parts. I further learned that she had no connection with the Mission Churches or any other, was self ordained, and peppery on the subject. In due time I found that she was the daughter of a man who had ventured to try his Christian prayers and faith against the magic of a local kahuna who had challenged him and had promised to pray his congregation of Hawaiians to death, one by one, to show that his beliefs were more practical and genuine than the superstitions of the Christians.

I even saw the diary of that earnest but misguided gentleman. In it he reported the death, one by one, of members of his flock, then the sudden desertion of the remaining members. The pages for many days were left blank in the diary at that point, but the daughter told me how the desperate missionary went afield, learned the use of the magic employed in the death prayer, and secretly made the death prayer for the challenging kahuna. The kahuna had not expected such a turning of the tables and had taken no precautions against attack. He died in three days.

The survivors of the flock rushed back to church ... and the diary resumed with the glad tidings of the return. But the missionary was never the same. He attended the next conclave of the mission body in Honolulu, and said or did things not recorded in any available records. He may only have answered scandalized charges. In any event, he was churched and never again attended a conclave. But the Hawaiians understood. A princess gave him a strip of land a half mile wide and running from the breakers to the high mountains. On this land at the beach where Captain Cook landed and was killed hardly fifty years earlier, there stood the remains of one of the finest native temples in the land—the one from which the gods were paraded each year over the road that is still called "The Pathway of the Gods." Farther back from the beach, but on the same grant of land, stood the little church of coral stone which the natives had built with their own hands and in which his daughter was to preside as minister sixty years later.

At the beginning of my fourth year in the Islands I moved to Honolulu, and after getting settled, took time out to visit the Bishop Museum, a famous institution founded by Hawaiian Royalty and endowed to support a school for children of Hawaiian blood.

The purpose of my visit was to try to find someone who could give me an authoritative answer to the question of the kahunas which had plagued me for so long. My bump of curiosity had grown too large to be comfortable, and I harbored an angry desire to have something done about it one way or another, definitely and decisively. I had heard that the curator of the museum had spent most of his years delving into things Hawaiian, and I had the hope that he would be able to give me the truth, coldly, scientifically and in an acceptable form.

At the entrance I met a charming Hawaiian woman, a Mrs. Webb, who listened to my blunt statement of the reason for my visit, studied me for a moment, then said, "You'd better go up and see Dr. Brigham. He's in his office on the next floor."

Dr. Brigham turned away from his desk, where he was studying some botanical material through a glass, to examine me with friendly blue eyes. He was a great scientist, an authority in his chosen field, recognized and respected in the British Museum for the perfection of his studies and printed reports on them. He was eighty-two, huge, bald and bearded. He was heavy with the weight of an incredibly varied mass of scientific knowledge—and he looked like Santa Claus. (See Who's Who in America for 1922-1923 for his record, under William Tufts Brigham.)

I took the chair which he offered, introduced myself, and went swiftly to the questions which had brought me to him. He listened attentively, asked questions about the things I had heard, the places where I had lived and the people I had come to know.

He countered my questions about the kahunas with questions as to what my conclusions had been. I explained that I was quite convinced that it was all superstition or suggestion, or poison, but admitted that I needed someone who spoke with the authority of real information to help me quiet the nagging little doubt in the back of my mind.

Some time passed. Dr. Brigham almost annoyed me with his questions. He seemed to forget the purpose of my visit and lose himself in the exploration of my background. He wanted to know what I had read, where I had studied, and what I thought about a dozen matters which were quite aside from the question I had raised.

I was beginning to grow impatient when he suddenly fixed me with so stern a glance that I was startled. "Can I trust you to respect my confidence?" he asked. "I have a little scientific standing which I wish to preserve," he smiled suddenly, "even in the vanity of my old age."

I assured him that what he might say would go no farther, then waited.

He thought for a moment, then said slowly: "For forty years I have been studying the kahunas to find the answer to the question you have asked. The kahunas do use what you have called magic. They do heal. They do kill. They do look into the future and change it for their clients. Many were impostors, but some were genuine. Some even used this magic to fire-walk across lava overflows barely cooled enough to carry the weight of a man." He broke off abruptly as if fearing he had said too much. Leaning back in his swivel chair he watched me moodily through half-closed eyes.

I am not sure, but I believe I muttered "thanks." I half rose from my chair and sank back on it. I must have stared at him blankly for an idiotically long time. My trouble was that there was no wind left in my sails. He had knocked the underpinning from under the world I had braced almost to solidity over a period of three years. I had confidently expected an official negation of the kahunas, and I had told myself that I would be able to wash my hands completely of them and their superstitions. Now I was back in the trackless swamp, and, not up to my ankles as before, but suddenly sunk to the tip of my curious nose in the mire of mystery.

I may have made inarticulate noises, I have never been quite sure, but finally I managed to find my tongue.

"Fire-walking?" I asked uncertainly. "Over hot lava? I never heard of that...." I swallowed a few times, then managed to ask, "How do they do it?"

Dr. Brigham's eyes popped open very wide, then narrowed down while his bushy brows climbed toward his bald dome. His white beard began to twitch, and suddenly he leaned back in his chair and let out a roar of laughter which shook the walls. He laughed until tears rolled down his pink cheeks.

"Forgive me," he gasped at last, placing a placating hand on my knee while he wiped his eyes. "The reason your question struck me as so funny was that I have been trying for forty years to answer it for myself—without success."

With that the ice was broken. Although I had a baffled and hollow feeling at being tossed back into the middle of the very problem I had thought to escape, we fell to talking. The old scientist had also been a teacher. He had a gift of simplicity and directness in discussing even the most complicated subjects. I did not realize it until weeks afterward, but in that hour he placed his finger on me, claiming me as his own, and like Elijah of old, preparing to cast his mantle across my shoulders before he took his departure.

He told me later that he had long watched for a young man to train in the scientific approach and to whom he could entrust the knowledge he had gained in the field—the new and unexplored field of magic. Often on a warm night when he sensed my feeling of discouragement over the seeming impossibility of learning the secret of magic, he would say:

"I've hardly made a beginning. Just because I'll never know the answer is no reason why you will not. Just think what has happened in my time. The science of Psychology has been born! We know the subconscious! Look at the new phenomena being observed and reported month by month by the Societies for Psychical Research. Keep everlastingly at it. No telling when you may find a clue or when some new discovery in psychology will help you to understand why the kahunas observed their various rites, and what went on in their minds while they observed them."

At other times he would open his heart to me. He was a great soul, and still simple. He had an almost childish yearning to know the secret of the kahunas and he was getting very old. The sand was almost sure to run out before success came. The kahunas had failed to get their sons and daughters to take the training and learn the ancient lore that was handed down under vows of inviolable secrecy only from parent to child. Those who could heal instantly or who could fire-walk had been gone since the year 1900—many of them old and dear friends. He was left almost alone in a field in which little was left to observe. Moreover, he was a little bewildered. It seemed so absurd to think that he had been able to watch the kahunas work, had become their friend, had fire-walked under their protection—and still had not been able to get the slightest inkling as to how they worked their magic except in the matter of the death prayer, which, as he explained, was not true magic, but a very advanced phenomenon of spiritualism.

Sometimes we would sit in the darkness with the mosquito punk burning on the lanai and he would go over various points in review, to be sure that I had remembered. Often he would say in ending:

"I have been able to prove that none of the popular explanations of kahuna magic will hold water. It is not suggestion, nor anything yet known in psychology. They use something that we have still to discover, and this is something inestimably important. We simply must find it. It will revolutionize the world if we can find it. It will change the entire concept of science. It would bring order into conflicting religious beliefs....

"Always keep watch for three things in the study of this magic. There must be some form of consciousness back of, and directing, the processes of magic. Controlling the heat in fire-walking, for example. There must also be some form of force used in exerting this control, if we can but recognize it. And last, there must be some form of substance, visible or invisible, through which the force can act. Watch always for these, and if you can find any one, it may lead to the others."

And so, gradually, I took over the materials which he had collected in this strange new field. I became thoroughly familiar with all the negations, all the speculations and all the verifications. I began the slow work of trying to find remaining kahunas and do what I could to learn from them the Secret. Upon hearing a story of what some kahuna had done, my invariable question would be, "Who told you that?" I would begin tracing back, and sometimes I would be able to find the person who had been the subject of the tale and get from him all the smallest details of what had been done. The greatest difficulty was to get an introduction to the kahuna who had exerted the magic. Usually this was utterly impossible. The kahunas had learned by hard knocks to shun the whites, and no Hawaiian dared to bring a white friend to them without their permission—and that was almost never given.

Four years after I met Dr. Brigham, he died, leaving me with a weight on my heart and with the frightened realization that I was perhaps the only white man in the world who knew enough to continue the investigation of the native magic which was vanishing so rapidly. And if I failed, the world might lose for all time a workable system that would be endlessly valuable to humanity if it could be recovered.

With Dr. Brigham I had been watching hopefully for some new discovery in Psychology or in the field of Psychic Science, and, discouraging as it was, had been forced to admit that both sciences showed signs of becoming stalemate.

With over a hundred recognized scientists engaged over a period of half a century in Psychical Research, not a single theory had been evolved which would explain even such simple things as telepathy or suggestion, to say nothing of ectoplasm, apports and materialization. More years passed. I ceased to make progress and, in 1931, admitted defeat. It was then that I left the Islands.

In California I continued half-heartedly to watch for any new psychological discovery that might again open up the problem. None came. Then, in 1935, quite unexpectedly, I awakened in the middle of the night with an idea that led directly to the clue which was eventually to give the answer.

If Dr. Brigham had been alive he certainly would have joined me in a scarlet flush of embarrassment. Both of us had overlooked a clue so simple and so obvious that it had continually passed unnoticed. It was the pair of spectacles pushed up on the forehead while we hunted for hours unable to find them.

The idea that had struck me in the middle of the night was that the kahunas must have had names for the elements in their magic. Without such names they could not have handed down their lore from one generation to the next. As the language they used was Hawaiian, the words must have appeared in that language. And, as the missionaries began making the Hawaiian-English dictionary as early as 1820—the one still in use—and as they certainly had not known enough about the native magic to translate correctly any names used to describe that magic, it was obvious that any attempted translations would have been either faulty or entirely wrong.

The Hawaiian language is made up of words which have been built from short root words. A translation of the roots will usually give the original meaning of a word. Presto! I would find the words used by the kahunas in recorded chants and prayers, and make a fresh translation of them from the roots.

On the following morning I recalled the fact that everyone agreed in Hawaii that the kahunas had taught that man had two spirits or souls. No one paid the slightest attention to this patently erroneous belief. How could a man have two souls? What absurdity! What dark superstition! ... So I hunted up the two words naming the two souls. As I suspected, they were both there in my copy of the old dictionary which had come off the presses in 1865, some years after the discovery of mesmerism, during the early days of Psychical Research, and a full two decades before the birth of our infant science of Psychology.

The dictionary said:

"U-ni-hi-pi-li, The leg and arm bones of a person. Unihipili was the name of one class of gods called akuanoho; aumakua was another; they were the departed spirits of deceased persons.

"U-ha-ne, The soul, the spirit of a person. The ghost or spirit of a deceased person. Note: The Hawaiians supposed that men had two souls each; that one died with the body, the other lived on, either visible or invisible as might be, but had no more connection with the person deceased than his shadow. These ghosts could talk, cry, complain, etc. There were those supposed to be skillful in entrapping or catching them." *

It was apparent that the earnest missionaries had consulted the Hawaiians to ascertain the meanings of these two words, and had been given conflicting information which they had done their best to order and include in the translations.

The outstanding feature of the unihipili was that it seemed to be connected with the arms and legs very definitely, and besides that it was a spirit. The uhane was also a spirit, but it was a ghost who could talk even if it were hardly more than a shadow in connection with the "person of the deceased."

As the first word was longer and had the most roots, I began work on it to get a root translation. There were seven roots in the word, counting overlaps of letters, and some of these roots had as many as ten meanings. My task was to sort meanings to see if I could find any that would apply to the magic used by the kahunas.

Here was my haystack before me, and all I needed to find was the needle. It seemed rather promising. I remembered Dr. Brigham's injunction to watch always for the consciousness involved in fire-walking and other magic, for the force used to produce the magical result, and for the visible or invisible physical substance through which the force might act. Yes, I would try to find three needles. (And I did find them eventually, the first two before the year was out, and the last one six years later.)

What I found immediately, and almost before lunch time, was the subconscious, but not as we know it. The subconscious of the magicians was twice as large and three times as natural. I was so surprised by the discovery that I went down for the full count of ten. It was incredible that the kahunas could have known the subconscious, but the evidence was undeniable.

Here is how the roots described the spirits named in the words unihipili and uhane:

Both are spirits (root u), and this root means to grieve, so both spirits were able to grieve.

But the root hane in uhane means to talk, so the spirit named in this word could talk. As only human beings talk, this spirit must be a human one. That raises the question as to the nature of the other spirit. It can grieve, and so can animals. It may not be a man who can talk, but at least it is an animal-like spirit that can grieve. The uhane cried and talked weakly. In the dictionary note it was said to be considered nothing more than a shadow connected with the deceased person. Evidently it was a weak and not very substantial talking spirit.

Unihipili, with an alternate spelling of "uhinipili," gives more roots to translate. Combined we get: A spirit which can grieve but may not be able to talk (u); it is something that covers up something else and hides it, or is itself hidden as by a cover or veil (uhi); it is a spirit which accompanies another, is joined to it, is sticky, and sticks or adheres to it. It attaches itself to another and acts as its servant (pili); it is a spirit which does things secretly, silently and very carefully, but does not do certain things because it is afraid of offending the gods (nihi); it is a spirit that can protrude from something, can rise up from that something, and which can also draw something out of something, as a coin from a pocket. It desires certain things most earnestly. It is stubborn and unwilling, disposed to refuse to do as told. It tinctures or impregnates or mixes completely with something else. It is connected with the slow dripping of water or with the manufacture and exudation of nourishing water, as the "breast water" or milk of the mother (u in its several meanings). (Note: Later on I was to learn that water is the symbol of the human electro-vital force, so there was one needle. The two conscious spirits of man are two-thirds of the other needle. But the third is only hinted at in the meaning of "sticky" or "to adhere.")

To summarize, the kahuna idea of the conscious and subconscious seems to be, judging from the root meanings of the names given them, a pair of spirits closely joined in a body which is controlled by the subconscious and used to cover and hide them both. The conscious spirit is more human and possesses the ability to talk. The grieving subconscious weeps tears, dribbles water and otherwise handles the vital force of the body. It does its work with secrecy and silent care, but it is stubborn and disposed to refuse to obey. It refuses to do things when it fears the gods (holds a complex or fixation of ideas), and it intermingles or tinctures the conscious spirit to give the impression of being one with it. (The use made in magic of the "sticky" element as a symbol, and the ability to "protrude" or to "draw something out of something else" will become clear later.)

Given this certainty that the kahunas had known for thousands of years all the psychology we had come to know in the last few years, I became quite sure that their ability to perform feats of magic stemmed from their knowledge of important psychological factors not yet discovered by us.

It soon became apparent that, in naming the elements of psychology and placing in their word roots symbol meanings to point to related elements, the kahunas of the dawn days had done a superb job. The only great stumbling block was the fact that the symbol words stood for elements whose nature I could not imagine.

Searching feverishly for the meanings of these symbols, I returned to the reports on Psychic Phenomena and, as I checked each type of phenomena in turn, endeavored to locate its counterpart symbol in the roots of the terms used by the kahunas.

After a few months it became plain that I had gone as far as I could in the first work of matching the more complete psychology with the external rites of kahuna magic. I decided that what I had found was too valuable to keep from the world, and forthwith wrote a report on my findings and the kahuna lore in general. *

The English publication brought me many letters. I had placed my name and address in the back of the report and had requested any reader who could offer pertinent information for the study to write to me. Almost no really helpful information arrived, although hundreds of letters contained speculative material and guesses.

Then, over a year after the publication of that book, there came a letter from a retired English journalist. His name was William Reginald Stewart, and what he had to say was very much to the point.

In my report, he had been greatly interested to find that I was describing the same magic that he, in his younger days, had found being used by a certain Berber tribe in the Atlas Mountains of North Africa. Also, to his surprise, he had found that the Hawaiian words used by the kahunas were the same, except for dialect differences, as those which had been used to describe the magic in Africa. He had, after reading my book, hunted up his yellowed notes and compared words which he had been told belonged to a secret magical language. The Hawaiian word kahuna appeared as quahuna among the Berbers, and the Hawaiian term for woman kahuna was changed from kahuna wahini to quahini. The word for a god was nearly the same in both languages—akua and atua—as were a number of other words we checked.

As the Berber tribes spoke a language not at all related to the Polynesian dialects, the discovery of the similarity of the magic and the language used to describe it offered definite proof that the two peoples had either come from the same original stock or had been in contact with each other in ancient times.

Stewart had heard tales of this Berber tribe and their magician while exploring for oil signs for a Dutch company, and corresponding for the Christian Science Monitor as a free lance writer and authority on North Africa. Taking a vacation, he hired guides and set out to find the tribe. Eventually he did find it and met the magician, a woman. By dint of much persuasion he got himself adopted and made her blood son so that he could become eligible to receive training in the secret magic. The magician, whose name was Lucchi, had a daughter aged seventeen who was just beginning to take the training, so Stewart was allowed to join in.

The training began with her explanations of legendary tribal history, in which it was related that twelve tribes of the people having kahunas, once lived in the Sahara Desert when it was still a green and fertile land of flowing rivers. The rivers dried up, and the tribes moved into the valley of the Nile. While there they used their magic to help cut, carry and place the building stones of the Great Pyramid. At that time they were rulers in Egypt and topped all others because of their magic.

The account continued with the recital of how it was foreseen that a time of intellectual darkness was due in the world, and that the secret of their magic was in danger of being lost. To preserve it, for it was as precious as it was secret, the twelve tribes decided to hunt for isolated lands to which they might go to preserve the "Secret" (Huna) until the time was ripe for its return to the world. Eleven of the tribes, after making a psychic exploration and finding the islands of the Pacific empty and waiting, moved off by way of a canal to the Red Sea, and thence along either the African coast or over to India and thence into the Pacific. After many years they became "lost" in so far as the twelfth tribe was concerned. This twelfth tribe had, for some unstated reason, decided to go north and settle in the Atlas Mountain fastnesses. They had lived there for centuries, always preserving the Secret and using its magic, but as modern times arrived, the kahunas had died out until only one remained. She was the teacher, Lucchi.

Stewart found the Berber tribe hospitable, clean, very intelligent, and in possession of a fine old culture. They spoke a conglomerate language peculiar to the Berber tribes, but when it came to teaching the ancient lore of magic, another language had to be employed because in it alone could be found the proper words to name the elements in man which made magic possible.

The young Englishman was already hampered by language difficulties, having to match his French with that of some of the Berbers, and having to delve endlessly to arrive at a proper understanding of what words in the so-called "Secret" language might mean.

Little by little he learned the basic philosophy of magic. His teacher made many demonstrations of her magic in healing and in the control of birds, beasts, serpents and weather. All was going well indeed, and the theoretical work had been covered and its practical application was about to follow. Then, on a misty afternoon, two raiding parties in the valley below the Berber camp began shooting at each other. A stray bullet struck Lucchi over the heart and she died almost instantly.

Left without a teacher, and with Lucchi's daughter knowing no more than he did, Stewart's training came to an abrupt end. He gathered up his notes, took leave of his blood brothers and sisters, and returned to his old rounds.

It was thirty years later that he read my report and recognized the Hawaiian words I mentioned as the same words—aside from dialect changes—which he had preserved so long in his notes.

This linked up the Hawaiian kahunas with North Africa and possibly with Egypt. Hawaiian legends contained the oral history of the people. In these it is told that the Hawaiians once lived in a home land far away. They saw by psychic sight the land of Hawaii and set out to find it. Their journey commenced at the "Red Sea of Kane," which fits neatly into the idea that they came from Egypt by way of the Red Sea, as it is called to this day in at least three languages. The history gives few details of the journey from that place on, except to tell how progress was made from land to land in large double canoes. When the eight unoccupied islands of Hawaii were found by the scouts who went ahead, they returned to the nearest islands to the west to fetch the others of the tribe who had remained there to rest. Trees, plants and animals were brought on subsequent voyages as the tribe moved in and took up its home in Hawaii. The voyages to the outside islands stopped for a long time and complete isolation reigned. Then the royal blood ran out and a voyage to the other islands was made to find and bring back a prince of the high blood. He brought with him his favorites and a kahuna. This kahuna, if we can credit the account, introduced into Hawaii a contaminated form of kahunaism which contained little magic, and commanded idol worship and temple building. This contamination remained, with its idols and temples, even though kahunas possessing knowledge of the workable and practical magic continued their work and preserved the Secret in almost uncontaminated form.

Attempts by scholars to trace Hawaiian origins through language and customs have been none too successful. There are eleven tribes of Polynesians, all speaking dialects of the same language, but some having words, customs and beliefs easily identified as of Indian origin. On the other hand Polynesian words may be found scattered all the way from the Pacific to the Near East. Madagascar has them, indicating the early contact with a people who spoke the Polynesian language. Even in Japan may be found Polynesian words and ideas. In India a number of the ideas connected with the kahuna magic are to be seen, greatly changed and now of no practical use, but still pointing in the same general direction.

With the invaluable help of Stewart, and by making full use of what he had learned in North Africa, I was able to continue the research. Little by little the "Secret" was reconstructed as its symbols and practices were matched against the observations made of the external acts or rites of the kahunas by Dr. Brigham and, in a lesser degree, by me.

It would, however, have been utterly impossible to grasp the meanings of words and the significance of rites, had modern Psychology and Psychical Research not already made certain basic discoveries upon which to rest fuller structures. Religions also played a valuable part because in them I found the battered remains of the original Huna philosophy. These remains, misshapen as they were, gave hints as to where to look next for certain bits of information, and helped to verify other uncertain materials as they came to light.

Soon after the publication of my report in England I had entered into a correspondence with a priest of the Church of England who had written me upon reading my book, and who was carrying on psychological studies of mental and spiritual healing. His interest in the kahuna lore grew, and shortly after my contact with Stewart, the clergyman and a group of his associates decided to try out some of the healing magic of the kahunas. This they did, after much writing back and forth. They were especially successful in obsessional cases. The family of a patient who was healed offered to supply money for extensive experimental work, and the clergyman and three of his group made the journey to California to spend some time with me in discussing the best ways to proceed. They left me, all plans complete even to a blueprint of the building to be erected. But on their way back to England, World War II broke out and the plans were dropped. With the war over, the funds are no longer available, and the healing group is scattered.

Such experimental work as has been done has gone far to prove that the reconstruction of the Huna system is sufficiently complete to be workable in the hands of individuals owning certain natural talents and able to give sufficient time to learning to use the system. Steady and continued practice under proper guidance seems to be the main thing needed.

In Hawaii there is little or no dependable literature covering the kahunas. What little there is available in books and articles and pamphlets, misses entirely the basic mechanisms of which I report. Each writer contradicts the others, and the muddle is never resolved.

My own studies and those of Dr. Brigham are almost unknown in the Islands, and copies of my first report are kept carefully locked away in the library in Honolulu, being brought out only if requested by one who knows that it is there. Because of misconceptions and because there was formerly a very real danger in the "death prayer," the general attitude of the residents is one which encourages denial of kahuna magic, or, failing that, a policy of letting sleeping dogs lie.

With these introductory remarks, I will now proceed with the task of presenting the Huna system with all its details, and with the available proofs of its correctness as a workable set of scientific facts.

CHAPTER II

FIRE-WALKING AS AN INTRODUCTION TO MAGIC

There are two features that make the psycho-religious system of the "Secret" (Huna) outstanding and set it apart from modern systems of either religion or psychology.

First and foremost, IT WORKS. It worked for the kahunas and it should work for us.

Second, and but slightly less significant, it works for men no matter what their religious beliefs.

The finest example of a workable piece of magic which functions perfectly in the hands of any and all religionists, or in the hands of heathens and savages, is FIRE-WALKING, which has been practiced for centuries and which continues to be practiced today in many parts of the world.

Fire-walking has another thing to recommend it. It involves feet, and burning coals or other burning hot materials, such as stone, or even pure flame. Now, there is nothing mysterious about feet, or hot things. Both are subject to the most painstaking examination, and neither is subject to the manipulations of trickery.

In addition to feet and heat, there is a third element which cannot be seen, tested or examined. But it is just as real and just as free from danger of trickery. This third element is what I call "MAGIC" for want of a better word.

This third element is certainly present when feet contact heat, and burns do not result in the usual way.

War has been waged steadily on superstitions for at least two centuries. The growth of the sciences was dependent on the ability of scientists to fight up through superstitions and religious dogmatic taboos. Today, however, scientific denial of psychic and psychological phenomena has turned out to be a dogmatic taboo of science itself. Our schools and our press have done their best for years to discredit all things which could not be explained, setting up the cry of "Black superstition!" Because of this attitude the average person has been led to believe that all magic, and especially such things as fire-walking, are the beginning and end of trickery.

If my report is to get a hearing, I must prove that magic is a fact. I shall prove that it is. But, for the reader who has already decided that no such proof can be given to his personal satisfaction, I say this: Read my report anyway. It offers much new and exciting material for thought, and will be found entertaining, if nothing else. And when you finish it, see if you can give a better set of answers to its puzzling questions than did the kahunas.

For convenience sake in my report, I shall place major units of evidential material under case headings, with preliminary notes of introduction and with a comment at the end.

For the first case I draw from Dr. Brigham's investigations and personal observations in the field.

Case 1 Dr. Brigham Fire-Walks on Red Hot Lava Preliminary Notes:

The usual explanation for fire-walking is that the feet are so calloused that they cannot be burned, or that they have been toughened by alum or other chemicals. Also, the coals or hot rocks are said to be covered with a layer of ashes, or not to be hot enough to burn. Harry Price, in trying to explain the fire-walking of Kuda Bux (a Kashmiri Mohammedan) before the University of London Council for Psychical Investigations in 1936, wrote:

"It is hardly necessary to point out that, in rapid walking, the whole of the foot is not put into contact with, or withdrawn from, the ground at one instant, so that no portion of the skin was in contact with the hot embers for as long as half a second."

In the case about to be presented, it will be noted that none of these explanations is adequate.

I give the account as I recorded it in my notes shortly after getting it at first hand from Dr. Brigham. To make it more visual I have tried to reproduce his own words and expressions.

The Case:

"When the flow started," related Dr. Brigham, "I was in South Kona, at Napoopoo. I waited a few days to see whether it promised to be a long one. When it continued steadily, I sent a message to my three kahuna friends, who had promised to let me do some fire-walking under their protection, asking them to meet me at

Napoopoo so we could go to the flow and try fire-walking.

"It was a week before they arrived, as they had to come around from Kau by canoe. And even when they came, we couldn't start at once. To them it was our reunion that counted and not so simple a matter as a bit of fire-walking. Nothing would do but that we get a pig and have a luau (native feast).

"It was a great luau. Half of Kona invited itself. When it was over I had to wait another day until one of the kahunas sobered up enough to travel.

"It was night when we finally got off after having to wait an entire afternoon to get rid of those who had heard what was up and wished to go along. I'd have taken them all had it not been that I was not too sure I would walk the hot lava when the time came. I had seen these three kahunas run barefooted over little overflows of lava at Kilauea, and the memory of the heat wasn't any too encouraging.

"The going was hard that night as we climbed the gentle slope and worked our way across old lava flows towards the upper rain forests. The kahunas had on sandals, but the sharp cindery particles on some of the old flows got next their feet. We were always having to wait while one or another sat down and removed the adhesive cinders.

"When we got up among the trees and ferns it was dark as pitch. We fell over roots and into holes. We gave it up after a time and bedded down in an old lava tube for the rest of the night. In the morning we ate some of our poi and dried fish, then set out to find more water. This took us some time as there are no springs or streams in those parts and we had to watch for puddles of rain water gathered in hollow places in the rocks.

"Until noon we climbed upward under a smoky sky and with the smell of sulphur fumes growing stronger and stronger. Then came more poi and fish. At about three o'clock we arrived at the source of the flow.

"It was a grand sight. The side of the mountain had broken open just above the timber line and the lava was spouting out of several vents—shooting with a roar as high as two hundred feet, and falling to make a great bubbling pool.

"The pool drained off at the lower end into the flow. An hour before sunset we started following it down in search of a place where we could try our experiment.

"As usual, the flow had followed the ridges instead of the valleys and had built itself up enclosing walls of clinker. These walls were up to a thousand yards in width and the hot lava ran between them in a channel it had cut to bed rock.

"We climbed up these walls several times and crossed them to have a look at the flow. The clinkery surface was cool enough by then for us to walk on it, but here and there we could look down into cracks and see the red glow below. Now and again we had to dodge places where colorless flames were spouting up like gas jets in the red light filtering through the smoke.

"Coming down to the rain forest without finding a place where the flow blocked up and overflowed periodically, we bedded down again for the night. In the morning we went on, and in a few hours found what we wanted. The flow crossed a more level strip perhaps a half-mile wide. Here the enclosing walls ran in flat terraces, with sharp drops from one level to the next. Now and again a floating boulder or mass of clinker would plug the flow just where a drop commenced, and then the lava would back up and spread out into a large pool. Soon the plug would be forced out and the lava would drain away, leaving behind a fine flat surface to walk on when sufficiently hardened.

"Stopping beside the largest of three overflows, we watched it fill and empty. The heat was intense, of course, even up on the clinkery wall. Down below us the lava was red and flowing like water, the only difference being that water couldn't get that hot and that the lava never made a sound even when going twenty miles an hour down a sharp grade. That silence always interests me when I see a flow. Where water has to run over rocky bottoms and rough projections, lava burns off everything and makes itself a channel as smooth as the inside of a crock.

"As we wanted to get back down to the coast that day, the kahunas wasted no time. They had brought ti leaves with them and were all ready for action as soon as the lava would bear our weight. (The leaves of the ti plant are universally used by fire-walkers where available in Polynesia. They are a foot or two long and fairly narrow, with cutting edges like saw-grass. They grow in a tuft on the top of a stalk resembling in size and shape a broomstick.)

"When the rocks we threw on the lava surface showed that it had hardened enough to bear our weight, the kahunas arose and clambered down the side of the wall. It was far worse than a bake oven when we got to the bottom. The lava was blackening on the surface, but all across it ran heat discolorations that came and went as they do on cooling iron before a blacksmith plunges it into his tub for tempering. I heartily wished that I had not been so curious. The very thought of running over that flat inferno to the other side made me tremble—and remember that I had seen all three of the kahunas scamper over hot lava at Kilauea.

"The kahunas took off their sandals and tied ti leaves around their feet, about three leaves to the foot. I sat down and began tying my ti leaves on outside my big hob-nailed boots. I wasn't taking any chances. But that wouldn't do at all—I must take off my boots and my two pairs of socks. The goddess Pele hadn't agreed to keep boots from burning and it might be an insult to her if I wore them.

"I argued hotly—and I say 'hotly' because we were all but roasted. I knew that Pele wasn't the one who made fire-magic possible, and I did my best to find out what or who was. As usual they grinned and said that of course the 'white' kahuna knew the trick of getting mana (power of some kind known to kahunas) out of air and water to use in kahuna work, and that we were wasting time talking about the thing no kahuna ever put into words—the secret handed down only from father to son.

"The upshot of the matter was that I sat tight and refused to take off my boots. In the back of my mind I figured that if the Hawaiians could walk over hot lava with bare calloused feet, I could do it with my heavy leather soles to protect me. Remember that this happened at a time when I still had an idea that there was some physical explanation for the thing. "The kahunas got to considering my boots a great joke. If I wanted to offer them as a sacrifice to the gods, it might be a good idea. They grinned at each other and left me to tie on my leaves while they began their chants.

"The chants were in an archaic Hawaiian which I could not follow. It was the usual 'god-talk' handed down word for word for countless generations. All I could make of it was that it consisted of simple little mentions of legendary history and was peppered with praise of some god or gods.

"I almost roasted alive before the kahunas had finished their chanting, although it could not have taken more than a few minutes. Suddenly the time was at hand. One of the kahunas beat at the shimmering surface of the lava with a bunch of ti leaves and then offered me the honor of crossing first. Instantly I remembered my manners; I was all for age before beauty.

"The matter was settled at once by deciding that the oldest kahuna should go first, I second and the others side by side. Without a moment of hesitation the oldest man trotted out on that terrifically hot surface. I was watching him with my mouth open and he was nearly across—a distance of about a hundred and fifty feet—when someone gave me a shove that resulted in my having a choice of falling on my face on the lava or catching a running stride.

"I still do not know what madness seized me, but I ran. The heat was unbelievable. I held my breath and my mind seemed to stop functioning. I was young then and could do my hundred-yard dash with the best. Did I run! I flew! I would have broken all records, but with my first few steps the soles of my boots began to burn. They curled and shrank, clamping down on my feet like a vise. The seams gave way and I found myself with one sole gone and the other flapping behind me from the leather strap at the heel.

"That flapping sole was almost the death of me. It tripped me repeatedly and slowed me down. Finally, after what seemed minutes, but could not have been more than a few seconds, I leaped off to safety.

"I looked down at my feet and found my socks burning at the edges of the curled leather uppers of my boots. I beat out the smouldering fire in the cotton fabric and looked up to find my three kahunas rocking with laughter as they pointed to the heel and sole of my left boot which lay smoking and burned to a crisp on the lava.

"I laughed too. I was never so relieved in my life as I was to find that I was safe and that there was not a blister on my feet—not even where I had beaten out the fire in the socks.

"There is little more that I can tell of this experience. I had a sensation of intense heat on my face and body, but almost no sensation in my feet. When I touched them with my hands they were hot on the bottoms, but they did not feel so except to my hands. None of the kahunas had a blister, although the ti leaves which they had tied on their feet had burned away long since.

"My return trip to the coast was a nightmare. Trying to make it in improvised sandals whittled from green wood has left me with an impression almost more vivid than my fire-walking."

Comment:

There you have Dr. Brigham's story. You will now doubtless be interested to know how this scientist tried to figure out the reason for his being able to do what he had done.

"It's magic," he assured me. "It's a part of the bulk of magic done by the kahunas and by other primitive peoples. It took me years to come to that understanding, but it is my final decision after long study and observation."

"But," I asked, "didn't you try to explain it some other way?"

The doctor smiled at me. "Certainly I did. It has been no easy task for me to come to believe magic possible. And even after I was dead-sure it was magic I still had a deep-seated doubt concerning my own conclusions. Even after doing the fire-walking I came back to the theory that lava might form a porous and insulating surface as it cooled. Twice I tested that theory at Kilauea when there were little overflows. I waited in one case until a small overflow had cooled quite black, then touched it with the tips of my fingers. But although the lava was much cooler than that I ran across, I burned my fingers badly—and I'd only just dabbed at the hot surface."

"And the other time?" I asked.

He shook his head and smiled guiltily. "I should have known better after that first set of blisters, but the old ideas were hard to down. I knew I had walked over hot lava, but still I couldn't always believe it possible that I could have done so. The second time I got excited about my insulating surface theory, I took up some hot lava on a stick as one would take up taffy. And I had to burn a finger again before I was satisfied.

No, there is no mistake. The kahunas use magic in their fire-walking as well as in many other things. There is one set of natural laws for the physical world and another for the other world. And— try to believe this if you can: The laws of the other side are so much the stronger that they can be used to neutralize and reverse the laws of the physical."

In this case we have an instance in which the magical control of heat was of such a nature that it did not protect the leather in Dr. Brigham's heavy boots, but did protect his feet. There was no chemical solution to protect the feet of the fire-walkers from heat. There was no layer of ashes on the lava to insulate it. The lava was so hot that, even in running steps where contact was momentary between boots and lava, the leather burned to a crisp. The heat was far more than enough to burn feet under ordinary circumstances.

Case 2 A Stage Magician Who Used Genuine Magic Preliminary Notes:

Startling as it may seem, there is real magic sometimes used on the stage instead of the supposed mechanical trickery which we universally believe to be in use.

In this case we have a man traveling with a carnival and saying nothing about the magic he uses, unless it be to those inclined and able to accept a statement of the true facts. This man and his wife performed in Honolulu and later were kind enough to try to explain their magic to me and try to tell how they had learned it. Just now we are interested only in what they did and not how they did it.

The so-called "fire-magic" usually seen on the stage or in circus and carnival is a very poor imitation of what I shall next describe. It consists mainly of such feats as holding a lighted cigarette on the tongue and inserting it into the mouth, with the coal held safely away from contact with the flesh, or of taking gasoline into the mouth and lighting its vapors as they are blown out—this being possible because the vapors burn only when well away from the lips and after mixing with air.

The Case:

The fire magician of whom I speak gave his performance in a small tent. A railing separated him from his audience by a distance of from three to six feet. His apparatus consisted of a pine table on which lay the few things he used. The only part of his performance in which real magic was not used was the part in which his little dog leaped delightedly through a small hoop soaked with oil and set afire. Everything was done at close range and the watchers encouraged to test the heat of every article before it was brought into contact with flesh. Every move was made slowly and with no attempt to "juggle" or conceal.

The following things were done by the magician in each of the two performances which I witnessed: (1) He boiled water in a cup and drank it down rapidly while it was still bubbling and steaming. (2) Finger-thick pieces of soft pine wood were held in the blaze of a gas burner until they were turned at one end to glowing charcoal.

He took up six of these, bit off the live ends, and chewed them. (3) He heated thick iron bars to a bright red heat in the middle and then passed his tongue along the red surface repeatedly—resulting in sizzling steam rising from his bare tongue. (4) He lighted an ordinary welding torch; drew the flame down to a cutting cone of blue-green; used the flame to cut through iron bars repeatedly; gave the bars and the torch to members of the audience for examination. Without adjusting the torch in any way, and seeming to have no protection or method of temporarily extinguishing the flame, he introduced it repeatedly into his mouth. His mouth remained open to its fullest extent and the flame could be seen playing from the end of the burner, even when it had been thrust in as far as his lips. (5) He heated an iron bar to redness and handled it with bare hands in a way which would have burned another severely indeed. He took a heavier flat bar and heated it to redness in the center. He took the heated part between his teeth and, holding the ends of the bar in his hands, bent it up and down twice from the center. Comment:

The bending of the bar held between the performer's teeth caused me to examine his teeth carefully. They were strong teeth and not false. This point interested me greatly, as the red-hot iron remained for a period of nearly ten seconds in close contact with the upper and lower front teeth. Although this was one of his stock "tricks" done several times in an evening, the enamel was not cracked on the teeth nor did they seem injured. Before the second performance a dentist joined me. He stated that contact with such heat would kill nerves and destroy teeth under ordinary circumstances, as well as cause intolerable pain while the nerves were still alive. Ulceration would result and the teeth have to be pulled out. We scraped the biting edges of the teeth with a penknife just before the second performance—this to make sure no invisible insulating substance, no matter how thin and transparent, could be present.

The question of some solution to insulate from heat seemed most improbable as the mouth was itself wet. Also the edges of the teeth would hardly take such a coating—one too thin to be detected or scraped off. *

Case 3 A Professor of Biblical History Reports Preliminary Notes:

On February 21, 1935, I attended a lecture at the Los Angeles Public Library. The speaker was Dr. John G. Hill, Professor of Biblical History at the University of Southern California. His subject was "Fire-Walking." He had spent four seasons in the South Seas and illustrated his lecture with moving pictures he had taken.

He told of voyaging from Tahiti to a neighboring island, and of traveling fourteen miles overland to see a fire-walking performance. A great pit had been dug, filled with logs and stones, and a fire had been burning among them for many hours until the stones were red-hot. Invocations were recited to "Nahine (woman) of the Skies," then the performers marched around the pit and made seven crossings back and forth. Ti leaves were used in the ceremony to carry and to "dust off" the rocks.

Dr. Hill exposed much film, taking close-up pictures of the feet and hot rocks, and pictures of the group walking in single file over the stones. He showed one native who had been forced to walk the hot stones as an "ordeal" to prove his guilt or innocence of a certain charge. As he was badly burned, the natives decided that he was guilty, despite his denials, and so had not merited the protection of "Nahine of the Skies."

The ceremony over, Dr. Hill and his white companions tested the heat of the rocks, the following results being reported: Length of time possible to hold the hand at a distance of three feet from the rocks: eleven seconds. Time required for a bundle of wet, green branches to take fire when thrown on the rocks: thirteen minutes.

While the testing of the heat was going on, the head magician was inviting his guests to cross the rocks under the protection of his magic. One of the white men joined the natives who were accepting the invitation. He walked across the rocks. Dr. Hill stated that they were almost red-hot even at that time. The man's shoes were not burned in any way, nor were his feet, but, oddly enough, the intense heat burned his face so badly that it peeled a few days later.

After the lecture I joined a group gathered to hear Dr. Hill answer questions. He was asked for any possible explanation of the feat. His answer was that he was totally at a loss for an explanation. He could only guess that there might be some superior form of mental activity used—some form which could keep heat from burning. He was very positive in his refusal to accept his own guess as a fact.

The usual questions were raised as to the possibility of some "undetectable solution" being used. This, the Doctor explained, was impossible for the simple reason that the white man's shoes had not been so treated and would certainly have been ruined by the heat under ordinary circumstances.

In an endeavor to throw further light on the mystery, Dr. Hill told of another fire-walking performance which he had seen but not photographed. There a young white man, described as being "quite a mystic," avowed that if the brown men's magic would protect them, his God would also protect him. He questioned the friendly magician in charge and was laughingly told to go on across the stones without fear. Disregarding the protests of other white travelers, the young man took off shoes and socks. He approached the fire-walk with set face—evidently trying to concentrate on his task and hold his faith in readiness. He followed the magician on to the rocks and was getting on perfectly when a wild dog-fight broke out close beside the pit. For a moment he glanced aside. He lifted one foot suddenly, but his face again became set and he continued his crossing. The foot lifted was found later to have a large blister on its sole. Dr. Hill vouched for this data, but made no comment on its possible significance.

Comment:

For those who may not have seen moving pictures of fire-walking shown in 1934 news reels at theatres, I mention the following sources of photographic or written information:

The book, The Colony of Fiji, edited by A. A. Wright and published by the Government of Fiji, contains several good illustrations of fire-walking. As a commentary on the influence of the scientific attitude in so far as any official publication is concerned, we find in this book only one lone paragraph to describe the finest tourist attraction in Fiji. This paragraph gives a meager statement of the facts of fire-walking, but nothing more.

Another book more easily procured in libraries is the Seatracks of the Speejacks. In its log, which is written by Jeanne Gowen, will be found both pictures and full descriptions of the fire-magicians and their work.

In Herbert MacQuarrie's book, Tahiti Days (George H. Doran Co., 1920), an entire chapter is given over to a report on fire-walking, and there are five pictures showing the fire-walkers, crowds and pit, as well as of the actual performance.

Case 4 Fire-Walking as a Religious Rite in Burma Preliminary

Notes:

In Hawaii I made my living for the greater part of my stay in the Islands by keeping a kodak and art store in Honolulu. Among my many customers there was, in the year 1929, an Englishman who had been making a trip around the world. He carried with him a 16 mm. moving picture camera and was especially anxious to photograph anything out of the ordinary.

I had known him several days when he came in one morning and asked me if there was anything in Hawaii which was very unusual and which he might "film." I certainly knew of many very unusual things in Hawaii, but it was impossible to tell him where he might go to get a picture of a kahuna at work with his magic.

In the course of our conversation he mentioned the fact that he had bribed the priests of a certain temple in Burma to let him hide on a temple balcony and photograph the mysterious and far-famed fire-walking of the devotees of the fire god, Agni.

I begged for the story and the opportunity to see his pictures. He went at once to his hotel and brought back the films. Let me give in detail what I saw and what was told that day in my little projection-room.

The Case:

"You see," said my friend, with all the glow of one about to present a wonder of wonders, "I don't just tell about the things I see, I photograph them. And it's a good thing I do. Now take this film I'm about to show you. If I didn't have the film I'd even think I hadn't seen it myself! What I saw is impossible! It's contrary to nature! Anyone will tell you it couldn't happen. I'll even tell you that—and I saw it with my own eyes not three months ago." He paused and waited for me to look up from threading the projector. I did my best to show the proper surprise and mystification.

"Well," he said grandly, "turn it on. See if you can believe what the camera got."

I pulled out a couple of chairs and threw in the switch. On the screen at the end of the projection-room lifelike shadows began to flicker and move.

"That," explained my new friend, "is the parade. It came before the service in the temple's courtyard. That bunch going past now are the candidates who had been getting ready for years to take the fire initiation of the Agni cult. Odd beggars, those brown people. See the funny looks on their faces. They all seemed to be thinking hard about something as they marched along. Never seemed to notice the crowd which had gone crazy with excitement just to see them. Seems everyone hopes some day to get ready to walk through the fire—great honor. Walk through once and you are set for life. You become some sort of priest or holy man. All the priests in the temple have had to walk through fire to get their jobs."

"How do they do it?" I asked as I watched the long parade move past with all its Oriental trappings.

"Wouldn't you jolly well like to know! And wouldn't I?"

"What do you think?" I urged.

"How should I know? I tried to get it out of the priests, but they spoofed me, I think. They said theirs was the one and only true religion and that the fire-walking proved it. Said no other faith could make it possible for the converts to walk through fire. What they wanted me to believe was that their god kept the feet of the pure and holy from being burned. Those who weren't quite pure enough got burned." He pointed suddenly to the screen. "See that chap? He's the priest I managed to get off to one side to talk to, at about the time the parade was done marching all over the city. Good sort. Really rather sporting. He was smart, too."

"How do you mean?" I asked.

"Not like most of the other beggars—suspicious and hating white skins. And by 'smart' I mean he was smart enough to pretend to believe me when I told him I'd studied his religion and wanted to join up. I thought he was going to laugh in my face at first, but I jingled money in my pocket and he began to take me seriously."

"Perhaps he did take you seriously," I suggested as I watched the parade continue to pass on the screen.

"He was no fool, not that one. He'd heard money. And when I told him I would join up and pay well if I could be allowed to see the fire-walking with my own eyes, he got my drift. I insisted on giving him a good donation for his church right there. He thanked me for it and told me to meet him in a little while at a side-door of the temple. Of course, I didn't say anything about bringing along my little movie camera."

The scene changed suddenly on the screen and the inner court-yard of the temple appeared. It was a large court surrounded by high walls. Below us and at one end was a long, high pile of burning charcoal which shimmered with intense heat. It was perhaps fifty feet long and about five feet high. Men were beginning to rake it out into a long, narrow platform of living coals as I watched.

"That's it!" cried my English friend. "I met my priest and got in with my camera case without his knowing what I was up to. He took me up to a balcony and hid me behind some bamboo screens. I paid some more church dues and he went off. In a minute I had a hole in the screen for the lens and one for the finder. My camera was all loaded and ready, so I had at it right away.

"I took the beginning and the end of the raking out of the coals," he continued as the scene changed. "See? Now they are all done and are smoothing down the bed. About six inches deep. The charcoal had been burning for ten hours, the priest told me. Hot as Hades! Made it so hot, even off there behind the bamboo screen, that I could hardly stand it. And see how the rakers have to keep their heads turned away and have to keep turning their bodies from side to side so they won't roast. Beastly hot!

"And now watch that gate in this scene. I began filming when I heard the noise outside. I knew the procession was about to come in. There they are! Priests in front and the candidates next. All men candidates—women are too sinful ever to get purified. Lots of the men are old. Forty-three I counted. And see their faces— look like they were going to afternoon tea—got on their most polite faces. Those big fellows in uniform are Sikh bobbies. Find them in all British possessions. They don't belong to the temple, but the authorities send them along to keep order. You'll see them keeping it right soon."

As I watched, the procession moved into the courtyard. The candidates gathered in a silent group at one end of the long bed of shimmering coals. Behind them gathered a mixed crowd of men, women and children, all greatly excited. The Sikhs moved slow-ly through the crowd, their clubs in hand. The priests had gone around the fire and met another group of six priests who had come from the temple and were taking their places at the opposite end of the bed of coals. In the hands of each of the six was a short whip with many lashes. Between them and the fire was a shallow water-filled indentation in the paving. It was about six feet wide, four inches deep and ten feet long, extending all across the end of the glowing platform.

"What are the whips for?" I asked. "Are they to keep the fire-walkers out of the water?"

"You'll see in a moment," was the hurried answer. "Seems that when they step out of the fire into the water, the priests have to beat them to keep their minds off their hot feet for a second. I asked the priest but didn't understand what he tried to tell me— something about an old custom."

"Do neither the whips nor the fire hurt them?" I demanded.

"The whips do. Lay their backs open sometimes. But keep your eyes on the picture. See? They are all praying now. Making a lot of funny gibberish. Praying to Agni to protect the pure and burn the impure. Gave me the creeps...."

The camera moved back to the silent group of candidates. They were taking no part in the prayers, but simply waiting. They wore only loin-cloths. Then a bent old man raised his hand, as in greeting, to someone in the crowd behind. He turned and walked slowly to the pathway which danced and shimmered before him. Clasping his hands and lifting his face as if in appeal to Heaven, he walked calmly into the bed of fire. I caught my breath. With a firm, steady stride he went wading through the coals toward the priests who waited at the far end.

I scarcely breathed as I watched. His feet were leaving black tracks which closed over and were lost in a moment after he had passed. On and on he went, never changing his pace. Made slightly misty and unreal by the heat waves rising all about him, he seemed more an apparition than a man. As I stared, my amazement was tinged with doubt. What I was seeing was an impossibility. But the end of that dreadful pacing came at last. The old man stepped from the living fire into the water and was instantly taken by the arms on either side by two priests. Their cruel whips flashed three times, cutting into the bare brown back. The old man writhed with pain. Two more priests took him and hurried him off to a bench beside the wall. They examined a foot each, nodded, and hurried back to their places.

The camera flashed around and caught another candidate just as he stepped into the coals. He was a thin, middle-aged man. His face was turned to the waiting priests and his hands were clenched and swinging at his sides. With long rapid strides he began his ordeal. His pace quickened. His head went up and his face lifted as if away from the heat. He was half-way through and walking more and more rapidly. Suddenly his pace broke and he went on at a rapid trot. The trot increased to a run, and as he came to the end of the fiery bed he leaped frantically for the water. Hardly had he leaped before the whips fell. They fell in flashing blows that doubled the candidate as he strained in the strong grasp of the two priests.

The camera flashed back again to catch the next candidate.

"Was that second man burned?" I faltered.

"No. Only three got burned out of the whole bunch," was the abstracted answer. "Watch this one," he commanded.

A very bent and feeble old man had entered the fire. His hands were stretched imploringly upward. After the first few steps he began staggering. He hesitated, leaped into the air, plunged wildly forward and fell. Instantly attendants were at the side of the bed of coals, long drag-hooks in their hands. They labored frantically, rolling the smoking body over and over. They dragged it clear, coals sticking to the burned flesh. A jar of water was dashed over the still form and it was lifted and carried swiftly away.

"Dead before they got him out ..." said a low voice at my elbow. I started slightly, having momentarily forgotten my friend. "But that didn't stop them; they kept going right through."

Again a splice ran through the projector and the camera swung back from a man being lashed. It picked up another man at the far end. He had just stepped into the fire and in his arms he carried a boy. The child was hardly more than six and dressed in loin-cloth only. I gasped in horror. Why should a child be endangered? What if the big lean man should fall? Again I held my breath. Would the man never start running? Was he insane?

"He'll make it," my friend encouraged me.

I sank back into my chair. On and on the man went, striding deliberately. The little boy became vague and clear by turns, as the heat shimmer was stirred or left stagnant by air currents. One small hand lay quietly and confidingly on the bare shoulder of the man. The boy gave no sign of fear or concern. Never quickening or slackening his pace, the man came at last to the end. He stepped into the water. The whips fell but once on his back. He lifted the boy high to keep him from being struck. In his gesture was something that hinted of a love great in its triumph. The camera followed as he set the child on his feet and led him away toward the wall.

Suddenly the film began to change rapidly from scene to scene. Men ran or walked a few feet through the fire before vanishing.

"I was running short of film," explained the voice in my ear. "I just took grab shots. But now watch—I got another of those who got burned.... There he goes! Off at the side—howling—now he's into the water. No use to beat him. The priest said he'd never walk again. Now keep an eye on this—see that Sikh? See what happened? The crowd went crazy—religious frenzy—they wanted to try it themselves. See those Sikhs with their clubs! What if they hadn't been there to lay them out? The whole crowd would have rushed into the fire!"

Suddenly the film clicked in the projector and the screen flickered blank and white. The picture was ended.

"How do you feel?" asked the Englishman curiously.

"Rather upset," I answered truthfully.

"And wasn't I!" he exclaimed. "I'd seen it with my own eyes! For a penny I'd have joined the temple. It gets you. I was a week trying to forget it. It's like seeing a ghost or something. Can't get your mind straightened out. You go giddy. Can't strike the old balance. Keep wondering if you have everything wrong.... Can't get over the idea that there's something in it besides a trick."

"Then you really believe it is a trick?" I asked.

There was a long moment of hesitation. "What else can it be? ... But how could the beggars put anything on their feet that wouldn't wear off in a half-day of parading barefoot? ... And how was it some of them got burned if they all had the same stuff on their feet to protect them?"

"Perhaps they know better than we do what's behind it," I suggested.

There was a slow nod. "I almost joined the temple ... just to find out if there was...."

Comment:

In this case it would seem that the priests did not use magic in behalf of the fire-walkers, but let them use their own powers as best they might. It is evident that some were not yet good magicians, regardless of the religious significance of the matter.

As we shall eventually consider a very important point concerning the nature of "purification" from' sin in its relation to the ability to perform fire-magic, I will now present a short case having to do with descendants of Igorot head-hunters.

Case 5 Descendants Prove that Their Head-Hunting Ancestors Did Fire-Walking Safely Preliminary Notes:

In the Philippines the Igorots have done fire-walking for centuries. They have also been head-hunters.

To waylay the enemy and take his head is not a business which the Burma devotees would consider a help to "purification," but the Igorots seem unaware of this. Here we see descendants of the little pink-brown people using fire-magic with the same success as did their forefathers.

The Case:

Some Igorot fire-walkers came to Los Angles some years ago and gave several performances at the old Chutes Park on Washington Street. My friend, Mr. George Dromgold, saw them at work, and his description of their feats gives us the usual picture of hot rocks, green branches in hands, and bare feet treading on intensely hot stones with no resultant burns.

Comment:

This case is mainly important to show that headhunters have done fire-walking and that the art has come down to the Igorots of our time.

Of secondary importance is the fact that magic can be practised in civilized countries and away from the favorite plant, ti, which is so largely used in the ceremonial throughout Polynesia.

Case 6 A Japanese Healer uses Fire-Magic Preliminary Notes:

In the preceding cases we have had the two best known forms of fire-magic. For the third we must look to a less widespread, but more practical form: fire-magic used in healing certain types of disease.

The Case:

In 1928-1929 there came to Honolulu a Japanese fire-healer. He advertised his powers and began his healing practice. His specialty was the treatment of arthritis. He would heat stones so hot that they would ordinarily burn flesh. By the use of magic—according to his later admission in court—the stones could be packed around an affected joint and the trouble cured. There were several cases which he had treated successfully, notably the case of a wealthy American who had been unable to walk for several months because of arthritis in the knees. After treatment with the hot stones by the Japanese healer he recovered the full use of his knees.

Comment:

This case is of importance to our study and proofs, because the records of it are preserved in court documents. After practicing for some time in Honolulu, the Japanese was arrested at the instigation of the medical men. He was charged with practicing medicine without a license, but, as he had administered no medicine, the charge pressed against him was that of being a kahuna. *

The court that tried him was not interested in evidence given to prove that his treatment was effective, when that of local doctors was not. The Japanese offered as his defense the fact that he was using magic and not medicine. Magic is not admitted in evidence in any civilized court. He admitted that he had used burning-hot stones to cure others. That was enough. He was fined and imprisoned as a kahuna. Later he was deported.

Had there been any trickery on the part of the Japanese healer, would it not seem that he would have acknowledged it rather than go to jail for a longer term, because he insisted that he had used real magic? Of course, to deny his magic it would have been necessary for the healer to show how he did the "trick," and this was something impossible for him to do as there was no trick.

Summary Under the classification of "fire-immunity through magic," there must be mentioned again the inconclusive tests of fire-walkers made before the World War II period by Harry Price and his associates in London. From the early printed reports on the tests made with Kuda Bux, it is to be seen that white men were severely burned on three attempts to duplicate, even in a small way, the fire-walk performed by the man from India. Later on, when the Price group tested another Indian who claimed to be a fire-walker, his feats were less spectacular and were safely duplicated by at least one white bystander. Price cautiously refuted his statements made after the Kuda Bux tests because of the later fiasco with Hassan.

Another excellent source of data on fire-immunity is to be found in the annals of Psychical Research. In these cases, dozens of which have been studied and reported, fire-immunity was supposedly given through the agency of "spirits." The famous medium, D. D. Home, at seances, was accustomed to take live coals from fires in fireplaces and hold them in his bare hands while blowing them to a white heat. He wrapped these coals in fine linen handkerchiefs without scorching the cloth. He held his head of bushy hair in the flames of the fireplace, burning not a hair. He held fresh flowers in the flames without having them wither. A recent book written around his life and experiences tells of these and other magical matters.

Fire-immunity, whether gained through prayer to a superhuman being, or through the agency of a deceased human "spirit," presumably making such a prayer, is the result of a supranormal action—is magic.

All supranormal actions are magic, whether they be instant healing, the production of psychic phenomena—telepathy, prevision, etc.—or the use of the "death prayer."

CHAPTER III

THE INCREDIBLE FORCE USED IN MAGIC, WHERE IT COMES FROM, AND SOME OF ITS USES

Before beginning the explanation of how fire-walking and other magic is performed through the use of three invisible elements which are still almost unknown in modern psychology, a few things need to be told about the religious beliefs of the kahunas.

The "Secret," or body of information handed down from one magician to another, was what may be called applied psychology for the most part. The element of religion was very small, especially if we accept the technical definitions of religion in the best modern sense.

Dr. Paul Tillich, Professor of Philosophical Theology at Union Theological Seminary writes, "Magic is a special kind of interrelation between finite powers; religion is the human relation to the infinite power and value.... Magic is the exercise of imminent power, religion is the subjection to the transcendent power."

All religions are mixed with magic. Prayer is magic. Everything we do to gain benefits for ourselves in this life or the next is a part of magic. Magic is getting something from supernormal sources. Religion is worship of a Supreme Being and an acceptance of whatever It gives us, whether pleasant or unpleasant.

While the kahunas got from the common source of such tales—the Nile Valley and neighboring lands—the stories of Adam and Eve, the Creation, the Flood and so on, and brought those tales with them to Polynesia, they did not share the concept of a personal and patriarchal God.

The kahunas taught that the human mind is not capable of understanding a form of consciousness unlike and superior to its own; therefore, all human efforts to imagine the characteristics of a final, ultimate and supreme God were a waste of time. They believed that there must be some Ultimate Creative Source, but they did not pray to It.

Take a flower, for example. It can have but a vague idea (if any) of the cow in the pasture. The cow can have a very vague idea of the nature and motives of the herder. The herder, therefore, when he has decided that there must be a Supreme Being who created the universe, can picture It only as another man. Although he cannot picture this Great Man except in the vaguest terms, he fears Him, prays to Him in hope of receiving favors, tries to bribe Him with sacrifices or sacrificial austerities, tries to obey such commands as he imagines this Supreme Man has laid down, and, last, worships him.

In a like manner, the invisible world of spirits and spiritual beings is to us much as our world is to a fish in the sea. The fish is hardly aware of a world above his watery realm. But as we ascend in the scale of intelligence, we of the realm of earth and air can know and understand the fish in his depths, even while remaining unable to share those depths as a place in which to live.

The kahunas, while supposing that there were levels above levels of consciousness above man, as there are levels below him, paid scant heed to any level other than the one directly above our own. On this level existed the thing we would call the superconscious part of mind. They called it by various names, one of which, the favorite, was Aumakua. This translates, "Older, parental, utterly trustworthy spirit." As it takes two to be a "parent," the Aumakua was considered to be a spirit composed of a male and female pair. All prayers and rites were addressed to this dual spirit, but because it was considered as much a part of ourselves as the conscious or subconscious is to the modern way of thinking, the Parental Spirit was worshiped not at all—it was LOVED. No sacrifices were made to it. No bribes were offered. It laid no commands on the lower selves. The relation was one of mutual love and trust—the parent and child relation.

Very logically, the kahunas taught that if any prayers to still Higher Beings were necessary, the Parental Spirit would know when they were needed and how to make them, doing for us such things as we are unable to do for ourselves because we have minds of a lower level of ability.

Because of this common sense attitude the kahunas remained simple and free from man-made dogmas to a surprising degree. They were direct and to the point. They could afford to be, for they possessed a system that actually WORKED. A workable system leaves little room for vagueness and dogmatic speculation.

This practical system by which magic was performed left no unfilled needs of a philosophical nature for the kahunas. They had, therefore, no saviors, no salvation, no heaven or hell, and no revealed religion with books in which were written, "Thus said God

..." In very fact, they had no books. Their language was never written until modern times.

While few of us may ever wish to fire-walk, this ancient rite is of great importance because it is a clear demonstration of the fact that there is a magical power that may be called into action if we know the methods to use.

Most of us pray for blessings of various kinds. The lore of the "Secret" brings definite and immediate results much superior to those we get. We cannot pray for fire-immunity and get it. Need more be said of the value to us of a study of the ancient lore?

Dr. Brigham, it will be recalled, had analyzed the basic nature of magic before understanding it. He had told me to watch for (1) a form of consciousness which used (2) some form of force, and (3) manipulated that force through some invisible kind of physical matter.

The Aumakua or superconscious part of mind is the consciousness involved in giving fire-immunity. The force it uses in this work is called mana by the kahunas, and is known to us as vital force. It is electrical in its nature and shows strong magnetic qualities. The invisible substance through which the vital force acts is called aka, or "shadowy body stuff."

As we already know that there is such a thing as vital force, let me begin my presentation of Huna (the "Secret") by pointing out some of the things already known about the uses and nature of this force, and then go on to things better known and explained by the kahunas.

It will be seen that the kahuna explanations also cover much that has been unexplained in the field of Psychical Research.

The three elements, consciousness, force and invisible matter, give us three measuring sticks with which to measure all magic. Notice how they apply more and more to magic as we come to see it unfold.

Case 7 (Mixed) The Three Invisibles Behind Magic Preliminary Notes:

In order to present a detailed and clear picture of the materials under discussion, I will cite some well known types of psychic phenomena, beginning with table tipping.

When we place our hands on a table and tip it, that is like a dog wagging its tail. When we place our hands on a table and some invisible being tips it, or when the table lifts or levitates from the floor with all hands on its top, that is the tail wagging the dog. However, when the table or other objects move of their own accord with no hands near them, the homely simile fails and we are face to face with one or the other of two forms of consciousness which may be involved in magic.

The first form of these two forms of consciousness is the ordinary "ghost." If it makes noises and bangs things around in a senseless or childish way, it is what the Germans called a poltergeist or "noisy ghost." But if the moving is done as if by a reasoning and adult ghost, it is normal psychic phenomena.

The second form of consciousness is that of a super-conscious type of being. Its work is characterized by the changing of an object into an invisible form before moving it—perhaps moving it many miles. This type of movement will be discussed later on. At present we are dealing mainly with the FORCE used to cause the movement.

The Cases:

The bulk of the cases which I shall cite in my report, unless it is specifically stated that they come from other sources, will have been drawn from the Encyclopaedia of Psychic Science, a monumental and authoritative book by Dr. Nandor Fodor who, with his staff, collected and digested all available reports and accounts relating to psychic phenomena during the hundred years prior to 1933. His evaluation of opinions and hypotheses has been both sane and wise. No better or more comprehensive source book will be found in any reference library.

(A) A famous psychical researcher, Gambier Bolton, in his book, Psychic Force, writes:

"During any meal with Mrs. Elgie Corner (Florence Cook, a famous and much studied medium), in one's own house, and whilst she is herself engaged in eating and drinking—both hands being visible all the time—the heavy dining table will commence first to quiver, setting all the glasses shaking, and plates, knives, forks and spoons in motion, and then to rock and sway from side to side, occasionally going so far as to tilt up at one end or at one side; and all the time raps and tappings will be heard in the table and in many different parts of the room. Taking a meal with her in a public restaurant is a somewhat serious matter."

(B) Sir William Crookes, in his Researches writes: "The instances in which heavy bodies, such as tables, chairs, sofas, etc., have been moved, when the medium was not touching them are very numerous. I will briefly mention a few of the most striking. My own chair has been twisted partly around, whilst my feet were off the floor. A chair was seen by all present to move slowly up to the table from a far corner, when all were watching it; on another occasion an armchair moved to where we were sitting, and then moved slowly back again (a distance of about three feet) at my request. On three successive evenings, a small table moved slowly across the room, under conditions which I had specially prearranged, so as to answer any objection which might be raised to the evidence."

(C) Cesar Lombroso, the famous Italian psychiatrist and criminal anthropologist described in La Stampa (of Turin) his observations in a wine cellar where, in the absence of any living person, bottles of wine were frequently broken. He wrote:

"I went into the cellar, at first in complete darkness, and heard a noise of broken glasses and bottles rolled at my feet. The bottles were ranged in six compartments, one above another. In the middle was a rough table on which I had six lighted candles placed, supposing that the spirit phenomena would cease in the bright light. But, on the contrary, I saw three empty bottles, standing on the ground, roll as though pushed by a finger, and break near the table. To obviate any trick, I felt and carefully examined by the light of a candle all the full bottles which were on the racks, and assured myself that there was no cord or string that could explain their movements. After a few minutes, first two, then four, then two other bottles on the second and third racks detached themselves and fell to the ground, not suddenly but as though carried by someone; and after their descent, rather than fall, six of them broke on the wet floor, already soaked with wine; only two remained whole. Then at the moment of leaving the cellar, just as I was going out, I heard another bottle break."

Comment:

Comment on the above cases, as well as on all cases which will later be cited, will fall into three parts. First we shall have to consider what is known in the modern world relative to such cases. Second, we shall have to consider what the lore of the kahunas may add to the information. And third, we shall have to weigh all evidence as best we can (in this period prior to exhaustive experimental work) and make our guesses—do our speculating.

While no effort will be made to divide comment into these three parts, the reader will do well to remember that there are these three very important methods of approach to the fascinating problems which confront us.

As there is nothing to be learned and nothing to be gained from those who still elect to deny all the phenomena around which this investigation revolves, no time will be wasted in argument unless there is some valid objection which must be noted for its possible significance.

Modern explanations of table tipping and the movement of objects by unseen agencies have not improved on the classical one that the spirits of the deceased, or similar disembodied spirits, are responsible for all the phenomena.

The kahunas heartily agree that spirits are responsible, but give added information as to the nature and classification of such spirits.

Efforts have been made to explain these mysterious occurrences without falling back on the spirit hypothesis. These efforts will bear consideration for the reason that they represent the alternative that we may accept if we discard the idea of spirits.

Dr. Nandor Fodor, in his Encyclopaedia of Psychic Science, writes: "Exteriorisation of motricity was postulated in the case of Eusapia Paladino (noted medium) by Morselli, Flournoy, Geley and Carrington."

This "motricity" is thought to be a combination of electricity and vital force or nervous energy. It is postulated that this force, whatever it is, can leave the body and enter the object which shows movement. (This covers the first unit of our kahuna measuring stick, that of the force or power involved. The second unit is the intelligence involved to put the force to use in moving the objects, and the third is the invisible substance used as a hand to let the force act upon the moving objects.)

The intelligence which causes the movement of the various objects is supposed to have the ability to cause this motricity or force to come out of the body of a living person and cause the movement.

The intelligence is also credited with the ability to draw invisible (sometimes slightly visible and slightly tangible) substance from the living body of a mediumistic person (or sitters at a seance) and make from it a hand or other limb through which to use the force. This substance is called "ectoplasm." A different explanation is to be found in the postulation that the intelligence is the subconscious part of mind of the living medium, and that it, under certain mysterious conditions, can cause the motricity to leave the body together with ectoplasmic substance, and then cause objects to move. The subconscious is said to be causing this activity for the reason that, were the conscious mind at work, the medium would certainly be aware of the activity and in control of it.

In the bulky literature which has grown up around psychic phenomena and spiritualism during the century just past, scattered postulations are to be found covering the possible part magnetism may have in the action of motricity on objects. This is a most exciting and promising line of thought and, because of the unexplored territory which it still surrounds, it is recommended to the reader as a fine place to begin working with a view to helping to forward the general investigation of magic.

We suppose that gravity is akin to magnetism, and that magnetism is to be found where there is a current of an electrical nature. There might be something of a push-and-pull nature involved in the movement of tables and other objects.

The kahunas recognized the magnetic and the opposite, repulsive, nature of vital force or motricity but, unfortunately, they left no detailed exposition of the subject. They knew the force as a thing which had to do with all thought processes and bodily activity. It was the essence of life itself. The kahuna symbol for this force was water. Water flows, so does the vital force. Water fills things. So does the vital force. Water may leak away—so may vital force.

Dr. Brigham spent a considerable time studying the ancient kahuna practice of holding heavy wooden sticks in the hands and, by an effort of mind, causing bodily electricity to enter a stick and charge it heavily.

These sticks were formerly used in battle, the kahunas standing in the rear lines, charging large sticks, and then throwing them at one of the enemy. Upon contact with the sticks, even the strongest warriors were often made unconscious.

Dr. Brigham had tested the power of such sticks, and had found them capable of giving what seemed to be an electric shock of a peculiar kind. The shock numbed the limb which was touched and made the head swim. It was recalled that the American Indians had a similar knowledge and practice. (They were also fire-handlers and some are today.) An early account in the government archives tells how a medicine man exhibited his magic power by touching a strong brave on the chest with a forefinger, knocking him to the ground in an unconscious condition.

While the chance of an element of hypnotic suggestion being mixed in such performances must not be overlooked, it would seem that there is a very definite shocking power to be found in excess accumulations of vital force. The part played by the mind and will in causing such an accumulation, either in a throwing stick or a forefinger, as above mentioned, seems very important.

W. R. Stewart, during his preliminary training under the Berber kahuna, was told that vital force could be stored in wood, stone, water and the human body, also in the invisible body of a "ghost." This force could be expended suddenly and thus move very heavy objects.

A demonstration of the magnetic nature of the force and of an intelligence or spirit of a sub-human or off-human level was made by Lucchi for Stewart's benefit at night and on a hillside where a large stone was covered by wooden doors resembling cellar doors. These doors were pulled up, and they descended steps cut into the soil. The rock projected from the end of the cellar-like cave at the bottom. By torchlight a hen was killed and its blood allowed to fall on the face of the stone. An invocation was spoken addressed to the spirit supposed to reside in the stone at times. The hen was then dropped on the ground before the stone, but it soon rose in the air and pressed against the stone. A moment later Stewart, who had approached closer and held his torch down to have a better look, felt a powerful magnetic pull which almost jerked him forward against the rock. He was caught and pulled back with some effort by Lucchi, who immediately insisted that they leave.

Stewart never learned what intelligence had been invoked or for what such invocations were used in the course of daily magical practice. His guess was that the spirit which had made its presence known in the rock was a "nature spirit" and that it had something to do with the soil or the pasturage or weather—all very important to the Berbers and their herds. It was his private opinion that this

spirit and its powers were inimical to man and probably dangerous to any but a skilled kahuna. Lucchi had made the statement
that all dealings with such spirits must follow a carefully observed
ritual, and that any change in the ritual might cause trouble. Stewart had changed the usual course of the rite by stepping close to
the rock at the wrong time. He was told that he should have stood
back until all the life force in the hen had been absorbed by the
spirit—the latter needing it to use in complying with the requests
made in the invocation, after which the body of the fowl would have
dropped. Stewart was reminded of the many tales of jinn or nature
demons current in Arab folklore.

If some types of movement of objects by unseen forces could
be proved to be largely dependent on the magnetic pull or push
of electrovital force, we should have made a discovery of the first
magnitude. The conclusion might be two-fold, (1) that the force
could push or pull objects here and there without guidance from
any spirit, living subconscious mind or other intelligence; (2) that
the force could act without visible or invisible substance to serve as
a hand, or even without invisible ectoplasmic substance to use—
but, with some etheric matter, perhaps, through which to move in
wave form. (The theory of the ethers is still controversial.

Today Science gives us ether to fill void space and interpen-
etrate full space, and tomorrow takes it away from us.)

Magnets pull iron objects to them, and in turn are pulled toward the objects. If a magnet were placed on a shingle in a tub of
water, and a nail placed on a second shingle quite near, the magnetic pull would cause both shingles to drift closer together. In
other words, one shingle would not remain stationary while the
other was pulled.

Animal magnetism or vital force is amazing in that it displays
a pull on the nail, but no balancing pull on the magnet, so to speak.
Mr. Arthur Spray, a cobbler near London, well known to a friend
of mine, is a powerful hypnotist. In his book, The Mysterious Cobbler, he tells of a most intriguing—and entirely inexplicable—phenomenon which he has frequently met in his practice as a hypnotic
healer.

He demonstrated this phenomenon before a group of newspaper correspondents on one notable occasion. Taking a young man
who was a good subject, he had him lie at full length on the floor,
then placed him in a deep hypnotic sleep in which his body be-

came rigid. Then, standing at the feet of the prone subject, he ordered him to open his eyes. When the eyes opened and looked up at him, he began beckoning with his right hand. Slowly the head and shoulders of the subject rose of their own accord into the air, the heels remaining on the floor. Inch by inch the rigid body lifted at the head until it stood suspended at a right angle a good four feet from the carpet. It was held there for a few seconds, then the beckoning of the hand was reversed and the body slowly descended to the floor.

During this experiment, Spray felt no pull on his body or hand. While the young man weighed over one hundred and forty pounds, Spray did not feel the need of lifting an ounce to cause him to rise.

This experiment has been duplicated by other hypnotists, so we may accept the evidence of a one-sided pulling nature in human magnetism. (Which seems to result from an accumulation of electrovital force charges—these charges being built up through some physical action set in motion by the willed command.)

Baron Eugene Ferson demonstrated this one-sided magnetic pull in Honolulu several years ago before large class groups. He believed that by making a mental command he could draw from the atmosphere an electrical force. There was no doubt that he did draw force from some source, and his pupils readily learned the knack of the process. Under his instruction, one pupil would make the mental command to himself to accumulate a surcharge of force. When satisfied that such a surcharge had been attracted (probably generated in the body from oxidization of foods) the charged pupil would place his hands on the shoulders of an uncharged pupil, then draw them slowly away. If the surcharge was sufficient, the uncharged pupil would be pulled strongly after the hands as they were removed. However, there was no sense of pull on the hands of the surcharged pupil.

I once saw Baron Ferson demonstrate the peculiarity of this form of magnetism by placing his hand on a light folding chair which stood in a row of similar chairs against a wall. He willed the magnetism to leave his body and enter the chair. He then called a sensitive young woman from the next room and asked her to walk along the row of chairs. She did so, and as she came opposite the magnetized chair she was almost violently pulled down upon it. The young lady weighed at least ten times as much as the chair, and one might naturally expect the chair to rise and press itself against her body. But the action was just the opposite. The rule seems to be that the object—regardless of its size or weight—which has the heavier charge of vito-magnetic force pulls to it the less charged object, feeling no corresponding pull on itself as a reaction.

This magnetic force acts over a space of several feet and through such obstacles as cement walls. Baron Ferson, after charging himself, took his place on one side of a ten-inch cement wall while his class stood in an arched opening where both sides of the wall could be seen. On the opposite side of the wall the sensitive young lady (found to be the most sensitive of the class to the magnetic pull) was placed, her back three feet from the wall, and with a man stationed on either side to hold her by the arms to keep her from being pulled too violently against the wall by the magnetic force exerted by Baron Ferson. Ferson raised his arms and stretched them toward the girl on the other side of the wall. Instantly she was so powerfully pulled that the men had to exert all their strength to keep her from touching the wall. Ferson, on the other hand, stood with heels together, very erect, and neither felt a pull nor showed even a slight sway in the girl's direction.

The part that suggestion might play in such a demonstration was discussed by members of the class, and to test the magnetic pull without the possible implication of suggestion, the pulling effect was tried by two of w on a small bull terrier. Dogs are not known to be suggestible. We went through the prescribed exercise of accumulating extra force, then placed our charged hands on the rump of the dog which was made to stand before us, head pointed away. Both the owner of the dog and myself were successful in exerting such a pull on the dog that it was drawn backwards several inches, despite its clawing at the rug to resist. We, in our turns, felt no pull at all on our hands or bodies.

Dr. Rhine, of Duke University, famous for his pioneering in Extra Sensory Perception, has published excellent evidence tending to prove that mind can exert an influence over matter without physical contact. In one of his experiments a machine is used to roll dice. As the cast is made, the experimenter wills the dice to turn up certain sides. A very definite effect has been noted as a result of the use of will.

The more one considers the strange action of mind in conjunction with what seems undoubtedly to be vital force, the more easily one can believe in the various phases of magic. For all our proud scientific advancement, we must admit that we are still darkly ignorant when it comes to the secrets of mind, vital forces, and invisible substances.

Down the long centuries there have been current legendary accounts of human flight through the air. The witches were supposed to travel magically to their meetings. The Greek gods flew through the air at will. The adepts of India and Tibet have been said to overcome gravity and float off through the air to distant places in the twinkling of an eye. Or, they simply fade out in one land and reappear in another. Polynesian folklore is replete with tales of such travels. In modern Psychical Research there are numerous instances in which men have been lifted bodily into the air. The famous medium, D. D. Home, floated horizontally out of the window of one room and back into the house through the open window of an adjoining room—this on the third floor of the building.

If mind has a certain control over matter, it is probably that the control is exerted in some way by means of directing the action of vital force, and through it, the action of magnetism or even gravity. A number of experiments have been carried on in which breathing and will were used in combination to affect gravity.

Dr. Hereward Carrington, dean of all psychical researchers, in his book, The Story of Psychic Science tells of his experiments with the lifting game, in which four people stand ready to lift a fifth with the fingers. All five inhale deeply several times, then hold the breath and make the lift. The person lifted feels lighter than usual. When this game was played on platform scales, the normal combined weight of the five people and a chair was 712 pounds. At the moment of the lifting the scales registered a loss of weight from 50 to 60 pounds respectively in several tests.

Baron Schrenck Nötzing recorded a case in which a young man practiced breath control and was able to lift himself free of the ground twenty-seven times.

The other side of this picture is more obscure, but numerous reports have it that individuals have been able, through the use of will and breathing control, to increase their weight greatly.

In Hawaii (as in Tibet, according to a fairly recent book) there was used a combination of will-breathing to gain magical aid in running long distances. There were specially trained messengers who sometimes held races of sorts. In carrying messages for the high chiefs, their speed and endurance surpassed by far that of men not able to use this form of magic.

Another angle of this problem of vital force and its strange motor and magnetic phases awaits exploration. This is the healing power. From time immemorial there has been the practice of the laying on of hands to cure the ailing. It was always apparent that some people had more of this healing power than others. Kings were supposed to have it as their natural right.

In religion, prayer accompanies the laying on of hands. In kahuna practice amongst the Berbers, W. R. Stewart describes cases of immediate relief from pain when his teacher laid her hands on the sick. She told him that her magical force was so strong that it left her body and went into the sick one through the simple process of touching with the hands. In more serious cases she said she would make a ritual prayer and take time to ready the patient with psychological and ritual cleansings.

In Hawaii the transfer of vital force from the kahuna to his patient, or to the spirits of the dead for special ends, was common.

Baron Ferson told in his Honolulu classes of a peculiar effect which he had noted frequently when placing his hands on another for healing or other reasons. There seemed to be a return flow of negative force. This negative return flow carried substances with it, such as alcohol and nicotine. Ferson told of having accumulated an excess charge of the force (he called it "The Universal Life Force") then placing his hands on the shoulders of an intoxicated man, with the amazing result that he himself became intoxicated to a degree, while the drunk man became almost entirely sober within a few moments.

Mediums at spiritualistic seances have reported such a strong transfer of nicotine from heavy smokers in the circle (hands joined to cause the flow) that they suffered all the symptoms of nicotine poisoning. With heavy smokers removed from the circle, the symptoms failed to appear at later sittings.

I have watched natural healers lay hands on the sick, making at the same time suggestions that they are drawing out the poisons and illnesses with strokes of their hands, and were shaking these off their hands (making gestures as of shaking water from finger tips). Nearly all such healers are convinced that they actually do draw invisible substances from the sick. Most of them, after finishing their treatment, wash their hands and arms in water, suggesting that they are cleansing themselves of any of the harmful invisible substances drawn from the patient.

From my personal observations and studies of this method of healing, I have become convinced that almost any healthy person can help the sick by laying hands on them and making a willed command that his force enter the patients and strengthen them. The use of the will, if accompanied by the spoken word, forms a suggestion which may be highly effective.

Mesmer, who discovered mesmerism over a century ago, was not aware of the potency of suggestion in connection with a transfer of what he called "animal magnetism." However, he had practiced accumulating a surcharge of vital force (while holding a magnet from which he thought he was getting the force) until he was highly proficient—if we are to believe the accounts of what he was able to do with the charges of force. He demonstrated healing powers so well that he became famous. At first he laid his hands on his patients directly. Later, when there were too many patients for individual treatment, he made the willed effort to transfer his force to tubs of water from which iron rods extended. The tubs of water once charged, the patients then approached and grasped the rods. The descriptions of the effect on the patients leave no doubt but that mesmerism was a working force. Patients reacted differently. Some did not react and Mesmer would touch these, usually getting the reaction. There was much healing, and much hysteria such as may be caused by light hypnotic suggestion.

The sudden transfer of vital force from throwing sticks must be kept in mind in following this line of thought, also the sudden stunning discharge demonstrated when the American Indian medicine man touched a brave with a forefinger and caused him to lose consciousness at the touch.

Hypnotists, after the advent of mesmerism, found that hypnotism could be practiced by suggestion, or even by having the patient gaze at a bright point of light. They claimed that no magnetism was needed and none transferred to the patient or subject. This seems to be a mistaken idea. The fact that a hypnotic reaction is expected of the patient is in itself a suggestion. The fact that the hypnotist is near can account for a transfer of a sufficient amount of the vital force to make the suggestion take effect.

Later on we shall look into the kahuna explanation of how the vital force can travel between people without actual physical contact (or between the living and the spirits of the dead). At the moment it is necessary only to call attention to the fact that there is such an exchange, and that what we learned from Phineas Quimby to call "absent treatment" is an apparent reality, thanks to the ability to send over a distance both the vital force and the healing suggestion.

CHAPTER IV

THE TWO SOULS OF MAN AND THE PROOFS THAT THERE ARE TWO INSTEAD OF ONE

One of the most intriguing and radically different elements in the system of psychology used by the kahunas, must be introduced at this point in the report in order to continue the presentation of the vastly important subject of vital force and accompanying magnetism.

Dr. Brigham was able to learn more about the magical methods used in the "death prayer" in Hawaii than about any other kahuna practice. In a moment I will present a case from his experience, but first we shall have to have some general notes.

The kahunas had a number of beliefs which they did not keep secret. For instance, they shared with the common people their knowledge of the fact that man has two souls or spirits instead of one. The early missionaries thought this a most droll and idiotic concept, worthy only of heathen and savages. To them, man had but one soul, and their job was to save it if possible. As they arrived in Hawaii in 1820, and the subconscious was not discovered by Freud until over half a century later, they can hardly be blamed for laughing at the kahuna beliefs.

The kahunas went a step farther than modern psychology has gone (except for some of the most advanced thinkers, amongst whom was William McDougall, early mentor of Dr. Rhine, and a pioneer in the field). The kahunas knew that the subconscious, as we call it, was one spirit, and the conscious mind another. They dwell together in the body, each soul (or spirit or self or psyche—call it what you will) performing its part in the general task of living and thinking.

Each of our two spirits has its own mental abilities. The subconscious (unihipili) can remember but has only elementary reasoning power such as a dog or horse may have. On the other hand, the conscious (uhane) cannot remember a thought once it has let it go out of its center of attention. It has to depend on the subconscious to give back any thought needed as a memory. Sometimes the subconscious cannot find the right memory when it is desired, and often it must be given time to make a search. We have all had the experience of being unable to remember a name, and then, some time later, having the name suddenly come to us. The conscious mind has two powers which are its very own, however. One is the power to use will of the hypnotic kind (more potent than the elementary will of the subconscious self). The second power is that of using the highest known form of reason, the inductive, which sets man apart as a superior animal in the animal kingdom.

The subconscious accepts and reacts to hypnotic suggestion (or mesmeric treatment). The conscious cannot be hypnotized. Under the influence of suggestion, the subconscious, being illogical to a large degree, will accept and react to even absurd suggestion. In the theatrical performances based on hypnotic demonstrations, people can be made to believe most absurd facts about themselves, and thus amuse the audience. (Unfortunately.)

Case 8 Data on the Use of Vital Force in the Kahuna "Death Prayer" as Related to the Belief that Man Has Two Spirits, the Subconscious and the Conscious Preliminary Notes:

During my years in Hawaii, the stage play, The Bird of Paradise, was advertising Hawaii, its volcano and the kahunas with their "death prayer," throughout the civilized world. Hardly a tourist arrived in Honolulu who had not seen the play and learned of the deadly use of magic by the native priests.

One of the questions most frequently asked by visitors concerned the verity of the "death prayer." Usually they were told that there was nothing to it. Or they might be treated to wild tales of death through this form of magic. The truth was that over a period of several years during which time I checked the data through doctors frequenting the Queen's Hospital in Honolulu, not a year passed but one or more victims of the potent magic died, despite all that the hospital could offer in the way of aid. And the old time doctors had recognized the familiar symptoms year after year.

There were several kinds of kahunas in Hawaii before they ceased almost entirely to understand the ancient lore. Some were hardly more than spiritualistic mediums. Some were prophets. Some labored to control winds and weather. A few were able to perform almost any part of the magic, be it healing or controlling the elements.

Among the specialists were kahunas who might have several magical abilities, but who also could use the "death prayer" (anana).

The ability to use the "death prayer" was based on a mechanism so strange, and to us so fantastic and incredible, that it stretches the imagination to grasp it before we understand the full details of kahuna lore.

As I have explained, the kahunas believed that man had two spirits, the lower or subconscious one being illogical and subject to the influence of hypnotic suggestion.

To become able to use the "death prayer" a kahuna had to inherit from another kahuna one or more ghostly subconscious spirits. (Or he might, if sufficiently psychic, locate subconscious spirits or ghosts, and use hypnotic suggestion to capture and enslave them.)

In very early Hawaii, prisoners of war or other unfortunates were sometimes given what apparently was hypnotic suggestion in a potent form, to cause their subconscious spirit, after death, to separate itself from its conscious mind spirit and remain as a ghost to serve as guard at sacred stone enclosures or native temples of the degraded form of Kahunaism. It is probable that some of these unfortunates were given orders to serve kahunas in the "death prayer" magic after they were executed.

In any event, the kahunas in question had one or more—usually about three—of these enslaved ghostly subconscious spirits. When a person was to be prayed to death for any one of many reasons, the kahuna called to him his enslaved spirits and gave them mesmeric orders to absorb mana from food and drink placed on a mat on the ground and surrounded with ceremonial objects such as small white stones and certain pieces of wood.

This mana was vital force such as we have been discussing. It was undoubtedly transferred from the body of the kahuna into the food, drink and ceremonial objects which were called the papa or "forbidden." It was thought that when the mana was taken from the food and drink, some of the substances were also taken, especially alcohol from gin set as the papa in later days. (Recall Baron Ferson's experience with the transfer of intoxication from a drunk person to himself.)

The spirits were also given very definite instructions as to what they were to do with the force. They were to catch the scent from a bit of hair or soiled garment belonging to the intended victim, and follow it much as a dog does a track. Upon reaching the victim they were to await their chance to enter his or her body. This they were able to do because of the power to use as a paralyzing shock the surcharge of vital force given them by their master. The order which the spirits were trained to obey was recorded in one case. It was:

"O Lono, Listen to my voice. This is the plan: Rush upon ――― and enter; Enter and curl up; Curl up and straighten out."

The "curl up" and "straighten out" had other meanings than we give the words in English. The process was one of entering the body of the intended victim or attaching themselves to it. That done, the vital force of the victim was taken by the intruding spirits and stored in their ghostly bodies (of which we have much to say in due time). As the vital forces of the victim were withdrawn from the feet a numbness came to them which rose gradually over a period of three days to knees, hips, and finally to the solar plexus or heart, at which time the victim died.

When the death had been accomplished, the spirits left the body, taking with them their great charges of vital force, and returned to their masters. If the victim had been rescued by another kahuna, and the spirits sent back by him to their owner with hypnotic orders to attack their master, they might make such an attack with fatal results. In order to avoid such a danger, a magic ritual of cleansing was usually performed by the kahuna sending out the spirits (kala). Or, as was most often the case, the person who had hired the kahuna to send the "death prayer" to another, and who had vouched for the fact that the intended victim deserved such drastic punishment, would be named as the one responsible and to be attacked should another kahuna send the spirits back before their task was accomplished.

In the event of a return from a successful mission, the kahuna ordered his spirit slaves to play until they used up the vital force they had taken in the process of killing the guilty one. Their play usually took the form of what we would call "poltergeist activities." They would move or throw objects, make loud noises and create a bedlam of some proportions. Dr. Brigham once heard a great commotion in the hut of a kahuna at night, and was later told that spirits were at play in this manner.

None of the usual explanations of the "death prayer," such as the use of a mysterious poison or of "dying of superstitious fear" were true. Almost never did the victim know that he was about to be killed by magic.

To illustrate this, let me tell of two cases in which the fear element could play no part.

The Cases:

(A) A young Irishman came to Honolulu with the first of the modern taxicabs. He was rough and ready, his hair was red and he was afraid of nothing.

Before he had been long in the city he had contrived to get a fine Hawaiian girl so much in love with him that she broke off her engagement to a Hawaiian boy. The girl's grandmother did her best to break up the new affair, seeing as she did that the Irishman had no good intentions. She even went so far as to make veiled threats that heaven would punish him if he did not leave the girl alone.

Very naturally, the Irishman had no fear of heaven. He was very much of the scientific attitude, and probably quite accustomed to the futile threats of angry mothers and grandmothers. It is certain that such threats could not have had the least effect on him. One day his feet "went to sleep." He did his best to right matters, but the prickling numbness crept slowly upward. In the course of a day he had passed through the hands of two doctors and landed in the hospital.

Every effort was made to discover the cause of the malady, but no cause was found and no treatment availed. In fifty hours the prickling had reached his waist. When several doctors had interested themselves in the case, including one of my friends, there came headshakings and grave suspicion. An old doctor who had practised long in the Islands was called in. He recognized the symptoms at once as those of the "death prayer."

Taking the patient in hand he questioned him closely and soon learned the story of the girl. More questioning brought back the memory of the grandmother's threats, which the boy regarded as piffle and as of no consequence in diagnosing his strange malady. Saying nothing, the wise old doctor set off to visit the grandmother. Later he gave the substance of the conversation he had with her.

"I know that you are not a kahuna and have had nothing to do with this case, Grandma," said the doctor. "But, just as a friend, will you tell me if you think anything could be done to save the man?"

"Well," said Grandma, "I know nothing about the matter, and

I am no kahuna—as you know. But I think that if the man would promise to take the next ship for America and never return or even write back, he might recover."

"I will guarantee that he will do just those things," said the doctor.

"All right," said Grandma imperturbably.

The situation had to be explained over and over again to the unbelieving Irishman, but when the idea finally was driven home to him, he became terrified and was willing to agree to any terms. That was in the early afternoon. That night he was on his feet again and able to catch a Japanese ship for the "Coast."

(B) I will give the next case as I transcribed it from my notes shortly after an evening spent with Dr. Brigham. I will use his words as nearly as possible.

"I went to Napoopoo on the Big Island," said Dr. Brigham, "soon after the Museum was built. I wanted to climb Mauna Loa to collect indigenous plants. It was to be a three-weeks' trip with native guides and a pack train.

"At Napoopoo I spent five days getting men and pack animals together, but finally set out with four Hawaiians and eight horses and mules. It was good weather, and aside from the usual difficulties of those days when trails were all but lacking, we got on very well.

"I had reached the barren country above the rain forests and was making for the summit crater of Mauna Loa when one of my boys became ill. He was a strong lad of twenty. I left him behind with a man to care for him and went on to the summit, thinking it was the altitude which was bothering him, and that he would soon be all right.

"We spent the day in the crater and got back to the lower camp and the sick boy early in the evening. He was stretched out on a blanket, now too weak to rise. I decided to move him to a lower level the next morning, and was about to sit down to my evening meal when one of the older men came to me.

"'That boy very sick,' he said. Then, after much beating about the bush, it came out that the Hawaiians had decided that he was being prayed to death. I was slow to believe, but went to the boy and questioned him.

"'Do you think you are being prayed to death?' I asked.

"'No! No!' He was instantly frightened within an inch of his life. I next asked him if he had any enemies who might want to have him killed. He could think of none, and was more than anxious to have me say that I still thought it was the altitude that was bothering him.

"I made another and more thorough examination, but found nothing significant except the usual symptoms of slow paralysis of the lower limbs and threatening general collapse, all of which symptoms belong to the death prayer. At last I became convinced that the old man was right and that some kahuna was at work. When I admitted this, all the men became frightened. For all they knew the whole party might be killed.

"I went back to my meal and thought things over. Meantime, one of the men kept on questioning the boy. After a while he got some interesting information. The boy's home was on the windward side of Hawaii in a little out-of-the-way village in a narrow valley which ran to the sea. There was little to bring the haoles (whites) to the village, and its old kahuna had endeavored to keep the people isolated and living in the old way. Among other things he had commanded them to have no dealings with the haoles under penalty of being prayed to death. The boy had left home and gone to live in Kona several months back. He had all but forgotten the command.

"Up to the time of my arrival at Napoopoo, the boy had lived entirely with his Hawaiian friends and had not come into contact with white men—at least not in a business way. When I was hiring men for my trip up the mountain, he had joined me without a second thought. It had not occurred to him that the command still held outside his village.

"As I heard about these things I became more and more angry. My temper was no better in those days than it is now when it comes to someone injuring my friends. I sat there wishing I could lay hands on the kahuna, and also facing the fact that my work would have to stop if the boy died and I had to take him down to the coast.

"While I was thinking things over, the old man came to me as spokesman for the others and made a perfectly natural suggestion.

He politely called my attention to the fact that all Hawaiians knew that I was a great kahuna and even a fire-walker. To him it seemed simple enough that I should adjust matters by praying the kahuna to death and saving the boy.

"The men waited expectantly, and I could see in their eyes their confidence that I would turn back the death prayer and that all would be well. On my part I was cornered. I had bluffed for years, and now my bluff had been called. I was most uncomfortable. If I refused to do the obvious thing they would be sure that I was afraid of the kahuna and not the strong fellow I pretended to be.

"Now I've always had a considerable pride, and at the thought of showing what might be mistaken for the white feather before my men, I decided there and then to try my hand at sending the death prayer back to the kahuna. This is perhaps the easiest thing an amateur magician could be called upon to do. The spell had been initiated and the trained spirits sent out. All I had to do was to put up the usual big arguments to talk the brainless things over to my side, and then exert all my will to send them back and make them attack the kahuna. I felt this would be fairly easy as the boy was guilty of no actual sin.

"I was a long way from the ti leaves which are usually brushed over the victim as a part of the ceremony to help drive out the spirits, but I had never believed them very necessary. Moreover, I was angry and impatient. I got up and said to the men: 'You all know that I am a very powerful kahuna?' They agreed most enthusiastically. 'Then watch me,' I growled. With that, I went over to the boy and set to work.

"The trick of the thing is to put up an argument of such cunning that the spirits will be made to think that their master must be a devil to send them to kill one so pure and innocent. I knew that if I could win them over and get them worked up to a high emotional state and ready to revolt, I would be successful. Of course, I had to chance the kahuna having kala-ed (cleansed) himself; but I thought that improbable as he would have no fear that I would send back his death prayer. I doubted if he had ever heard of me over on that side of the island.

"I stood over the boy and began to advance arguments to the spirits. I was smoother than a politician. I praised them and told them what fine fellows they were, how deserving and clever. Little by little I worked around to tell them how sad it was that they had been made slaves by a kahuna instead of being allowed to go on to the beautiful heaven that awaited. I explained just how they had been captured by the kahuna and imposed upon. I told them how pure and innocent and good the boy was and how black and vile the kahuna was. I still consider that argument a masterpiece. The Hawaiians blubbered from time to time as I described the pathetic condition of the spirits.

"Finally I decided that I must have the spirits ready to pull the kahuna limb from limb. I was ready to give them the command to return and visit the kahuna with ten times the punishment he had ordered for the boy. I could bull-roar in those days with the best. I can yet! [The doctor threw back his head and gave a roar that shook the house.] Well, I gave my commands in about such a tone. I yelled so loudly that I frightened the pack animals. The men drew back hurriedly and the boy whimpered like a frightened child.

"It was a supreme effort, mentally, emotionally and physically with me. I put every particle of will and concentration into that command. When I had repeated it three times, I sat down by the boy, trembling and dripping.

"I continued to keep my mind fastened like a vise on the project in hand, never letting it waver from my willed determination to see that the spirits obeyed my orders. The light faded and the stars came out. The boy lay silently waiting. From a safe distance the men watched me with faces now expectant and now reflecting horrible fear of the unseen. At times the air about us seemed to tremble with the fury of some unearthly conflict of forces.

"The longest hour in history was about gone, when I suddenly felt an odd sensation. It was as if the tension in the air had gone in a flash. I drew a deep breath. A few minutes later there came a whisper from the boy. 'Wawae ... maikai' (Legs ... good).

"I could have shouted in my triumph as I set to work to massage the twitching limbs which seemed to react as if they had been frozen and were gradually becoming warm again. Little by little circulation was restored and the toes began to wiggle. The men crowded around me to offer timid congratulations. It was the high point in my career as a kahuna. In an hour the boy was up and eating his poi.

"But that isn't the end of the story. I had a pleasant conviction that I had killed something deadly. I wanted to check on my performance and see what had happened to the kahuna. I decided to cut my trip short so I could go down to the boy's village—the collecting had been less successful than I had hoped, anyway.

"We covered the ground rapidly in the few days we stayed on the mountain-tops. We camped one night at the lake on Mauna Kea, and explored the crater of Mauna Loa. We roasted by day and froze by night.

"In due time we pulled out for the lower country on the north side of the mountains. Water was easier to get, but the country was badly cut up and the forests heavy. At last, however, we got down to the ocean and struck a trail which took us along the bluffs and up and down through valleys and ravines. Always we followed the sea.

"Late one afternoon we came straggling out of the brush into a clearing in a fair valley. An old woman and a girl were working in a taro patch as we came along. They took one look at me and the boy, then flew screaming before us. We followed and soon came to a cluster of grass houses. Not a person was to be seen. I sat down outside the big hut where the kahuna had lived, and waited while the boy went to see if he could find someone.

"I heard him shouting for a time and then it was quiet for several minutes. Pretty soon he came back with news. On the night I had sent back the death prayer to the kahuna he had been asleep. He had awakened with a scream and rushed around to get ti leaves and began to fan himself to fight off his spirits. Between gasps he told the people what had happened. He had neglected to kala himself and the white kahuna had taken a low advantage of him. In a very short time he had fallen to the ground and lay there groaning and frothing at the mouth. He was dead by morning.

"The people were certain that I had come to wipe out the entire village. I told the boy to go back and tell them that I had taken my revenge and that if they behaved themselves I would consider them my friends.

"We waited some time before the head man came back with his flock. He wasn't at all happy, and most of the women were frightened nearly to death. However, I soon reassured them, and in no time we were all great friends. In fact, they seemed to consider me quite a fellow. No one seemed to resent my having killed their kahuna—that was all a part of the game to them.

"Some of the horses were tired out, so we accepted an invitation to stay and be fêted. They gave us a luau (feast), which, considering the poverty of the village, was not bad. They had no pigs, but the dog was as tasty as you please—being poi-fed meat. I had never taken kindly to dog, but as a full-fledged kahuna, I no longer hesitated. We parted blood brothers.

"The one thing which I could never understand about the matter is this: The old kahuna had found out that I had hired the boy— and by psychic means—but he had not found out that I had turned kahuna and was sending his death prayer back to him. The only way I can account for this is that he must have turned in for the night at dusk and gone at once to sleep.

"Another thing which seems certain is that the kahuna was of a fairly powerful class. Only those well up in their art can see at a distance. Just why he had not seen into the future, I cannot say, unless he was not quite up to that."

Comment:

There is another kahuna method of causing death by magic, known as kuni or the burning. It seems to be one seldom used in the old days, but was said to consist of the rite of burning a hair or other part of the victim's body and casting the ash into the sea. I have no reliable data to offer in this matter, and simply mention it in passing lest there be something of importance in this practice which later investigators might overlook if left unmentioned.

The killing of a person by magic was thought by the kahunas to depend upon whether or not the victim had a deep sense of guilt which was caused by wrongs done others. Such a guilt sense (complex) made the attack of the unihipili or subconscious spirits successful. Without this sense of guilt, the subconscious of the victim would successfully ward off the attacking spirits.

Down the centuries there has been a form of magic practiced (or tried) which consisted of making a doll or image of the intended victim, then thrusting pins into the image, a fresh pin each day. The idea was that some form of sympathetic connection was established with the victim, and that a magical reaction would be set up to cause death in due course of time. While this practice may have little potency, it cannot be tossed aside contemptuously. We are on the far forward fringe of exploration in a field which has not been fully explored. We must consider all possible sources of information lest we overlook some important clue to the full understanding of such things as instant healing.

The vital force or mana of the kahunas has three strengths. If it is electrical in nature, as modern experiments have demonstrated, we may safely say that the three strengths of mana known to the kahunas equal three voltages.

The kahuna words for the three voltages were mana, for the low voltage used by the subconscious spirit, and mana-mana for the higher voltage used by the conscious spirit as "will" or hypnotic force. There was a still higher voltage known as mana-loa or "strongest force," and this was thought to be used only by a superconscious spirit associated with the two lesser spirits to complete the triune man.

Modern studies of the vital electricity have been made by attaching wires to the skin of the body and of the scalp, then using very sensitive instruments to measure the electrical discharges carried by the wires.

Life magazine files show in the issue of October 18, 1937, some pictures of tests with charts and graphs. Two voltages of electricity have been found, a low voltage in the body tissues and a higher voltage in the brain. From this it has been discovered that all thinking involves electrical activity of the higher voltage of vital force.

The kahunas associated all thinking processes with mana. The word mana-o means "to think," the "o" added to show that the process is one of using mana to produce thought.

From the foregoing it will be seen that the ancient kahunas were good psychologists. They knew the subconscious and conscious as two spirits, and they knew the two strengths of vital electrical force which we call "body waves" and "brain waves." The kahunas also knew a superconscious spirit and a voltage of vital force used by it, this voltage being the highest. Although these last two elements are not yet known to modern science, they probably will be in time. In our present investigation there is much evidence to be considered which points to the correctness of the kahuna psychology. (One must always remember that the kahuna system of psychology, even if not complete and accurate in its smallest details, made possible such things as fire-walking. It was a workable system, and we cannot rest on our oars until we find one equally workable.)

Either the vital force or the magnetic force generated by the presence of vital force in bodily tissues, has been found to exert other strange effects on various things.

Experiments carried on in France with a famous medium showed that meat and fish could be prevented from decaying by being held in the hands and treated to a "magnetizing" process. Oranges and other fruits, as well as vegetables, so treated, did not decay but slowly dried up.

Other experiments showed that the vital force could be stored for a time in various substances such as wood, paper and cloth. Water took and held charges. Glass did not.

CHAPTER V

THE KAHUNA SYSTEM AND THE THREE "SOULS" OR
SPIRITS OF MAN, EACH USING ITS OWN VOLTAGE
OF VITAL FORCE. THESE SPIRITS IN UNION AND IN
SEPARATION

To return to our illustration of the measuring stick of the ancient system called the Secret, we have been considering the first unit, that of FORCE. The second unit to be measured is that of the CONSCIOUSNESS which directs the force. (Later we shall take up the third unit, that of the SUBSTANCE through which CONSCIOUSNESS exerts FORCE.)

If the kahunas were right in their idea that human consciousness is composed of two separate spirits on this level, with a third or superconscious spirit acting as a guardian angel, so to speak, we have in that concept an addition to psychological knowledge which is of such importance as to be hard to estimate.

This concept must cause us to reconsider our religious theories of the human soul. If the kahunas are right in stating that we have in us a less evolved lower spirit just up from the animal kingdom, as well as a more evolved spirit which has long been up out of the animal kingdom, our ideas of salvation will also have to be remodeled. Two salvations will be required, one for each soul because they are of a different level of development.

The religious concept of karma and reincarnation will also have to be revised in the same way and for the same reason—that of having to fit the theories to two unequally developed spirits, to say nothing of fitting them to the superconscious, which is the oldest and most highly evolved of men's three selves or spirits (the aumakua or "parental spirit").

Under this older and more workable system of psychology, we come to see ourselves in a clearer light, although we trade simplicity for the complication of triplicity of being. In religion we are accustomed to consider God a triplicity, but we have apparently lost sight of man as a similar triplicity.

This complication becomes even clearer and easier to grasp if we keep always in mind the fact that the low or animal spirit in us, the unihipili, does all the remembering for the man but has inferior powers of reason. The conscious mind spirit or uhane cannot remember for itself but can use the full power of inductive reason.

In addition to the evidential data to be found in the "death prayer," we find other proofs.

While modern Psychical Research has identified the spirits of the deceased only under the classification of "poltergeists" and ordinary "spirits," the information which has been gathered concerning the activities of spirits as a whole shows very plainly that there must be several grades of them, each grade having its own voltage of vital force, and its own mental abilities (or lack of certain abilities).

On the other hand, the kahunas have long since classified the several kinds of spirits. As this is quite new to us of the West, and as this classification is of great interest as well as of great importance, let me list the several ghostly spirits one may meet in the seance room:

KINDS OF GHOSTS OR SPIRITS LISTED ACCORDING TO
THE KAHUNA LORE.

1. The ordinary normal spirit of one deceased. This spirit is made up of a subconscious and a conscious spirit, as in life. It thinks and remembers like any ordinary normal living man. It uses the same forces.

2. The subconscious spirit of a man, cut off from its conscious companion by some accident or illness before or after death. This spirit remembers very well indeed but is illogical, having only animal-like deductive reason. It responds to hypnotic suggestion. It is like a child and is often a playful "poltergeist" or noisy ghost. It loves to attend seances and make tables tip. It tries to answer questions, and usually gives such answers as make it appear to be a liar or worse. It loves to imitate one's deceased relatives.

3. The conscious mind spirit of man, cut off from its companion subconscious spirit before or after physical death. This spirit cannot remember, therefore it is a nearly helpless wraith, wandering about aimlessly, sometimes making its presence known, sometimes seen psychically, but acting the part of the true "lost soul" until rescued eventually and paired off again with a subconscious spirit who can furnish it with remembering powers—often with a set of memories of a former life in which the rescued conscious spirit or uhane had no part.

4. Spirits of the superconscious order, including what may be called "nature spirits or group souls," after the Theosophical termi-

nology. Only vague information is given as to this class of spirits, although it is concluded that they frequently take a hand in the activities of the two lower spirits, the unihipili and uhane, helping them to do things of a spectacular nature at times.

Not until the rediscovery of the kahuna system of psychology have we had a remotely plausible and satisfying explanation of the phenomena of dual and multiple personality (or of obsessional or split-personality types of insanity).

It is exciting, therefore, to see how the old system fits in with what we know of such cases. Let me present some standard data:

Case 9 Multiple Personality Preliminary Notes:

Source books: Outline of Abnormal Psychology, by William McDougall (Scribner's, 1926); Encyclopaedia Britannica (13th Edition), Article on Multiple Personality.

The word personality as used here is one not too well defined by Psychology. Jung, who has followed Freud in his investigations of the complex, describes the word and takes us back to its Latin origin: persona, the mask worn by actors when they change from one character to another in a play. This describes the thing changed in cases of multiple personality. It is the individuality, or traits, which distinguish one human being from another.

In describing the changes of personality in a body, little distinction is made between the subconscious and conscious—these being considered by most investigators to be component parts of personality. Jung, however, leads the way in his work by making the distinction of anima (Latin for breath or soul, and corrupted in French to animal) for the subconscious, and persona for the conscious.

The correct description of the phenomenon we are now to investigate should be "multiple anima and persona" instead of "multiple personality."

There are three points which we must watch in the following cases: (1) The appearance or disappearance of either the conscious or subconscious alone, with corresponding changes in personality; (2) The appearance or disappearance of both units combined as a pair; (3) The memories retained by the personalities as they come and go.

If the kahuna theory is correct—that the subconscious alone can remember—then by watching memory we should be able to tell which unit goes or remains.

Webster's International Dictionary speaks of this phenomenon as an abnormal condition of "mind." I prefer to think of it as an abnormal condition of body in which minds come and go, rather than of the various minds involved. Each mind observed is found perfectly normal while in possession of the body—unless lack of memory of its state when out of the body or asleep within it may be considered abnormalities.

The terms used in describing the elements of consciousness involved and the states of consciousness are: A personality cut off from control of the body and brain is said to be "dissociated"; the original personality in a body is the "primary" one, and those that come in to replace it are "secondary"; the personality in temporary control of the body and brain is said to be "dominant," while those who have once appeared and have gone, or who have not yet appeared, are said to be "latent."

In cases of "alternating personalities" two personalities only are involved in the change. If there is "reciprocal amnesia," neither personality remembers anything the other did while in possession of the body. If there is not reciprocal amnesia, one or both may be able to remember what was done in the body during its absence. Under the influence of hypnosis, one or more of these personalities can usually be brought from the latent state and made to answer the questions of the operator. The answers are none too logical as a rule, but they tell such things as could be remembered by any subconscious mind if such memories were stored in it.

This phenomenon is not a new one. Down the ages men have changed personalities or become "possessed." This usually refers to conditions of insanity, but not always. Our attention is now to be fixed on cases where insane personalities were not observed.

The Case:

I will condense a few typical cases which McDougall discusses in the source book mentioned.

Rev. W. S. Plumer first described the following case in Harper's Magazine in 1860: Mary Reynolds, a normal girl of eighteen, was subject to fits for a year. Then, while reading in a meadow one day, she became unconscious. She awoke blind and deaf. This affliction passed in three months. One morning she could not be awakened. Some hours later she awoke of her own accord—to all seeming a new-born baby. She could, however, repeat a few words. Learning with great rapidity, the "baby" began to grow mentally and use the adult brain. In a few weeks the primary personality came back and the secondary one disappeared. This alternation continued for years, the "baby" personality growing up in the process. Neither personality, when dominant, had any knowledge or memory of what the other had done while in possession of body and brain.

Professor Janet describes a case in which one of the alternating personalities knew the memories of the other: Félida began changing personalities at the age of thirteen. She was an hysterical child, but the secondary personality was very different. The secondary personality could remember all the memories of the primary, but the primary none of the memories of the secondary.

Dr. Morton Prince's most famous study was the "Beauchamp Case." At eighteen years of age a young lady began changing personalities. This changing continued for years, five personalities being identified in all—each considering itself a separate individual, and the mutual memories being a tangle.

The childhood of the girl, B, was one marked by emotional stresses and nervousness. Matured, she became a nurse, and received an emotional shock in the course of a love affair. Suddenly "all her peculiarities became exaggerated" and she became ultra-religious. The memory remained unimpaired, but there was a distinct change in characteristics. This change lasted some six years, during which time another personality named "Sally" came and showed her presence only during sleep. At night this Sally talked through the body and took it on sleep-walking excursions.

At the end of the six-year period there came another emotional shock, and a personality called B4 became dominant. This B4 could remember all the events of the life of the original B, but not those of the life of B1.

In the following year B1 and B4 alternated with reciprocal amnesia. Both remembered all that B had done, but knew nothing of the doings of each other. B1 was sickly and mild. B4 was more healthy and far more aggressive. Both were very emotional.

Dr. Prince used hypnosis on the patient. Under hypnotic influence another personality was brought to light. It conversed freely.

However, this very interesting personality puzzled the investigator. He was inclined to think she was the original B restored to normal condition and much improved. She resembled both B1 and B4 to some extent, seeming to be a mixture of them and of herself. She is described as "A person of even temperament, frank and open in address—one who seemed to be natural and simple in her mode of thought and manner." She had all the memories. B, B1 and B4 continued to alternate—B now commanding the memories of B1 and B4. During this time B1 and B4 seemed at times to partake of the "emotional characteristics" of each other—a trading back and forth.

After some years the original B became dominant and grew healthy and normal.

Sally was interesting. She could be contacted in hypnosis and questioned, although she would alternate with one of the other personalities and often upset the procedure initiated during hypnotic investigation. She considered herself a separate and distinct personality and remembered all the things she had done through or with the body at night. She said she had learned what the other personalities (except B4) were doing by reading their minds when she found their thoughts interesting. When they were reading a book which she disliked, she stopped reading their minds and amused herself with her own thoughts. She disliked B1 and often forced upon her visual hallucinations and certain motor automatisms. At times she took control of B1's voice; often she forced B1 to do things she did not wish to do—things such as telling lies.

When Sally took over the body she could not open her eyes. One of the automatic actions she forced on the others was the rubbing of the eyes. In this way she eventually got her own eyes open and so was able to see, and to dominate the whole organism. Her first success in this came in a moment when the then dominant B1 was drowsily resting. Thereafter, Sally was able at will to displace B1 in normal as well as in hypnotized states. At such times, B1 returned with no memory of what Sally had been doing with the body. In struggles of will, Sally seemed to be able to "paralyze" the will of BI who, although seemingly dominant, was forced to obey orders much like a hypnotized subject, which resulted in Sally's being able to play practical jokes on B1. Unravelling the knitting was a favorite joke. Neither B1 nor B4 had any memory of Sally or her periods of dominance. Sally could not read the thoughts of B4, and could not often force automatisms on her; this, she said, was because B4 had heard of her and fought against any control. At certain times when Sally became dominant she could not get the eyes of the body open; and the skin, deep tissues, and "muscular sense" were all in a condition resembling that of the body when in sleep.

Comment:

Dr. Prince holds that all the various personalities using one body are "split off" parts of the one real personality. His method of treatment was that of blending two or more personalities to get a dominant third. In this he was none too successful.

Professor McDougall, in his study (our source book), decides that each personality is a separate "monad" or entity in itself.

None of the psychologists are willing to admit that these personalities can come and go in and out of the body, and that the subconscious mind can be used by one or more personalities or changed in the body.

My own study of multiple personality data resulted in my accepting the kahuna system of psychology as one better explaining complicated changes which take place.

In some cases which have been reported, a "baby" personality arrives and becomes dominant; in others, an adult personality comes and brings with it a complete change in health—even a paralyzed limb—and a definite memory of a past life in another body.

As psychologists and kahunas disagree, let us go on to see what proof we can find that a "personality" actually can leave a body and return to it.

Case 10 Did the Conscious and Subconscious Minds of General Lees Mother Leave the Body and Return? Preliminary Notes:

This case was reported in the Hollywood Citizen, December 14, 1934, in the Strange As It May Seem daily feature. I take it that it can be authenticated by the originator of the feature. In any event, there are many more similar cases which are perfectly authenticated.

The Case:

Fourteen months before the famous Confederate soldier, General Robert E. Lee, was born, his mother seemingly died. The doctors found that her heart had stopped beating and that she had turned stiff and cold. Thinking she was dead, funeral services were held and her body placed in the family vault. Fortunately in those parts at that time, bodies were not embalmed.

A week later the keeper of the cemetery went into the vault to remove withered floral offerings, and was startled to hear a moan from inside the casket. Hurriedly he opened the coffin. Inside it he found Mrs. Lee—again back in her body, alive. Apparently she had but then returned, for she had not smothered. She recovered and lived to give birth to the son who was later to become so famous.

Comment:

In this and many similar cases we have proof of the cessation of all activities of the conscious mind in the body. Those of the subconscious all but ceased. To account for absence of decay in the body we are forced to conclude that there was a slight connection—perhaps by an ectoplasmic thread—between the body and the subconscious which must have been partly removed because of the death-like state of the body.

In this connection it is well to remember the yogis of India. These "holy men" use some form of autosuggestion to throw their bodies into a death-like state while the conscious mind goes away for long periods of time and the subconscious becomes dormant.

In the two cases we have just examined there are data which will later be of value, but in the next two we will come upon the data which finally showed me the significance of all data—pointed me to the secret of secrets of the kahunas.

Case 11 The Strangest Personality of All Appears Preliminary Notes:

One of the early members of the Society for Psychic Research, and one who has taken part in many investigations, was a resident of Honolulu when I was there. He was Dr. Leapsley, a brilliantly educated man who was as trustworthy as he was wise. He made frequent journeys away from Honolulu, on this quest and that. Often he lectured to a group of friends to give them the findings of his latest investigation. I give this case from notes taken at one of the lectures.

The Case:

Dr. Leapsley (Ph.D. and a biologist), in company with two medical doctors, was called in as a ranking expert in matters of multiple personality—the case to be investigated and treated being that of a young lady twenty-eight years old, the daughter of a prominent California attorney.

From the age of four, this young lady had alternated personalities regularly every four years. Only two personalities were involved and there was complete reciprocal amnesia.

The change of personalities which came with such regularity would be made in a moment of deep sleep. The secondary personality had been a "baby" when it first arrived, but had learned very rapidly and soon equalled the mental growth of the primary personality.

Through the years, each of the two personalities had continued its growth and education in its times of dominance, and each was able to learn with amazing rapidity anything the other had learned before it. Neither had the slightest memory of the experiences of the other. Upon returning to the body, neither personality could remember what it had done or where it had been while away. There was always surprise and momentary bewilderment at the time of returning to a body grown four years older and unfamiliarly dressed.

The primary personality was quiet and studious. It loved to sew and was shy and retiring. The secondary personality was an aggressive and unabashed tomboy. Their tastes and recreations were different.

One of the changes took place one afternoon while the mother was reading to her twelve-year-old daughter. They were in the sitting-room and the primary personality, whom we may call Miss First, was then dominant. The child was listening quietly and happily to the reading when she suddenly fell asleep. It was little Miss Second who awakened in the body a moment later.

Four years passed. Miss Second, now sixteen, was in the same room with the mother. The mother was reading another book, but this time not aloud, as Miss Second did not care for books. The body fell asleep, as it happened, in the same big chair in which it had sat four years before and on much the same kind of sunny afternoon.

Suddenly the eyes opened and Miss First looked wonderingly out. "Why did you stop reading, Mother?" she asked. She was unaware that four years had passed. She thought she had dropped off to sleep and that the reading of four years before had suddenly stopped. When told what had happened, she knew by remembering similar experiences what must have occurred. Also she could see that her body was larger and that it wore a dress much too colorful to suit her quiet taste.

So, every four years the girls changed places in the body. At the age of twenty-eight, or nearing it, each girl had lived fourteen years in the body. With each change, the wardrobe had to be made over to suit the personality which took over the body. Amusements were instantly changed, as well as diet, habits and occupational hobbies.

At last the parents decided to call in experts to see if there was not some way in which the secondary personality could be forced to leave the body to the primary. In this the parents were much perturbed as they had come to love both personalities as they would two different daughters, as indeed the girl seemed to have become to them.

The investigators took the young lady and explained to her that they were going to hypnotize her and endeavor either to cause both personalities to blend into one, or to get Miss Second to leave the body entirely to Miss First who now had possession, but feared the approach of the usual time for the change. Most eagerly she submitted to the treatment.

Under hypnosis the usual thing occurred. Both personalities appeared in turn and could be questioned. Each personality showed a complete memory of its own periods of life in the body, and each said that it knew all about the activities of the other— not by sharing those experiences but by "reading" what was in the memory of the other. They were not sure whether they stayed in the body or not, when latent, and they showed the usual lack of reasoning power. When the subconscious of Miss Second was told that she must go away and leave the body, the reply was vague and unsatisfactory. The order seemed to be accepted, but the doctors were convinced that nothing would come of such a command. So convinced were they that they also gave the usual hypnotic suggestion aimed at forcing a blending of the two personalities. (Note: As the subconscious alone can be hypnotized and made to act upon given suggestions, the blending must be between two subconscious entities. Such a blend would give the dominant conscious entity a double set of memories and so imitate a completely blended pair of personalities. It would seem quite impossible—if the kahunas are right in their postulations—that two conscious entities could blend without becoming instantly aware of their duality.)

After the first treatment it was found that no blending of personalities had resulted. The treatments were continued daily until the usual time of the change drew near.

It was hoped that with Miss First well aware of the fact that they desired her to stay in the body and blend consciously and subconsciously with Miss Second, something would be accomplished. However, when the change occurred, Miss First was not blended with Miss Second.

Hypnosis was applied again, after the new arrival had heard what was being done. Again the subconscious minds were questioned. Miss First remembered the instructions given her to try to blend with Miss Second, but said she seemed unable to do anything about it. When asked where she was, she answered only, "Here."

Suggestion was next tried in an attempt to drive Miss Second out of the body. Then a startling thing happened. The body became as if dead. No response from either subconscious could be obtained. The doctors and parents became much alarmed. It was their desire to be rid of the invading personality, but now it seemed that they had driven it out but could not recall Miss First. While suggestion was being laboriously continued, a still more startling thing happened. The lips opened and an entirely unfamiliar personality spoke to them with such wisdom and authority that they were confounded.

This new personality spoke with a resounding voice which had in it an evasive but undeniable masculine quality. It was much like the gentle but very firm voice of some old man. The group about the girl's body listened in amazement. Immediately the doctors realized that they were hearing still another personality addressing them. To add to their confusion, they realized that this new personality did not think as they thought. It seemed not to be logical, but superlogical. It seemed to know definitely and to the smallest detail what had gone before and what was being attempted. It asked no questions but began at once giving one statement after another concerning the girls and their lives. Each statement was precise and covered ground with which parents and doctors were familiar. As soon as the new personality had summed up the condition, it became silent.

The doctors asked who the speaker might be. The answer was another statement, and it was to the effect that this personality was one which had the two girls and the one body under its care and guardianship. In answer to more questions, more facts were stated—always without arguments such as a conscious mind might use, and always without explaining reasons. The group was told that the two girls were using one body for the purposes of living.

The doctors then contrived their best arguments. They told in full the way in which the change of personalities was ruining the life of the girl. She could not marry and could not live a normal life. To this the new personality answered with statements, the logic of which was apparent without argument or reasoning.

Statement followed statement, each giving some definite purpose of living—the various purposes of growth and experience.

The learned doctors were helpless. Each statement was so profound and perfectly reasonable that they could find no logical argument to advance against it. They were like children before age-old wisdom. The type of thinking with which they were confronted was not human. The doctors would have been able to produce arguments in favor of the statements which were given them seemingly as eternal verities, but they could not have given arguments against them.

In a very short time they lapsed into silence. The personality which addressed them had left them helpless.

In desperation one of the doctors cried out that if Miss First was not allowed to have the body, they would keep it hypnotized indefinitely. To this the answer was another statement to the effect that no one would do anything to injure the body. Still another statement was then given—a final one which closed the interview forever. This statement was simple and to the point: "If you interfere with my work, I shall withdraw the girls and leave you the corpse."

There was a long silence. Not one in the group doubted for an instant that the wise old personality would fulfil its threat. There had been a conviction of truth and serene power in every word. At last someone ventured to ask another question ... but no answer carne. More time passed. Suggestion was made to release the body from hypnosis. Miss Second opened her eyes and smiled. Doctors and parents gave up. They had been confronted as if by God himself. They realized the futility of their efforts.

Comment:

In the old man personality we find something quite different from either the subconscious or the conscious. The difference lies in its assumption of the duties assigned by the kahunas to the superconscious or "parental" spirit, also there is a decided difference in the mode of thought.

The superconscious uses, according to my conclusions, a form of thinking higher than either memory or reason, although it seems capable of remembering and reasoning. The only word in English to describe this thinking process is "realization"—a process of knowing things without going through the labor of remembering and applying logic to what is remembered and what is being observed.

The superconscious spirit, it will be recalled, uses a superior voltage of vital force. It is evident that it also has and uses a superior form of mentation. According to the lore of the kahunas, this form of mentation makes it possible for the superconscious to see into that part of the future which has become crystallized.

The best proof of the kahuna theory of the three selves and of their different forms of mentation, is found in checking multiple personality cases with obsessional insanity or schizophrenia. In the first, the patient remains sane because he or she is obsessed or controlled by a normal ghostly intruder who has his own subconscious and conscious selves, and who can, therefore, both remember and use reason. Only personality (conscious self) may change, or only memories may change (subconscious self), or both may change— and still there is sanity because a reasoning conscious self is always in control of the body regardless of changes. In the second case, insanity results from the changes because the conscious self is displaced and a new one does not take over the body. This leaves the resident subconscious in charge, and, lacking reason, it keeps the body alive but in a condition of lack-of-reason, or insanity. Or, an invading subconscious self may obsess or take over the body after the resident two selves have been driven out. Cases of insanity are common in which a foreign subconscious self obsesses a body. We know that it is foreign because it brings with it a foreign set of memories and convictions, even when illogical. The insane who believe themselves to be Napoleons are of this type, often not dangerous, often being able to remember from day to day, but never able to use the type of reason characteristic of the conscious self.

Later we will consider obsession in connection with a study of Huna healing methods. For the moment the important thing is to understand that the kahunas believed that there were three separate and independent spirits making the man, and that these were known to be SEPARATE AND INDEPENDENT BECAUSE THEY COULD BE SEPARATED BY ACCIDENT OR INTENTION.

Of only slightly less importance is the knowledge that the subconscious alone can remember, and that only the conscious can reason, while the superconscious has a still higher form of mentation which gives it exact knowledge of the past, the present and the part of the future that has been determined in advance.

CHAPTER VI

TAKING THE MEASURE OF THE THIRD ELEMENT IN MAGIC, THAT OF THE INVISIBLE SUBSTANCE THROUGH WHICH CONSCIOUSNESS ACTS BY MEANS OF FORCE

As I have explained, the kahuna system gives us three units or measures of magic; first, the consciousness at work in any given operation; second, the force used; and third, the invisible substance through which the force operates—through which this electrical type of energy is conducted and brought into play.

We have seen the three spirits or selves in the composition of a man, each self having its own peculiar mental powers, and each using its own particular voltage of vital force.

If to this we add THREE INVISIBLE ASTRAL—ETHERIC—GHOST bodies, the picture will be fairly complete—at least as I now am able to see it.

In Theosophy, as borrowed from the religionists of India, we have a strong resemblance to the kahuna idea of the three bodies which are made of invisible substance, and which serve each of man's three spirits as a ghostly body or vehicle presumably before the birth of the physical body, and after its death. I have used the terms astral and etheric, borrowing from Theosophy, for the want of better English words. The Hawaiian word is kino (body) aka (shadowy). Each of our three spirits has a shadowy body, but that of the conscious spirit is finer and thinner than that of the subconscious. That of the superconscious is the finest and thinnest of the three.

The word aka has also the meaning of a luminous extension away from the body or a halo of light around the moon or sun, or a circle of light extending from the moon or sun before it rises above the horizon.

The shadowy bodies of the conscious and subconscious spirits blend with the living physical body (they can come and go), interpenetrating it. The shadowy body of the subconscious interpenetrates the entire body, being a mold of every tiny cell and tissue of it. The shadowy body of the conscious spirit centers around the fore-brain and is pictured in the mediaeval paintings of the saints as the inner circle of the halo around the head. (Or, perhaps it was the shadowy body of the superconscious of the saint which was intended.) In the early Greek religious writings we have, according to James Morgan Pryse in his Restored New Testament introduction, a belief in two invisible bodies: a sun body, a moon body, and then also, the physical. In the Upanishads of India we find two invisible bodies, the "causal" and the "subtile" (kārana sharīra and sūkshma sharīra) as well as the gross physical.

In book after book, one reads the conclusions of learned men who have searched for the truth behind religion and psychology. They put into words whit Thornton Wilder called the "vast, vague intimations" of religion. In these intimations one can, once he is familiar with the kahuna system, begin to pick out a few cold and substantial facts. Let me quote a typical paragraph from the work of Pryse:

"Semi-latent within this (the) pneumatic ovum (of the aura) is the paraklete, the Light of the Logos, which in energizing becomes what may be described as living, conscious electricity, of incredible voltage and hardly comparable to the form of electricity known to the physicist.... The solar body, so called because in its visible appearance it is self-luminous like the sun, has a golden radiance. This solar body is of atomic, non-molecular substance.... The psyche, or lunar body, through which the Nous acts in the psychic world, is molecular in structure, but of a far finer substance than the elements composing the gross physical form, to whose organism it closely corresponds, having organs of sight, hearing and the rest. In appearance it has a silvery lustre, tinged with delicate violet; and its aura is of the palest blue, with an interchanging play of all the prismatic colors, rendering it iridescent."

In Egypt, as we might expect after learning from the Berber kahuna the legendary history of the stay of the kahunas on the Nile, there are very definite traces of the kahuna system to be found.

E. V. Straiton, wrote in Vol. II of The Celestial Ship of the North, glossary, (in describing ancient Egyptian beliefs):

"Many entities were supposed to comprise man, each functioning in a separate life in the tomb with the mummy. Man was thought to consist of the Sahy, the Ka, the Ba, the Khoo, the Khaibit, the Sekhem and the Ren. The Ka was said to come into being when the body to which it belonged was born, and it lived in the body until it died. It was the ethereal projection, the divine image or double of Eternal Being, image of the Spiritual Ego, the glorified second self as a type of the higher mortal self, the genius, depicted as being born with the mortal into this life. It was the perfect likeness, whether as a child, the man or the woman. The Ka separated and united with the body at will, and when uniting or coming to the body, says, 'Thou hast let my Eternal Soul see my body.' There was a special chamber [in the tomb] for the Ka.... Ba, the Heart-Soul [was the] most refined and ethereal in substance. The Ba could enter heaven at will. It would revisit the body in the tomb and reanimate it, and like the other entities was thought to decay if not well nourished, so food was supplied it by man or the gods. The Ba could transpose itself.... The Khoo was the Spark of the Divine Fire, the Luminous Spark, and dwelt in heaven as well as in man's body. It was the translucent Spirit Soul that ascended to heaven.... The Khaibit [or] Shadow was regarded as a part of the human economy. It held an independent existence, and could separate from the body, visiting it at will. It was thought to be always near to or with the soul.... Sekhem, [or] 'Vital Power' usually mentioned with the Khoo and the Soul. It also had its existence in heaven. Ren [was] the name, and had its existence and was thought to be in heaven.... All these were said to be indissolubly bound together, although in primeval times they were thought to be separate and independent parts in man's mortal nature.... The Osiris [or] assembling of the spiritual parts of man. The Osiris of a man attained spiritual bliss after the ceremonies for the dead. These spiritual parts when gathered together resembled him exactly.... The deceased was called the Osiris and continued to be so called until the Roman period."

In these fragmentary remnants of the older system of the kahunas, one may pick out indications of the tradition of the three spirits of man, the three voltages of mana or vital force and the three aka-s or shadowy bodies. The psychic vision of the seers and mediums all point to the fact that the superconscious self, in its subtle body, and charged with the incredibly high voltage of vital force, appears strongly illuminated as with white light.

In the kahuna lore the "TRUE LIGHT" was the Secret psychology and especially that part of it that had to do with the superconscious, which was called the Light. It was also called the Way or Path. In Christianity there are to be found numerous remnants of the Secret. The rites of baptism with the use of water, the confessional, exorcism, and the ritual forgiving of sin, all had their fuller and more significant counterparts in the magic of the kahunas. This would be natural, if the tradition placing the kahunas in Egypt before the time of Moses is approximately correct. Christianity stems from earlier religions originating in or near Egypt. As no other source of the rituals of the Church of Rome or the Greek branch of the Church has been discovered, with the possible exception of the Mass itself, it is significant, to say the least, to find the kahunas in far Hawaii, who knew the Bible stories of the Old Testament but not a thing of the New Testament, making daily use of rites and ceremonies of the early Church in their healing magic.

It is probable that the kahunas, in the migration to Hawaii from Egypt, passed on to the priests of India some of their basic beliefs. But it is evident that in India a similarly ancient set of doctrines had already developed, and that, in grafting the kahuna beliefs to the native beliefs of India, a greater contamination of kahuna ideas resulted.

For example, take the idea of FORCE as represented in Indian lore by the pranas or pranic energies. While the kahunas recognized but three voltages of mana (note the similarity of the two words for force), the Hindus divided and divided again, giving a special force or pranic energy to each known action of mind and body. This tendency to analyze everything into many fine parts resulted in there being forty-nine pranas in some Indian systems. All modes of thinking and sensing were likewise divided to make "seven times seven," giving us the dhātus and dharmas as a part of the scheme. The proof of any pudding is always in the eating. Despite the more complicated and more elaborate system evolved in India, their psycho-religious system remained far less practical than that of the kahunas.

Moreover, the doctrines of karma and reincarnation, as held in India, and as applied to man as if he were made up of a single spirit, hindered the use of magic for healing, as it hindered many other normal activities, and as it fostered the oppressive caste system.

We need not quarrel with the strictly religious element in any religious system, but, like modern Psychology (infant though it is), we must, perforce, question the older psychological systems where they are at variance with the recent discoveries.

When I first came upon the meaning of "stickiness" as part of the root (pili) meaning of unihipili, the kahuna word for the subconscious spirit, I could make nothing of it. But, when I had associated the shadowy body or aka with the subconscious spirit, and had considered the several root meanings of a-ka, I discovered that the thing that was "sticky" was the shadowy body. It sticks to anything we contact or see (even to things we contact by hearing, I am inclined to believe). It is like touching fly-paper with a finger and, when the finger is pulled away, a long fine thread of the adhesive substance is drawn out.

Absurd as this may sound at first telling, that is exactly the way the kahunas found the shadowy body of the subconscious worked.

The idea of an aka thread or cord is closely related to the idea of a flow of mana or vital force. The root ka means a cord, and also means a vine which branches out. The vine is the symbol of mana, as is water.

The astral cord is described in Theosophical literature as a cord of invisible stuff which connects the spirit in one of its thin bodies to the gross physical body when the spirit leaves it at the time of death, or during a condition of trance.

Modern Psychology has no slightest hint of such a thing as a shadowy body which is connected to things once touched by thousands and thousands of tiny invisible threads, but here and there in the reports of the Psychical Research records and writings of mediums, one meets evidence of the existence of such threads or cords. They can be seen and felt psychically. When heavily charged with vital force, they seem to become solid enough to feel with the fingers.

Before going on to show the part these invisible threads play in magic, let me mention a kahuna belief that all things, be they men, animals, flowers, chairs or THOUGHTS, have shadowy bodies, and these remain after the thing in its gross physical form has been destroyed. At this point we are particularly interested in the theory that thoughts have shadowy bodies—that they are substantial and enduring things, although microscopic and invisible, as are the shadowy threads.

When we think thoughts, the kahunas believed, we make thought forms. As most thoughts come in a train and in relation to other thoughts, the thought shadowy bodies or "thought forms" (recognized by Theosophists), form clusters. These clusters are likened by the kahuna system to bunches of grapes (a symbol of such clusters of thoughts in their shadowy bodies).

One of the most common uses of magic is that of sending messages by telepathy. Close friends, relatives, husbands and wives, frequently find that they get telepathic impressions one from another.

As before mentioned, Dr. Rhine of Duke University has done splendid service in studying telepathy under laboratory conditions. In fact, so well has telepathy been demonstrated that few deny its possibility.

In recent years telepathic messages were sent out by an arctic explorer almost daily, and were recorded by his friend in New York. The messages were accurately received over a distance of half way around the globe.

It is well known that the theory of radio broadcasting of mental messages from mind to mind will not hold water. Such a broadcast would depend upon an electrical discharge to carry the message, and as the power of such a discharge varies inversely as the square of the distance, a telepathic message sent half way around the world would be necessarily very much fainter than one sent across the street. The experimental studies have proved that distance makes no appreciable difference in the strength or clearness of the messages. As this cancels all modern theories made in an attempt to explain the mechanism of telepathy, we must fall back on the kahuna explanation.

This is a simple and logical explanation. It is that the threads of shadowy body substance connecting friends who send telepathic messages back and forth, are perfect conductors of vital electrical force.

In physics we know of no perfect conductors of electricity. All metals offer resistance to the passage of a current and the farther the current travels along a wire, the weaker it becomes. The higher the voltage of the current, the less the loss seems to be.

Through late experiments with "body waves" and "mind waves," we have come to know that vital force is electrical in nature and that it is flowing or leaping in infinitesimally small charges along our nerves and from cell to cell in the body. The voltage was reported by Drs. Libet and Gerard of the University of Chicago to be a millionth of a volt or less in the brain cell interchanges, but the action of the charges that of "million volt potentials of current."

Not only did the kahunas believe that the vital force passed unimpeded over aka threads, they believed that on the flow of the current there could be carried back and forth the thought forms which were clustered together to make complete messages or impressions.

As the subconscious spirit has control of all threads of shadowy body substance, all thought forms after they are created in the course of "thinking," and of all flows of the low mana or "body electricity," we cannot send and receive telepathic messages at will. We must give the subconscious a mental order to do the sending and receiving for us, then relax and wait for it to set to work. We can tell it what messages to send, but we can only wait for it to receive messages and push them to the center of consciousness so that we can become aware of them—the process is similar to that of recalling a memory, in so far as any sensation accompanying the receiving of a message is concerned.

Little by little, thanks to the recovered knowledge of the kahunas, we can see the explanation of telepathy take form. This explanation would mean little or nothing to us, however, were we not advanced in modern sciences to the point of being able to understand the ancient lore and the mechanisms described by it.

CHAPTER VII

PSYCHOMETRY, CRYSTAL GAZING, VISIONS OF THE PAST,
VISIONS OF THE FUTURE, ETC., EXPLAINED BY THE
ANCIENT LORE OF THE KAHUNAS

Telepathy is the sending of messages (as thought forms) along the connecting cords of invisible shadowy body substance which connect one person with another. The messages are sent by the subconscious self and received by it, to be given to the conscious self in due time.

Psychometry, and its related phenomena, depend on the same mechanisms except that the shadowy cord or thread does not connect two similar persons. A psychometrist usually sits quietly and touches a letter, a ring or some object about which he wishes to get psychic information, such as the past of the object held, or the contents of a letter and the nature and surroundings of its writer.

The fact which I wish to stress is that one practicing this form of magic reaches out along the shadowy threads which are attached to an object, following them to their ends, and finding there the things and people formerly associated with the object. Or, if the object is a stone such as has fallen in a meteorite, the thread will lead only to the source of the stone—the meteorite.

Case 12 (Mixed) Psychometry, Crystal Gazing and Related Phenomena Preliminary Notes: None

The Cases:

(A) A piece of lava was psychometrized by Mrs. Cridge, and the impression she received of the volcano was so vivid and frightening that she was seized with a feeling of terror that lasted for over an hour.

(B) Mrs. Denton psychometrized a fragment of mastodon tooth and described the sensations which resulted: "I feel like a perfect monster, with heavy legs, unwieldy head, and very large body. I go down to a shallow stream to drink. I can hardly speak, my jaws are so heavy. I feel like getting down on all fours. What a noise comes through the wood. I have an impulse to answer it. My ears are very large and leathery, and I can almost fancy they flap my face as I move my head. There are some older ones than I.... They are dark brown, as if they had been completely tanned. There is one old fellow, with large tusks, that looks very tough. I see several younger ones; in fact, there is a whole herd."

Note: Ossowiecki, one of the foremost psychometrists of our time, gives an excellent description of his sensations during the practice of this form of magic:

"I begin by stopping all reasoning, and I throw all my inner power into perception of spiritual sensation. I affirm that this condition is brought about by my unshakable faith in the spiritual unity of all humanity.

I then find myself in a new and special state in which I see and hear outside time and space.... Whether I am reading a sealed letter, or finding a lost object, or psychometrizing, the sensations are nearly the same. I seem to lose some energy; my temperature becomes febrile, and the heartbeats unequal. I am confirmed in this supposition because, as soon as I cease from reasoning, something like electricity flows through my extremities for a few seconds. This lasts a moment only, and then lucidity takes possession of me, pictures arise, usually from the past. I see the man who wrote the letter and I know what he wrote. I see the object at the moment of its loss, with details of the event; or again I perceive or feel the history of the thing I am holding in my hands. The vision is misty and needs great tension. Considerable effort is required to perceive some details and conditions of the scenes presented. The lucid state sometimes arises in a few minutes, and sometimes it takes hours of waiting. This largely depends on the surroundings; scepticism, incredulity, or even attention, too much concentrated on my person, paralyzes quick success in reading or sensations."

There are various phases to psychometry. Some do their best work when hypnotized before various objects are handed them to be psychometrized. Some see into the distant past, sensing the ancient surroundings of an object. Some follow psychically the deceased into the "beyond" and see their present condition and actions as disembodied spirits. Some, and these instances are rare, even see the future events which will be associated with the object which is held in their hands.

In just over a century of Psychical Research and of effort to explain how psychometry is accomplished, several theories have been advanced. Dr. Pagenstecher offered the following:

"The associated object which practically witnessed certain events of the past, acting in the way of a tuning fork, automatically starts in our brain the specific vibrations corresponding to the said events; furthermore, the vibrations of our brain once being set in tune with certain parts of the Cosmic Brain already stricken by the same events, call forth sympathetic vibrations between the human brain and the Cosmic Brain, giving birth to thought pictures which reproduce the events in question."

Sir Arthur Conan Doyle offered the explanation that all events and circumstances impressed themselves on some form of invisible and permanent, unchangeable ether. This imprinted ether, he supposed, was read by psychic vision by the psychometrist when attention was centered on a part of the ether connected with the object held in the hands.

Theosophists, building on ideas found in India, propound (see the works of Blavatsky) the theory that there is a World-Soul or Akasa, upon whose memory is impressed all that happens. Psychometry, under this theory, becomes more definitely mechanical. One uses the object held in the hands to make a psychic connection with the part of the memory of the World-Soul having to do with the object's past. By a form of psychic telepathy, or—better yet—mind reading, the psychometrist "reads the Akashic Records."

Another angle of the problem of psychometry is to be found in visions of a psychometric nature which occur in the vicinity of past battles or other less exciting events. These visions appear to a number of persons gathered on the scene, and all agree as to what they see—however, there are usually present people who see not a thing. Dr. Nandor Fodor gives some of the instances which have been recorded and which are widely accepted as true. The following case is one of them:

(C) "The Battle of Edge Hill ... was fought on October 22, 1624. Two months later a number of shepherds and village people witnessed an aerial reenactment of the battle with all the noises of the guns, the neighing of the horses and the groans of the wounded. The vision lasted for hours, and was witnessed by people of reputation for several consecutive days and when its rumor reached the ears of Charles I., a commission (sent out to investigate) not only reported to have seen the vision, on two occasions, but actually recognized fallen friends of theirs among the fighters, among others Sir Edmund Varney."

Dr. Fodor also calls attention to a well-verified case of Psychometric Premonition experienced by Count Buerger Moerner in recent times, and described in a German psychological periodical in 1931:

(D) "Passing through the little garden and glancing in at the window as he approached the house ... the Count was horrified to see the body of an old woman hanging from a ceiling beam... but once across the threshold was stunned with amazement to find the old woman rising startled from her chair, demanding the reason for his surprising intrusion.... Some days later ... he decided to visit the hut once more, curious to see if by some peculiarity of the windowpane he might not have been observing an optical illusion. Nearing the hut ... as before, the same terrible sight met his eye. This time, however ... he entered to find what he saw this time was no vision. The old woman's body was indeed hanging from the beam. She had committed suicide."

Crystal gazing is akin to psychometry with the difference that instead of an object to hold in the hands, the thought of a certain person may be held in mind while gazing into the crystal in expectation of seeing a vision form in its depths. This form of psychometry, while not generally recognized as such, is not to be overlooked in a study of the problem.

Comment:

To make the matter of this particular magical practice all inclusive, one has but to include dreams in which the future is seen. Here we have not even a thought to be held in mind (as in crystal gazing) to form the seed of the psychometric action.

In the premonitory dream the same elements are contained as in the other examples which have been given. (1) Evidence of an impress on some intangible medium capable of recording impressions of events. (2) Evidence of some form of consciousness or intelligence which directs this recording process. (2A) Evidence—in the case of events recorded on such a medium before they occur—that this Intelligence has some form of mentation superior to ours in so far as it enables it to see into the future, to say nothing of the past or of the happenings of the moment at distant places. (3) Evidence of some mechanism by which the psychometrist, the crystal gazer, or the dreamer of premonitory dreams comes into contact with the postulated recording substance, or reads a postulated memory and pre-memory in the mind of the postulated Intelligence. (4) Evidence that this connection is of a telepathic nature, or is related to clairvoyance and mind reading. (5) Evidence—because the psychometrist cannot command the visions but must wait until they rise before his consciousness—that the subconscious is the one who does this mysterious work of making telepathic contact, not the conscious.

I have, in order to pull together the scattered and seemingly unrelated phenomena just discussed, made several points in such rapid order that the report may seem confusing at this place. However, the reader will now have a general picture of the ancient magic of the kahunas, and if it can be kept in mind that there are three sets of three things, and a physical body, as I list them below for ease in checking back, the picture will grow clearer as the several phenomena related to psychometry are taken up in cases and examined in detail.

The Ten Elements in Kahuna Magic or Psychology I. Three spirits which compose the man (living or deceased).

A. The subconscious. Remembers but has defective reason. Creates all emotions.

B. The conscious. Cannot remember but has full reasoning power.

C. The superconscious. It has a form of mentation by which it knows by a process of "realizing." It knows the past, the present and as much of the future as has been crystallized or definitely planned, created or projected on its level.

II. The three voltages of vital force (mana) used by the three spirits of man.

A. The body waves or low voltage vital electrical force. It is used by the subconscious and can flow over threads of shadowy body substance (aka. Similar to "astral cords"). It can carry chemical substances with it as it flows from person to person. It can take the form of magnetism and can be stored in wood and other porous substances. A large discharge of this low voltage vital force, commanded by the "will" can exert a paralyzing effect, or a mesmeric effect resulting in unconsciousness, sleep and the rigid or cataleptic state.

B. The brain waves or vital force of the next higher voltage, used by the conscious mind spirit in us in all its thinking and "willing" activities. Used as will, it can be mesmeric or hypnotic force, provided that a thought form is introduced into the mind of the subject. It cannot travel over the shadowy substance threads, as can the lower voltage. (Or at least it seems not to do so.)

C. The high voltage of vital force (not discovered by science as yet), that thought by the kahunas to be used by the superconscious for its various purposes. It is of the atom-smashing voltage of electrical energy, in all probability.

III. The invisible or shadowy substance (etheric or astral) bodies in which the three spirits composing man reside. The lower two usually interblend with each other and with the body, during life. They remain interblended after death unless separated by some unfortunate circumstance.

A. The shadowy body of the subconscious. It is the most dense of the three. It is of such a nature that it sticks to whatever we touch (or perhaps see or hear), and when removed from the contact, draws out a long invisible thread of itself which connects one with the thing contacted, in a form of semi-permanent union. (It is not known how permanent this thread or the main body itself may be, but it seems to survive far longer than dense physical substances.) All things were supposed by the kahunas to have a shadowy body, be they crystals, plants, animals, fabricated articles, men or gods— even thoughts (the latter being very important to the magical system and its practices). This substance is an ideal conductor of vital electrical force or currents, and can be used as a storage place for it. When heavily charged with the low voltage of the force it becomes rigid and firm enough to be used as a "hand" or instrument to move or affect physical objects—as in table tipping, etc.

B. The shadowy body of the conscious mind spirit of man is less dense than that of the subconscious. It seems not to be sticky or to pull out into threads. It may or may not be a conductor of low voltage vital force, but undoubtedly is a conductor of the middle voltage—its own peculiar voltage as used in its form of mentation and "will." It forms the ghostly body in which the spirit functions as a spirit after death.

C. The shadowy body of the superconscious spirit of man. The superconscious is supposed to reside in this invisible and very light body at all times, seldom making direct contact with the physical body by entering it. By analogy, it is supposed to have characteristics somewhat resembling the shadowy bodies of the two lower spirits.

The use of terms familiar to us through modern Psychology is difficult, and a simpler set of terms, patterned after the terminology of the kahunas, will be handier. Below I give the simpler terms (near the above check list of the ten elements, for convenience in referring to them):

Simplified Terms for the Ten Elements in the Ancient Psychological System

I. Low spirit or low self: the subconscious. A separate spirit.

II. Low mana or low voltage of vital force. Used by the low spirit.

III. Low aka or low shadowy body (low astral or etheric double) of the low self.

IV. Middle spirit or self: the conscious mind, spirit or entity. It is a separate spirit and not a permanent part of the low self.

V. Middle mana or middle voltage of vital force. Used only by the middle spirit.

p. 140

VI. The middle aka or middle shadowy body, inhabited by the middle spirit.

VII. The High Self or Spirit: the superconscious. A separate spirit or self connected distantly with the low and middle selves, and acting as an "over-self," or parental guardian spirit.

VIII. The High Aka or high shadowy body of the High Self, in which it lives.

IX. The High Mana or high voltage of vital force, used by the High Self or High Spirit.

X. The body: the physical body which is entered by the low and middle spirits or selves in their aka bodies and used by them during life. The High Self is distantly connected to the physical body, probably, for the most part, by aka threads issued by the low self from its shadowy body.

The corresponding terms in Hawaiian are listed below for convenient checking:

I. Low self: unihipili.

II. Low vital force: mana.

III. Low shadowy body: kino aka.

IV. Middle self or spirit: uhane.

V. Middle voltage of vital force: mana-mana (a symbol, meaning "to spread out as a vine"). (Doubling the root often indicates an increase in the strength of the meaning.)

VI. Middle shadowy body: kino aka. (No differentiation of term.)

VII. High Self or Spirit: Aumakua (meaning older, parental and perfectly trustworthy spirit). There are a number of other names also used to indicate the High Self in its various activities, and it is obvious that the kahunas paid it much attention.

VIII. High voltage of vital force: mana-loa (meaning strongest or greatest force). The symbol of the High Self was the sun, and its force was symbolized by the light.

IX. High shadow body: kino aka, with no differentiation of the term as applied to the two lower spirits, although there seems to have been some use of symbolic terms to indicate it. The Berber kahuna thought its symbol was the moon.

X. The physical body: kino.

CHAPTER VIII

MIND READING, CLAIRVOYANCE, VISION, PREVISION,
CRYSTAL GAZING, AND ALL OF THE PSYCHOMETRICALLY
RELATED PHENOMENA, AS EXPLAINED IN TERMS OF THE
TEN ELEMENTS OF THE ANCIENT HUNA SYSTEM

Case 13 Mind Reading Preliminary Notes:

If one sits down in a quiet place where others are assembled, as in a study-hall, and attempts to read the thoughts of others, he must have (1) some way to contact the person whose mind is to be read across a space of several yards, and (2) contact once made, he must have a means of seeing or sensing the thoughts in the mind of the other and bringing back those impressions to himself.

Modern Psychology and Psychic Science offer no explanation of these two mechanisms. The idea of mental broadcast has been discredited by the fact that distance makes no difference in telepathic communication as it does in broadcasting. The idea of mental "vibration," which was taken from the theory of sound vibrating air, has not been of the slightest practical help. The idea that disembodied spirits might get the thoughts of another and bring them to us, is likewise impractical as an explanation. That leaves us with the one explanation which can cover the conditions—the explanations of Huna.

The Case:

I once undertook to test the possibility of reading the thoughts of others. I chose a study-hall for my laboratory. My method was to fix my eyes on the back of a student's head, quiet my own thoughts, and wait for impressions. I practiced thus for ten-minute intervals for several days before I began to get results.

Moments would come when a thought or impression would float into my mind as if I had remembered something. Knowing that these memories had nothing to do with my own past, I accepted them as things coming from the mind I was trying to read. To a few of my closest friends I dared confess my activities, that I might ask them whether I had read aright. I picked up trifling things for the most part—things being thought of aimlessly when the conscious mind was not actively engaged. I received memory-like impressions of a new dress which was being planned; of a desire to go skating; of a young man's bashful love for a girl.

Soon I exhausted my friends, or rather made them wary of my glance and so of no use to my experiment. I concentrated my attention next on a youth who seemed much given to reverie.

At first I read from his thoughts the picture of a strange room, small and dimly lighted and close—but desirable, despite its crude furnishings and bunk beds. Later I got an impression of a little old Chinese who had prominent teeth, but almost no chin. He seemed to be talking with my subject about something I could not get clearly. Later I got the name of the Chinese as "Squirrel." This amused me and made me think I had supplied that descriptive name myself because of the teeth and chin.

Finally came a reading which told me that my subject longed almost continually for that room and the Chinese—longed for something to be had and tasted, because of the room and the man "Squirrel."

Having accumulated sufficient data and a sufficient picture of what was heavy on my subject's mind, I took him aside one day, introduced myself and began to question him. I got nothing but the stoutest and

most angry denials. My next step in the rather long experiment happened to be related to this one of the room and the Chinese, but I did not realize that it was related when I began it.

In setting myself to read the thoughts of another young man, I was amazed one day to read in his thoughts the same longing and the same picture of the room and the Chinese. However, I read more fear than longing. The fear was at war with the longing for the peculiar "deep taste" I had sensed or felt as in my own body. What surprised me most was the recurrence of the name "Squirrel" in connection with the same Chinese.

I approached the second student and questioned him. I told him I had a feeling he was afraid of something, and asked if this could be so. He paled and said that in a way I was right. I next began to tell him of the room and the Chinese. He began to tremble and asked who had "squealed." I then assured him that I had no information directly. I explained my mind-reading test and told him how I had found a startling similarity between his thoughts and those of one who seemed to be his friend. My subject considered the matter—still white and shaken—then laughed nervously and denied everything, even that he was afraid. Also, he asked me to mind my own business.

It was some months before I got to the bottom of the matter and learned that what I was convinced I had "read" was correct. A group of young men had taken to smoking opium out of curiosity. The Chinese to whose rooms they were in the habit of going was indeed called "Squirrel." I had seen his face correctly. The opium-smoking group had, one by one, contracted the opium habit. The two young men whose minds I had read so successfully in the study-hall were part of the group. The first was not afraid; he was only desirous of his "smoke." The second was not only desirous of his "smoke," but was afraid that he had formed the habit and could not break it.

Comment:

In the above case we see that the subconscious or low self is the one which must, at our command, set about learning to read the thoughts of others. The proof of this is that the conscious self or middle spirit cannot read minds itself by any effort it may make. One must let go the hold on the low self and relax mentally, assuming an expectant attitude and waiting to see what the subconscious is able to do after it has been given our order to attempt the experiment.

Most people have the ability to learn to use the simple psychic actions of consciousness. However, it takes practice. Some learn more rapidly than others, and some seem to have the ability naturally. The same thing applies to learning to use hypnotic suggestion, telepathy, crystal gazing and premonitions (to a lesser extent is this true of all premonitory activities, for the reason that the information concerning the future must be had from the High Self, if it is at the moment crystallized and on its way to becoming a fact in the future. The uncrystallized future is not to be seen, according to Huna.)

In order to make contact with the person whose mind is to be read (according to Huna theory), the subconscious self must first send out a thread of the aka or shadowy body stuff to connect itself with the subconscious of the person acting as the subject. (This must be done in telepathy and hypnosis, absent treatment and prayer—in the latter case the connection is with the High Self. All prayer is telepathic.)

The subconscious has the strange ability to project a portion of its shadowy body, something like an amoeba projects a part of its body to make a hand with which to grasp a particle of food. The kahuna vocabulary gives us several words to use in describing this act. First a "hand" is made and extended toward the person we wish to contact. Second, upon reaching the person, it is necessary to "pierce" and enter the shadowy body of the subject, as a spear would pierce a dense physical body.

It must be remembered that, according to the Huna theory, the subject, if aware of the effort to touch and pierce through into its invisible body, can usually cause its subconscious to repel such an approach. This would be done by an effort of the "will" of the subject's middle self or conscious mind. (In the same way, hypnotic suggestion can be repelled.)

The third step, once the contact has been made with a subject who does not resist, a thread of shadowy stuff connects the two individuals. Along it travels a flow of the low mana or low voltage of vital force.

Connected in this way by an electrically charged invisible wire, the subconscious of the mind-reader projects a tiny part of its sensory organs to the far end of the thread and observes what thoughts are passing through the mind of the subject, duplicating these thoughts as thought forms or thoughts in their individual shadowy bodies, and sends them back on the flow of vital force to the mind-reader's center of consciousness—where the thoughts are presented to the focus of consciousness of the middle self (much as a memory is presented by the low self when desired) and become known to the mind-reader proper, who is the middle self.

The above paragraph contains information of inestimable value. It has taken years to dig out the hidden meanings of the words used by the kahunas and to see at last just what takes place. To make this important mechanism clear, it must be reviewed in some detail.

The first and most important thing to understand is that the low self has in its shadowy body duplicates of every cell and tissue of the physical body, thus duplicating all sensory organs. If this were not so, the spirits who communicate with us through mediums would have to report that they are deaf, dumb and blind—which is quite contrary to the facts.

Proof that the sensory organs are duplicated in the low shadowy body is to be had from various experiments carried out with people who have taught their low selves to reach out a projection of their shadowy bodies and sense things without depending on the bodily eyes, ears, touch, etc. Kuda Bux, the fire-walker spoken of earlier, was able to project his visual sense from his physical eyes to the skin of his back, reading (while carefully blindfolded) newspaper headlines placed against his bare back.

I have watched a certain blind attorney walk into a store and slowly weave his way through a maze of counters and display stands, depending only on his trained ability to project his shadowy body's duplicate sensory organs to locate obstacles. The men blinded in the war have recently been taught to sense obstacles in their path, the work being based on a supposed heightening of the sense of hearing. A small snapper is used and the learner listens as for an echo of the snapping sound, being told that there is a faint echo, and that he can learn to hear it in time and judge by it his distance from wall, door or object. It has been observed that when snow is falling, the ability to measure distances to objects is lost. Snowflakes do not muffle sound sufficiently to account for this failure, but if a projection of shadowy body stuff is being sent out, it would contact the snowflakes and report them instead of the more distant objects. Of course, there may be a very distinct ability on the part of a well trained subconscious, to catch the echoes of sound from distant objects and so measure the distance, but in this case, the physical ear would hardly seem a sufficiently sensitive organ in itself—demanding the projection explanation as a further aid.

Mediums at Spiritualistic seances have frequently had the experience of leaving their physical bodies for a time, and under certain circumstances (which we will examine later on). During these moments (usually while the physical body is in a deep trance or insensate condition) the mediums find their senses much keener than when used through the dense physical organs. They also find that they think more rapidly and more clearly when out of the physical in their shadowy bodies.

If a person leaves the body for more extended periods and goes to more distant places, they are said to do "astral traveling." Much has been written to prove this form of traveling possible and a fact. In such travels distant places and persons are seen correctly.

The difference between mind-reading and astral travel is dependent on how much of the low shadowy body is projected. If only a small part is projected, the center of consciousness remains in the physical body, which contains the mass of the low shadowy body. But if the mass of the low shadowy body is projected, leaving only a thickish thread of shadowy substance to connect it with the physical body (astral cord), the center of consciousness necessarily moves with the greater part of the shadowy body and becomes actually present at the distant place which is visited.

This brings up the matter of being able to remember what has been seen after returning from the astral travel journey. Huna explains how memories are made—and so far we moderns have no other explanation to consider. A memory is a thought which has been preserved by being in some way impressed on a microscopic particle of the shadowy body substance.

Creating a thought seems to be possible to all three spirits of man as well as to animals and even lower forms of life. All thinking is done by means of vital force of some voltage. As each thought is formed, it is given its shadowy body and is fastened by a thread of the same substance (or by direct contact, perhaps) to thoughts which came before or after it (association of ideas in terms of modern Psychology is thus explained).

When a thought has been created and impressed on its bit of shadowy body substance, it is taken by the low self and stored in that part of the low shadowy body which usually interpenetrates those sections of the brain which we know are related to the act of remembering. In our normal and waking conditions, these thought forms are actually in the tissues of the brain, and when the middle self desires a memory, such as a friend's name, the low self finds it in the place where it is stored in the combined brain-shadowy-body brain-duplicate-organ and presents it to the middle self to be sensed. Memories are recalled in chain form, associated memories being presented as they are dragged up with the memory desired.

For instance, when we remember the name of a chance acquaintance, we also remember how he looks, how his voice sounds and where we are accustomed to see him. Memory can be increased by careful attention to these associated ideas or thought-forms. The kahunas, we remember, spoke of these associated thought forms as "clusters"—clusters as of berries or grapes. A bunch of grapes seems to have illustrated the mechanism very well in that each grape is fastened to a stem, the stems to a central stem, and this to the vine and its root, and to the earth, and through it to all other things rooted in the earth.

The fact that vital force is used in the process of thinking has been well demonstrated through the experiments with the body and brain waves. These are not waves as in radio projection—a very important point to us—but are confined to the body very closely. Graphs made of the movement of waves of tiny electrical discharges through nerve and other tissues of the body show that when one is asleep there is a different graph marked on the charts. This indicates that the low self uses a different voltage of vital force in a different way in its thinking during sleep and dreams. The most marked and irregular graphs are caused by the combined thinking of both the low and middle selves during waking hours. During unconsciousness the needle of the recording machine shows almost no electrical action, allowing the graph lines to flatten out completely. In epileptic seizures the graph lines run very high before the peak of the attack, and flatten to nothing after the typical "fall," when unconsciousness ensues (and, presumably, the low and middle selves leave the physical body temporarily.)

(May I suggest here, for the benefit of students of these matters, that epilepsy is the result of habitual attacks by disembodied low spirits who are able to overcome the resident low self of the afflicted individual and absorb the vital force from his body in a matter of a few minutes, despite the struggle to prevent such robbery. It is evident that the vital force is removed, as shown by the final loss of consciousness, and the slow recovery of consciousness and strength in the following period. Vital force is made from the food we consume, and it is to be thought that after the robbery of vital force by a low self or even a subhuman spirit, the blood sugar is gradually oxidized to create more vital force. It is possible that the resident low and middle selves are forced out of the body while the robbery is taking place, and that they return only after a time, being guided back by a connecting cord or strong set of threads of shadowy body substance holding fast between them and the dense physical body. Hypnosis has been used with marked success, in cases which I have studied and observed, to stiffen the resistance of the patient to the periodic attacks. The problem is closely related to that of changes of "selves" in multiple personality cases, and to cases of obsession by spirits in which insanity results, and in which the invading spirit is often made so uncomfortable in its stolen body through insulin shock methods that it departs and allows the rightful owners of the body to return.)

The mechanism of projection of a part or of the main mass of the shadowy body (low or combined with the middle as in conscious astral travel), is something which will bear close study. At the present stage of this investigation upon which I am reporting, it cannot be said just how one is able to project a thread of shadowy body substance across the room, or the whole shadowy body mass across half a continent. The best guess seems to be that the magnetic nature of shadowy body stuff, when charged with vital force, and acted upon by the consciousness, results in the use of attraction or repulsion as a motive force. By analogy we can consider the action one of extending a "hand"—as the kahunas did. But when the mechanism is finally understood in its fullness, magnetism may play a large part, especially when it comes to explaining the almost violent attraction exerted to jerk the astral traveler back to his body when the latter is disturbed.

In mind-reading, as in telepathy, the thought forms of one person are not taken from him by another. It is evident that duplicate thought forms are created by the very act of sensing what thoughts are present in the mind of the subject or of a fellow operator in a telepathic exchange. It is also evident that, each time we recall a memory, we create a duplicate of it in the process of considering that memory. Thus a poem is learned by repeated remembering of its lines, and a repeated reduplication of the memories of the words and lines—until all associated thought form clusters are very strong and permanent and easily found and brought to the focus of consciousness by the low self. (Remember that the middle self cannot remember. It cannot store thought forms in its shadowy body, and, if separated at death from its partner low self, is unable to remember who or what it is or has been. It is indeed a sorry ghost in the separated condition.)

The low self stores all our memories in its low shadowy body, and after death, we are able to use those memories. They do not die with the decay of the brain tissues of the dead physical body. The annals of Psychical Research are replete with cases in which the dead returned to communicate with the living through mediumistic persons, or otherwise, and the very proof of a survival after physical death is based on the endless proofs that the dead remember the events of their physical life.

Case 14 Telepathy or Thought Transference Preliminary Notes:

Telepathy, like mind-reading, is a simple use of psychic powers which involves neither the spirits of the deceased nor the cooperation of the Superconscious or High Self.

It is surprising how little practice it takes to develop slight telepathic abilities in most people.

Detailed studies and reports on telepathic experiments may be found in any good library. Outstanding are books by Eileen Garrett, Upton Sinclair and Dunninger, the mind-reader of the stage who has endeavored to send telepathic impressions to those listening to his radio broadcasts. (There seems to be conflicting evidence as to the success of the radio experiment. If proved successful, it would mean that, if we apply the Huna theories, the human voice, even when turned into radio waves, and then back to sound by receiving sets, can still carry across a thread of shadowy body substance to connect the broadcaster and his listeners. This would seem to be an incredible mechanism, but there are others equally incredible which have been fairly well verified. In any event, we must not overlook even the slightest possibilities or clues to the ancient magical practices.)

In Tahiti there has been a famous use of telepathy for some years. It is called the "cocoanut radio," and appears to be a systematic sending of news by telepathy around the main island, beginning at the port village of Papeete. When events of news value occur at the port, the messages are sent telepathically to natives living at various places around the island, most of them elderly women. In various accounts which have been written, instances have been given in which the names and descriptions of visiting tourists were sent ahead of them as they journeyed around the island. They were expected wherever they arrived.

In far places in Africa news of British political decisions has been received hours and sometimes days before the official word has arrived, the natives acting as telepathic receivers, or as astral travelers bent upon gaining news of events important to their lives.

Dr. Rhine of Duke University has done more than any one man to make telepathy scientifically acceptable, and extrasensory perception a recognized part of Psychology.

The Case:

Checking Dr. Rhine's experiments with my friends in a group meeting each week in 1946, I found that several individuals had natural telepathic abilities. This increased during some months of weekly practice.

One evening, using the cards devised by Dr. Rhine, each bearing a simple figure or symbol, I seated myself at one end of a long room, and at the other end, facing me, placed a lady of good ability to act as recipient of my telepathic messages. I shuffled the cards, then turned them up one by one, glancing at each as it was turned up, and holding the intention to send a telepathic impression of the symbol to the recipient.

Nine cards were turned up and the symbol on each was promptly named. As this was the most perfect score yet attained in the group, those who formed the audience became excited and began to make distracting exclamations after the ninth consecutive correct call. The tenth card was mistaken. But nine out of nine is conclusive proof for our purposes, especially when there is so much proof of telepathy that our interest now fastens more on how it is done than on the fact that it is done.

Comment:

The mechanism of telepathic communication is the same as that of mind-reading except that both parties are aware of an effort to send thoughts from one to the other. Here we see again the relaxed and receptive state of the recipient, and the need for a connecting thread of shadowy body substance along which impressions or thought forms travel on a current of low voltage vital force.

At this point nothing will be said about the telepathic messages in which future events have been sensed by t the recipient, who took them to be impressions of present events. This will come later.

Case 15 Crystal Gazing and its Significance Preliminary Notes:

Crystal gazing or scrying is a very ancient practice in magic. The kahunas often placed round black stones in calabashes of water, swished the water over the stones to make their rounded surface shine, then gazed on the shining surface, and soon saw the characteristic visual images appear.

There is nothing about the crystal which makes it peculiarly useful for gazing purposes. Any bright and rounded surface will serve the purpose, as a water-filled round container, for instance. Images have been seen in like fashion in pools of ink poured in saucers, or even on blank plastered walls.

The images seen in the crystal by a relaxed and expectantly observing experimenter show every evidence of being dream images rather than actual images which could be photographed or which could be seen by several people at once.

In cases in which several people have reportedly seen the same image in the crystal, the image would become something similar to the visions seen by groups of people over battlefields or other places where past events were to be observed in process of visual reenactment.

The purely dream-like image is seen only by one individual, the actively engaged crystal gazer. The images are visual and they move, as in dreams, sometimes they are accompanied by impressions of sound, as in dreams.

The desire to see a given thing, place or person, acts to give the psychometric quality to crystal gazing, causing the projection of the shadowy body substance to contact some one or thing at a distance. Usually the projection follows an older thread which already connects the gazer with the thing to be seen. While this mechanism is not yet fully worked out, it seems that the image in the crystal is a dream impression produced by the subconscious self after it has extended its sensory perceptions as in mind-reading or telepathy, and has made observations of distant things or scenes and has brought back thought forms of the impressions, reconstructing them in the dream image centering around the crystal.

The Case:

Some years ago in Lovelock, Nevada, I carried on a series of experiments with a friend who had, under my instruction, developed in a few weeks very excellent abilities in crystal gazing.

The gazing crystal was a magnifying glass in the form of a paper weight. It was laid on dark cloth and was looked into while relaxed and desiring to see certain places or people. The best results were obtained if the gazer touched with her fingers a letter or some other object which had been in contact with the person she wished to see in the crystal.

Several of her friends and mine were seen in this way in the crystal, and by writing these friends to ask whether or not they had been seen correctly, a check was made on the results. The check showed a surprisingly accurate performance. One of my friends was seen to approach a mine tunnel with a camera and tripod. He sat down and read from a small black book until the miners came out of the mine, whereupon he photographed them and went away. This is a good example of a distant scene, people and set of actions, all correctly seen over a distance of about five hundred miles. The event took place at the time it was being seen in the crystal. (Sometimes events were seen before or after they actually took place.)

After I left Lovelock, I received daily letters from my crystal-gazing friend telling me what I had been seen to do each morning at a little before a given hour. Places and people seen by me were accurately described. One peculiarity was noted: When I went down into a mine, the vision in the crystal seemed unable to follow, but remained stationary on the ground surface and equipment at the head of the shaft. Later the image faded.

Comment:

There are cases on record which also show that the spirits of the deceased may play a part in creating and exhibiting the visual images associated with crystal gazing. A most interesting account (see Fodor) of such a case was given before the Dialectical Society by a Mr. F. Fusedale. His children were discovered crystal gazing with a silvered ball from their Christmas tree, having found by accident that they could see pictures in the ball. The children were able to sense the presence of a friendly spirit who was producing the images. The scenes were of distant lands and of landscapes in the spirit world, so the children stated. The parents also saw the images. Soon the ball was broken, and thereafter the spirit obligingly showed the moving and colored pictures on a white plaster wall. The parents were impressed by arctic scenes in which people and dogs moved as in life. A ship was caught in the ice.

Messages in writing have been seen in crystals.

The relation of crystal gazing to astral travel is apparent in cases in which a distant place is seen in the crystal, and then at the wish of the operator, the scenes are explored, as in one case by moving from room to room and observing what things and what people were in various parts of a large house.

The dream characteristic is seen in the nature of the image, it frequently being such as to give the impression of viewing actual scenes at close range, even standing in the midst of the scenes. A further suggestive angle is to be found in reported instances in which the operator imagined a scene or event, and it then built up as a visual image in the crystal, the event continuing to unfold. In this way an author was able to imagine an opening scene of a book she was to write, and when the image developed in the crystal, she sat back and watched the characters in her proposed novel enact step by step the action of unwritten and unplotted chapters. A few years ago in Hollywood one of my friends who was among the highest paid scenario writers of the day, told me that his ability to turn out such a large amount of screen material was the result of having the knack of beginning a story, then watching a plaster wall until images appeared there and moved through the length of the whole film. He would watch to the end, then write in scenario form what had been seen.

A sharp distinction, therefore, must be drawn between three kinds of images seen in the crystal or on a blank wall. (1) The dream-like image of a distant place or scene (or future event), (2) the visual images produced by spirits and which may be seen by several people at once (indicating a more substantial image than the subjective or dream image), and (3) the purely dream-like image produced first as imaginings (but with the creation of thought forms which may be used in producing a later image in the crystal) which have no relation to actual places or events at a distance or to future events which will take place in the surroundings foreseen.

The nature of the substance from which images are created, in cases where they are seen by several people at once, is uncertain. It is probable that the substance is similar to that from which thought forms are made, that is, shadowy body substance. (Later we will consider this substance in its relation to ectoplasm.)

CHAPTER IX

THE SIGNIFICANCE OF SEEING INTO THE FUTURE IN THE
PSYCHOMETRIC PHENOMENA AND IN DREAMS

To be able to see a future event before it occurs is even more
amazing than fire-walking. One can, by stretching a point,
imagine that there are physical explanations for fire-immunity,
but by no stretch of the imagination can a physical explanation be
given for seeing into the future.

It is all as clear as day. A future event has not yet transpired,
therefore it is utterly impossible to see it or know in exact detail
what that event will be. But, the impossible and incredible happens.
We actually see events before they occur, in dreams or visions. We
sense future occurrences and call this sensing "premonition."

There is a third "impossibility" which stands beside fire-immunity and prevision as proof that there are higher and little known
powers at work in this world of ours. This third thing is instant
healing—a matter which will be considered at much length later
on because of its great importance.

As a secondary, but most desirable and practical part of the
Huna lore of seeing future events, there is to be considered the
magical practice of changing the future in order to better events
which are seen and found to be undesirable. This magical art was
a large part of the work of the kahunas, for they healed both body
and purse—social and economic tangles.

While it is of the utmost importance that we recover Huna and
so add to our priceless store of human knowledge, it is even more
important that we learn the ancient methods of calling down instant healing and of gaining the help of the High Selves in changing and reconstructing the accidental future so that it becomes ordered, planned and fortunate.

As a matter of fact, it may be said that instant healing, or even
the slower psychological healing practiced by the kahunas, is directly related to changing the future. If a patient is very ill and is
suddenly healed, that change in itself marks a change in the ordinary course of the future in which the illness might have resulted
in eventual death.

Aside from the usual explanation that "God knows and shows
the future" in dreams, prevision, premonition or clairvoyance, call

it what we will, we moderns have nothing faintly resembling an explanation to offer. However, we have accumulated considerable information as to the occurrence of these glimpses of the future, and this information can be used to check against the theories of Huna—which are the only detailed and logical explanations mankind has ever evolved.

There are several items of popular belief or disbelief that need to be discussed briefly before going on. The first of these is part and parcel of most religions, and raises a question which only the kahunas can answer in a conclusive manner.

The Problem of Free Will and Premonition In religions, war has long raged between those who taught that man had free will to do as he pleased, and those who taught that, because God must (if rightly understood and evaluated as a Creator) know everything that each one of us will do in future, we have no free will—our every act being decided upon in advance by a Supreme Being, and, therefore, predestined, unchangeable and inevitable.

Science, in grappling with the problem, has taught that everything happens in a purely accidental manner and that free will is the answer. (Overlooking the fact which bothers the religionists, that the future can be, and often is, seen.)

The bare and uncompromising records of the Psychical Research Societies tell of many instances in which events have been foreseen, and have been avoided by what cannot be described as anything but the exercise of "free will" on the part of those who were warned. In "my own experience I had such a case.

One evening at a Spiritualistic seance I was told by an entranced medium that I was slated to have a bad auto accident in the near future. I countered by asking whether my friend, Bob, sitting at my right, was also to have an accident. After a pause, the answer came as, "No." I asked my friend to accompany me and help me watch for an accident-potent situation for the next few days. Three days later, we were driving through Honolulu, when, at a busy intersection, a drunken truck driver drove his truck at high speed from behind a street car and came directly at me. I happened at that instant to be watching a car crossing ahead of me on the opposite side. Bob, however, caught sight of the truck rushing toward us, seized the wheel and twisted it around, and at the same time shouted a warning. The result was that the partial turn made by my car allowed the truck driver to squeeze in ahead of me, crumpling a front fender instead of striking a disastrous blow full on the side of the car where I sat.

This incident is typical of the evidence which shows that the future which would normally occur can be foreseen, and that it is not unavoidable, providing one is able to take the proper steps to circumvent the aforeseen incident.

The question of the value of seeing future events is settled by the mass of proofs (my own experience being only one of thousands) showing that, once forewarned, we can take steps to change or evade future events. A moment's thought will show how valuable to humanity an extension of the faculty of premonition would be.

General or world conditions can be seen ahead and the individual can profit by such foresight. I have a friend who saw in a dream the financial crash of 1929, and who sold out all his stocks and invested in government bonds. He warned several acquaintances, but his warnings were not heeded, (the warnings were three months ahead of the crash, and all looked rosy) and some of the acquaintances were ruined.

THE KAHUNA EXPLANATION OF THE PROBLEM OF FREE WILL VERSUS PREDESTINATION is that the Aumakua or Superconscious "parental pair" of each of us has a form of mentation, or mental power, unlike our own. It is higher than the power of remembering which characterizes the low self, or the power of inductive reason which characterizes the middle self. It is such that (among other things) it enables the High Self to see those parts of the future which have been crystallized or "set." Much of the future is in a fluid or uncrystallized and unset state, and so cannot be seen. Great world events seem crystallized farthest in advance. In a like way the long-term events in the lives of individuals are set and may be seen—such events as marriage, accidents and death.

There is a very distinct philosophy in the kahuna beliefs concerning the element of free will enjoyed by the low and middle selves which live together in the human body to make the man. The High Self, which is connected to the body by a thread of the aka (kino mea) or invisible "shadowy body stuff" (and through this connection maintains contact) is under some compulsion to let the lower selves exercise free will and learn by experience UNLESS they desire and request guidance and help from the High Self, in which case the Aumakua takes a hand in the affairs of the man. Only in planning the long-term events in the life of the man is free will seemingly denied, but even then, if proper steps are taken to change those events, it is possible to circumvent them to a degree.

There seem to be two kinds of free will, one for the low self in its less highly evolved state as an animal, and, therefore, under the rule of some High Self which presides over physical growth and operations connected with the body itself. Because of this direct supervision, the body conforms to definite and set patterns, while the conscious mind or middle self, having more complete free will, has the privilege of dictating the external activities of the body, although not its internal vital functions.

It might be said that man has two High Selves, one for the low self and its guidance, and one for the middle self. The "group soul" idea of Theosophy closely checks with the High Self guiding the an- imal man, and with the idea that the lesser animals and creatures are also guided and informed through "instincts" by High Selves watching over them in groups. As we cannot penetrate the plane of consciousness just above ours—that of the High Selves—we cannot know to a certainty what the real state is in this relation. However, we can observe the many acts and conditions of living things on our levels and draw our conclusions. This also holds for our obser- vations when we see some mysterious Consciousness using some mysterious force, through some mysterious form of invisible mat- ter, to produce fire-immunity, instant healing, prevision, the mate- rial phenomena of Spiritualism, and so on and so forth.

The kahunas also believed that ALL PREMONITION COMES FROM THE HIGH SELF BY WAY OF THE LOW SELF or sub- conscious. This agrees with the known fact that we cannot, by any effort of the will, force ourselves to see into the future or dream of it. In hypnotized subjects, the order to look into the future is seldom obeyed, thus causing us to conclude that the subconscious (which alone is suggestible) does not have the ability to look into the future. If neither the low nor the middle self can see ahead at will and as a result of its own natural ability, we must look for another source of prevision—look to the Super-conscious or similar Higher Beings.

A proof that the kahunas were right in saying that all pre- monition must come through the low self, lies in the fact that we get visions, dreams or other forms of knowledge concerning future events, through the subconscious when it is relaxed—when it is let alone by the middle self. The most relaxed state for the low self, and the time when it is most completely free from the domination of the middle self, is during sleep. For this reason it is natural that premonitory dreams are the most common sources of knowledge of future events. In crystal gazing there is a similar relaxation but of a lesser degree. The middle self stands by in a waking state to observe what is sensed by the low self through the images centering around the crystal. In telepathy the low self is also the agent performing all the work, and it has to be allowed to slip the ordinary control of the middle self and relax in order to project its "finger" of invisible shadowy substance, and so contact the person from whom a telepathic or mind-reading impression is to be gained.

The verification of the kahuna belief that the low self is the one which performs all psychic acts, always comes back to the indisputable fact that our best known self, the middle self or conscious mind, cannot, under any circumstance, use its will to force us to produce psychic action. We can only give the order to the low self and then let go of it so that, in a relaxed condition, it can set to work, exercise its psychic abilities, and present to us through our mutual center of consciousness the information obtained.

In getting information concerning the present, the low self can reach out and read minds or gather telepathic impressions directed to it by another, and otherwise act on its own initiative; but when it comes to the future, it must contact (as in telepathy) the High Self, and ask that it be given glimpses of the part of the future which has crystallized and which would, therefore, be visible.

THE MAKING OF THE FUTURE, according to the kahunas, depends upon the plans and desires of the lesser selves. These plans and desires, (and, unfortunately our fears) are made into thought forms (composed also of shadowy body stuff) and are used by the High Self in some seemingly automatic process of constructing the future for the individual. Just how this mechanism works is uncertain, as it belongs to the next higher level of consciousness, but the kahunas spoke of the thought forms as "seeds," which were taken by the Aumakua and made to grow into future events or conditions.

The kahunas considered it of great importance for the individual to take time out at frequent intervals to think about his life and decide in exact terms what he wished to do or wished to have happen. The average person is too much inclined to let the low self take the helm, which is dangerous because it lives under the domination of the animal world where things happen illogically and as if by accident. It is the business and duty of the middle self, as guide for the low self, to use its power of inductive reason and its will (to control the low self) in making plans for the task of living, and seeing that proper efforts are made to work according to those plans.

The average person, especially if emotional (an indication that the low self is too much in charge) changes plans too often, also changes desires. The result is the making of a mixture of contradictory thought forms of plans, wishes and fears, from which the High Self, perforce, makes a mixture of future events fully as unsatisfactory and inconclusive.

A large part of the kahuna's magical practice in days gone was aimed at seeing what crystallized future lay ahead for the client, then procuring changes in that future to make it more desirable. (Later on we will take up exhaustively the methods used by the kahunas and the nature of the difficulties to be overcome.)

Dreams are the open door to premonition. Research has disclosed the fact that in our dreams we are given to see the future almost nightly, but that we do not remember the dreams, and so remain unaware of what is to come except by vague uneasiness stemming from the depths of the low self.

Little is known of dreams, although there has been much conjecture and much muddled thinking about dream conditions. One thing, however, stands out clearly, and that is the fact that the low self has a peculiar knack of confusing things sensed in dreams with things familiar to it, frequently joining one idea to another through a process of association, to make a SYMBOL.

The practice of psychoanalysis is largely based upon a study of these symbols as they appear in remembered dreams, or in thoughts which come into the mind of the patient when he is in a state of relaxation brought about (in some cases) by suggestion or mild drugs.

Dr. Nandor Fodor, one of the leaders in this field and now practicing in New York, writes in his many articles on the subject, of a curious thing observed in psychoanalysis. It is that certain symbols mean the same thing even when found in the dreams of many different people, none of whom are acquainted with the others. This seems to be more than a coincidence, and points in the direction of the group soul, as do similar instincts with similar reactions in creatures lower than man.

It is to be concluded that a direct "seeing" of a future event may be passed on to us by the low self, or, it may pause to mix what it sees or senses with things already known to it, thus producing a symbol which the middle self will have to try to understand.

In her valuable book, Telepathy, Eileen J. Garrett tells of the frequency with which telepathic messages are received in a form which is partly symbolic. She found that her pupils, in learning telepathy, soon became expert in grasping the meaning behind the symbols which came to them repeatedly.

Mrs. Garrett describes her sensations when sending telepathic messages, and writes that she has the feeling that her five senses are tied to something like a white beam which she sends here and there with an effort of will to contact those to whom a message is to be sent. When this "white beam" (she does not speak of it as a beam of light) meets an obstacle, it bends around it.

The obstacle is felt but not seen, as a rule. This "white beam" corresponds to the kahuna idea of a "finger" of shadowy body substance which is projected by the low self, feeling or following with great speed along the threads of shadowy substance which already have been fastened and established as contact or connecting mechanisms between individuals who have once met.

Mrs. Garrett also describes the sensation experienced frequently by those who practice telepathy—the sensation of faint electric tingling or warmth, often accompanied by a tactile response of "goose-flesh" when a working contact has been made. In her own case these sensations often warn her that a message is being projected to her by someone and that her attention is needed to receive it.

Deep breathing is a common preliminary to telepathic practice or other forms of psychometrizing—all these related forms depending on the movement of thought forms along a thread of connecting shadowy body stuff. Deep breathing seems to help in getting the low self to relax and set to work. Impressions come frequently as from below the solar plexus, which has been considered the main seat of the low self when sending out or receiving messages or sensory impressions.

A slightly different phase of telepathy is one in which distant scenes appear before the inner eye. This is often called "clairvoyance," and it occasionally includes glimpses of events that will transpire in the future.

According to the kahunas, any glimpse or knowledge of the future which comes in connection with psychic practices, must be given by the High Self. Mrs. Garrett writes very clearly of her sense of greater alertness and of her quickening perceptions when she makes contact with what she has called the "superconscious," and from her statements, it is to be deduced that she contacts the same High Self described in the Huna philosophy. A similar increase in lucidity and a similar sharpening of the senses and perceptions has been mentioned by other psychics, particularly when they were fully or partially out of the physical body, either in a state known as "astral projection" or when they had left the body while a controlling spirit used it during trance states.

After these explanations and comments a better understanding of the case materials given in the next chapter will be possible. It must always be kept in mind that this is a very important part of magic, and that it needs understanding in careful detail to become practical in our hands, as it was in the hands of the kahunas.

CHAPTER X

THE EASY WAY TO DREAM INTO THE FUTURE

Case 16 Learning to Dream into the Future Preliminary Notes:

J. W. Dunn, in his popular book, An Experiment with Time, describes a simple and very easy method which he learned to use to dream into the future. The method is based on the fact that most of us dream of future events but do not remember the dreams upon awakening.

A pencil and paper is taken to bed with the experimenter and he impresses upon himself the determination to write down his dreams whenever he awakens during the night and can recall what he was dreaming.

(Most people dream from the moment they fall asleep until they awaken, even if they seldom remember a dream and so conclude that they seldom dream.)

Mr. Dunn kept a record of dreams which he had written down in the night, and found in some instances that he had dreamed of certain events in his life fifteen years before they occurred. One of these events was important enough to have been crystallized long in advance. It was a dream of flying over a pasture in one of the crude planes of the early experimental years of flight. He also tabulated the results obtained by his friends, and concluded that almost anyone can use the method successfully.

In passing, it may be noted that he met the problem of the impossibility of seeing what had not yet happened, by the simple expedient of deciding that the past, present and future of time are all right here with us, but that we cannot see beyond the instant of the present when events become momentarily actualized. Like Ouspensky in his Tertium Organum, Mr. Dunn falls back on the idea of a "space-time complex," leaps from that to a fourth dimension, and ends with little more than a play on words.

The Case:

I read An Experiment with Time on a Sunday afternoon in Honolulu in 1926. That night I took pencil and paper to bed with me, determined to write down all my dreams in order that I might watch for those relating, not to the past or present, but to the future. It was a restless night and I arose in the morning with several dreams and one drawing of a crude kind on my pad of paper. My notes ran like this: (I omit all dreams which did not come true.)

Strange, big, fattish man. Came to me and asked if I would help him on an invention—something of an optical nature.... Was at my desk. Had before me a piece of a smallish machine, about two feet six inches by four inches in size. Black electrical cord and white one running from the rear end of the thing. It looked like a black enamelled lid. In a side of this lid, or cap, was a square hole about four inches by four inches. On the top of the lid was an hourglass-shaped setscrew of blued steel. (I made the rough drawing here, of the lid.) ... I was in a latticed, low kitchen. Fat man there. Stranger also there, tall, slim, light, and about forty. Small Hawaiian woman there. I took sensitive paper from a box and placed it in a small opening in the machine. The thin man touched a switch and a light flashed. I took out the paper and developed it in one of three strange little white photo trays. The developed image was a scale, and a pointer which indicated a large number. I looked at the men. We laughed. I said, "Well, it works."

That was on Sunday night. On the following Thursday afternoon the dreams began to come true. The fat man I had seen in my dreams came into my camera store. He wanted help in splitting a ray of light to get an image of a weight-scale on a ground glass screen and a strip of recording photo paper at the same time. The top of the mechanism of the scale was described to me. It checked with the "lid" I had seen in my dream. I agreed to help him.

The next part of my dream was wrong. The lid was never brought to me and I never had it before me on my desk. I did not see it until after the mechanism I worked out, and which was built in a local machine shop, was completed. I saw it later, however, in the latticed kitchen of my dream. The tall, light man of my dream was the mechanic on the job, and it was his kitchen. The small Hawaiian woman was also there. She was his wife. The machine was used for weighing sugar syrup in sugar refineries.

When the problem had been solved and the mechanic had made changes in the machine at my direction, I went for the last time to the latticed kitchen to test the machine with sensitized paper. As it happened, I had acquired the unfamiliar little white photo trays in a trade only the day before. They were of Japanese manufacture and of a type and material I had never seen.

The results of the test were exactly as I dreamed them, except that we all exclaimed laughingly, "Well, it works!" for I had told of my dreams by then and had exhibited the notes.

I also dreamed of several other future events during this period of experimentation, but no dream sequence was ever again so filled with people, mechanisms and places so strange to me as to be entirely beyond the chance of imagining them beforehand.

Comment:

It will be noted that dreams of the future are not given primarily as warnings of accidents, deaths or other troubles. The ordinary life with its normal daily events are seen for the most part. It is for this reason that the average person finds little more than a temporary interest in using the Dunn method, and soon finds that a night of unbroken sleep is preferable to seeing into the future in a hit and miss fashion.

While my own interest was keen for a time, I, like most others, soon tired of the experiment. I then made the mistake of grumbling to myself when sleepily struggling to write down a dream. The light, when turned on so that I could see to write, hurt my eyes, and soon my low self got the idea that the whole matter was undesirable. It formed a complexed opinion of the matter, and thereafter seemed to refuse to pass on to me any picture of a future event which it obtained.

In the light of my experience, I strongly advise the beginner to provide himself with a weak night light which will not hurt the eyes when turned on. Above all, tell your sleep self what a pleasure it is to awaken and write down dreams. Of course, if one has a recording instrument and can press the button and speak the description of the dreams into the mouthpiece, that is the ideal equipment. Also, if my experience is a criterion, one will learn inside a month to know by some inward sense whether a dream belongs to the future and is worth recording or whether it is a common dream with little or no significance.

The field of the sleep state offers great possibilities for experimentation in other ways. There seems to be no better time for suggestion to enter the low self than during normal sleep. And this form of suggestion does not need the hypnotic force which we associate with hypnotic suggestion. The spoken word is enough. It may be spoken by a machine on which a carefully prepared record is placed. The record may be started during the night by a clock, made to repeat, or play through and stop. An under-the-pillow speaker may be used. In any event the words are to be played with low volume, and in a few nights they will cease to awaken one. The low self, which remains sensitive to sound during sleep, seems to hear the worded suggestion and make thought forms automatically of those words. These thought forms lodge in the shadowy body of the low self and remain there unaffected by the usual rationalizing process to which they would be subjected during wakening moments.

Rationalizing by the middle self is a process of tying to the words and thoughts of a suggestion a contradictory string of thought forms saying that the suggestion is not workable. For this reason, one using the recorded suggestions during sleep will do well to assure himself that the things which he elects to have read as suggestions by the machine during his sleep are acceptable, and that the low self will respond and make them workable. This attitude of the middle self, which is one of confident expectancy, leaves the low self freely open to accept the suggestions made at night and to react to them more and more fully as the nightly repetition goes on.

Most of us are smothered by our inhibitions and habits. From childhood our failures build in us complexed beliefs in our inability. We suffer from fear complexes. We are afraid of people, or even of God. The list is long. Much illness results from fixations. For this reason the recorded suggestion given through sleep needs careful consideration, and, when it comes to learning to cause the low self to deliver our telepathic prayers for instant healing to the High Self, the records may play a splendid part in the high magic.

While mention should be made of the fact that hypnotized subjects have often been reported as telling of events before they occurred, it is only as by accident that such prevision comes. It cannot be had upon command of the hypnotic operator, which again offers proof that the subconscious—which responds to suggestion—does not have the ability to see the future, but must have the future shown it by a being of superior mental powers—the kahunas say by the Aumakua or High Self.

For the student wishing to examine the record of premonitory abilities infrequently displayed by hypnotized subjects, the book by Richet, Thirty Years of Psychic Research, is available in most good libraries.

Case 17 Foreknowledge in Ordinary Dreaming Preliminary Notes:

Dreams which foretell the future are of several kinds. One of the most common is that in which the dreamer dreams of a symbol, and, when awake, translates the symbol and predicts the general nature of the event. For instance, a gentleman of my acquaintance would sometimes dream of seeing a fine red bull. This was for him the symbol of a lucky happening to come, and it was seldom that a fortuitous event did not follow soon after such a dream.

Another kind of dream mixes symbols with events from both past and future. Often the mixing distorts the events appearing in the dream. I once dreamed of seeing a store window filled with leaping monkeys who flourished fountain pens and wrote very long marks with them on moving curls of paper. Later in the same week I recognized the store window of my dreams when I saw a toy monkey dancing on a revolving table. In the opposite window a small machine was on display in which a paper cylinder revolved under the point of a fountain pen making miles of line to show the large ink capacity.

The dream which touches only the future event and shows it clearly and unmixed, may also move from one point in time ahead to others. This type of dream is the most deserving of study and cultivation. My father, at a certain time in my boyhood, had many such dreams. He would recount them at the breakfast table and ask us to remember them and help him check later to see how accurate they were—he recognized them by an inner sensing as dreams belonging to the future.

The Case:

My father dreamed of a valley in which sheep moved through the Wyoming sage. This time progressed, and in the same valley he saw a railroad being built. Another leap forward, and a town occupied the valley on one side of the railroad. On the opposite side a coal mine was opened and working. Behind the town an oil derrick stood. The final step ahead in time showed the same valley, but with everything gone except the rail line and the foundations of the vanished buildings.

This dream of a single night covered a period of about ten years. Father later recognized the valley and saw the new rail line pass through it, then a town, Spring Valley, Wyo., rise, the coal mine open, the oil well drilled near the town and later plugged. Soon the mine proved too dangerous to work because of gas, and the Union Pacific, which owned everything, removed all structures, leaving the valley as last seen in the dream. (I personally saw the valley in these various stages.)

Comment:

At the time my father had this dream, the coal vein at Spring Valley had not been discovered. It was only after the rail line had been laid that the discovery was made and the mine opened. It may be said with authority that in this dream there was no reading of the mind of another person. It was a straight, clear and detailed viewing of events of which no living man could have had knowledge at the time.

We are forced to conclude (1) that some intelligent being or form of consciousness had been able to foresee the future of the valley, and, in doing so, it demonstrated a form of mental power much superior to that of the conscious or subconscious selves. (This checks with the High Self of the kahuna system.) Or, (2) we have the alternative of concluding that the subconscious has the ability to see into the future, but this is a fallacy proven by its inability to see the future under hypnotic command.

Case 18 Seeing the Future Through Crystal Gazing Preliminary Notes:

Crystal gazing produces a condition of relaxation in which the low self is able to enter a state similar to that of sleep, with the difference that the middle self is able to stand by and observe the dream-like images which appear in the crystal.

The Case:

(A) I have already mentioned the lady who lived at Lovelock, Nevada, and who learned the art of "scrying" as it was called in ancient times. Not only was she able to find my friends at a distance and see what they were doing, she was also able to make a spoken request for vision of future events and, frequently, to get them in her crystal.

Two sittings were devoted to trying to look into the future to see what lay ahead for me. At that time I was traveling from town to town making photographs, and I was about to go to places which I had not visited before. In fact, I had not decided what those places were to be. During these sittings she saw two detailed and complete parts of my future, each covering a period of about a week.

Looking into her crystal, she saw a picture begin to take form in color and motion. She described it to me as it moved and changed from scene to scene. First there was a small town, laid out in neat streets on either side of a railroad line. There was a station and she saw me getting off a train with bags and cameras. The picture changed and she saw me entering a modern brick hotel. Next she saw me standing on a cottage porch talking to a red-haired young woman dressed in white, and holding on her arm a baby with red hair. A following scene showed Indians encamped not far from the hotel and holding some kind of a meeting. I was taking pictures of the camp.

This foreseeing proved to be correct in every detail in less than a month. I took a train to Mason, Nevada, and, upon arriving, recognized the town and hotel as ones which had been described. During my stay I met the woman dressed in white who had red hair, and made photographs of her red-headed baby. Two days after my arrival, Indians began to pour into the town for the annual conclave of the tribes of the Carson Sink region. They camped near the hotel and I made many pictures of the camp and of the Indians.

(B) A second town, which I visited after leaving Mason, was Yerrington, Nevada. It was exactly as it had been seen in the crystal. I left the railroad in a stage and traveled a couple of miles to find the town just as described, one built along an old main road, with almost no side streets. I watched for a rooming house bearing a sign, "Globe Rooming House," with a picture of a globe painted underneath, and it soon came into sight. I knew that this was the place where I was to stay, and, after getting down and ringing the bell, I watched hopefully to see whether or not the woman with "dark hair and slightly crossed eyes" would appear. She did, and, as it turned out, she became my good friend, helping me to get business and lending me some much appreciated books on occultism.

Comment:

The advantage of crystal gazing over ordinary dreaming is apparent. In the former one decides what is desired in the way of forevision, and in the latter, one has to take what can be intercepted in haphazard manner from dreams.

An interesting angle is to be seen in this mechanism through which the future is seen. While in other sittings no vision of the future appeared in answer to a request, there were other times when prevision came without request. The requests were spoken aloud without knowing to whom they were to be addressed, and it is surprising that there were any answers at all.

Seeing into the future is contrary to present scientific beliefs, as are fire-walking and instant healing. Science has no explanation to offer and is stalemate on these points, but the kahunas show the way ahead for those of open mind who are ready to investigate the evidence which has been accumulated.

Case 19 Premonitory Information Through Spirits of the Dead
Preliminary Notes:

According to the kahunas, all contact with the spirits of the dead—as with the High Self—is made by the low self. This applies in particular to the spirits in their invisible state in which they must be seen or sensed by what we may call "psychic" ability, which is nothing more nor less than the ability to relax and let the low self see and report anything from ordinary dreams, to "seeings" of the past, the present or the future.

It is reasonable to believe that when we die and become "spirits" we have only the mental powers we had during life. The act of dying does not make the lower selves into a Superconscious with the ability to look into the future. However, we have the same ability to contact the High Self and ask for vision of the future, and, if we are able to make our presence known to the low self of a living person, we may be able to pass on, through it, information we have obtained on the other side.

There is an alternate method by which one relaxes and lets the spirit of a dead person enter the body and speak through its lips. This is not an uncommon method. It is used by "mediums," and is highly approved by Spiritualism. It is studied by Psychical Research, and condemned by the Church and by reactionary Science.

In this state of trance when spirits are speaking through the medium, they are, as if by accident, sometimes able to foretell the future correctly. They cannot do so at will, which tends to prove that the High Self must give such information to the spirits of the dead as well as to the low selves of the living.

The records of Psychical Research are replete with instances in which spirits have correctly foretold the future, and with instances in which they have tried to do so and failed dismally. The failure has been so frequent that it has caused Spiritualism to be looked upon with question.

At spiritualistic seances as well as with the Ouija Board and similar mechanisms, the low self of a dead person, when it has been cut off from its middle self by some accident of dying, loves to communicate with the living. Being unable to use good reasoning powers (inductive), it tries to answer any question put to it, usually guessing (or reading the mind) what the sitters expect to hear by way of an answer. In this fashion no end of seeming lies are told by the spirits and Spiritualism given a black eye. When we learn to tell the difference between these isolated low self visitors and the regulation normal spirit having both a low and middle self, we will not be deceived so often.

The Case:

(A) At breakfast, when I was a lad, my mother told the family that she had awakened in the night and had seen her sister, May, who lived in San Francisco. (We lived in Wyoming). She had appeared misty and had said that she had died and that it was her wish that her two children be taken and reared by my mother. The next day a telegram came telling of the sudden death of May. The two children were, as requested by the ghostly mother, taken into our family to be reared.

(B) A spirit speaking through the well-known Australian medium, Mrs. Foster Turner, at a seance in February, in 1914 with Sir Arthur Conan Doyle, gave the following premonitory information (which later turned out to be correct).

"Now, though at present there is not a whisper of a great European war at hand, yet I want to warn you that before this year, 1914, has run its course, Europe will be deluged in blood. Great Britain, our beloved nation, will be drawn into the most awful war the world has ever known. Germany will be the great antagonist, and will draw other nations in her train. Austria will totter to its ruin. Kings and kingdoms will fall. Millions of precious lives will be slaughtered, but Britain will finally triumph and emerge victorious."

This sitting was in a hall and the prediction was heard by nearly a thousand people composing the audience.

Comment:

Knowing that the future can be foreseen, it takes no great
stretch of imagination to grasp the kahuna idea of a High Self with
superior mental powers which enable it to see ahead. But, and this
is far more difficult, we cannot so easily imagine this ability at
work when it passes from a general prediction, such as we might
make by guessing at the outcome of present conditions, to the detailed prediction. If the High Self used the type of reason that we
middle selves use, it could only guess, and as it gives small details,
there is either a magnificently superior form of reasoning or super-
reasoning brought into play, or, as the kahunas believed, the future event or condition is actually a real thing, formed though it is
of invisible shadowy body (aka or mea) substance similar to that of
which thought forms are composed.

If the High Selves, working in a UNION or ONENESS quite
beyond our comprehension, take the deeds and thoughts and desires of the world of middle and low self humanity, and, averaging
all these, produce the pattern of the future, then that pattern is visible on the High Self plane of consciousness, and all its details are
crystallized and set in so far as the main pattern is determined.

These conditions bring home to us the fact that the High Self
has powers of mentation so greatly superior to ours that we can
hardly conceive of them, to say nothing of the impossibility of understanding how they work. We can know so little. We must speculate so much. However, all we really need to know to be able to
make practical use of our semi-knowledge is the part we must play
to gain the aid of the High Self to shape our future toward health,
success, and more kindly living and service.

The kahunas believed that the great events of the future were
set and could be foreseen far ahead. World or national events might
be seen hundreds or even thousands of years ahead. The future of
the individual, because of the shortness of a human life time, could
be seen only months or years ahead.

The kahunas demonstrated constantly their ability to foresee
the future of the individual and gain the aid of the High Self to
change it for the better. From this we can conclude that the future
of the world and nations might also be foreseen and changed by
concerted effort, were we sufficiently enlightened. Today, when we
consider the possible use of the atom bomb as a weapon, we might,
if greed did not rule the world, still be able to take such concerted

action as to change what appears—even to our blind eyes—to be inevitable disaster.

Unfortunately, the majority of mankind is moved by greed and the animal instincts of the low self with its complexed and unreasoning hates and fears, rather than by the unemotional logic of the middle self. Few indeed listen to the promptings of the High Self where the rule of Love and Service holds sway.

Our conscious mind selves may be said to rule the world, but they are dominated by the low selves which are still animals, willful, savage and unthinking. As middle selves we have been given free will, but until our cumulative world experience is sufficient to teach us the lessons we must learn, we will use that gift of free will very badly, both as individuals and as nations.

The kahunas taught that there was an ideal condition to which the individual might aspire. It was a condition in which the aid and guidance of the High Self was requested, received, and then acted upon. The one rule of life that must be obeyed was that we should do nothing to hurt another. For those more advanced, the rule included loving service. Love can unite men and enable them to do great works for the good of all. Hate and fear can unite men only for war and destruction.

When the kahunas were at their best in Polynesia, they taught the people to live without hurting others. Those who willfully hurt others were considered worthy of death, and were frequently punished with the death prayer. It was the means of developing in Polynesia the most friendly and considerate people in the entire world. All the early explorers marveled at this and mentioned it in their writings without exception. It was the nearest approach to a Golden Age during the span of time covered by recorded history.

CHAPTER XI

INSTANT HEALING THROUGH THE HIGH SELF. THE PROOFS AND METHODS

At the Christian shrine at Lourdes, doctors have examined those who have come hoping to be healed. For over fifty years records have been kept of those who have been healed. These records detail the afflictions, give the time consumed in the healing, and the condition after healing.

There are two kinds of miraculous healing. The first is so rapid that it may be called instant healing. In a matter of seconds, or, at most, minutes, the diseased or deformed parts or tissues of the body are changed to healthy normal ones.

The second kind of healing is like the first except that the process of replacing abnormal tissues may take a few days. It seems to depend upon a great speeding up of normal healing processes.

Those who come to pray for others, rather than for themselves, seem more apt to be healed than those who pray for themselves alone.

Nearly all the ills common to man have been healed in this way. Cancers have vanished, deformed bones have been straightened, sight and hearing have been restored—the list is blessedly long.

Case 20 A Kahuna Heals A Broken Bone Instantly Preliminary Notes:

Religion explains the miracle by saying that God or a Saint or other Superhuman Being performs the miracle of instant healing, but, as in the case of fire-walking and seeing the future (and changing it), only the kahunas have offered detailed explanations of how such things are accomplished. Our one and only hope of learning to get miracles performed by the Higher Beings, as a matter of daily occurrence, in any place, lies in close study and understanding of the beliefs and practices of the kahunas. It may well be objected that praying Christians and Mental Healers sometimes get miraculous cures of both body and purse. This is, happily, true. But they do not get them with certitude. There are a million failures to one successful demonstration. While the kahunas did not always succeed in gaining the help of a High Self each time they asked, their average of success was so high that there can be little comparison.

Dr. Brigham was fortunate enough to be able to study several cases of instant healing performed by kahunas, but the most simple case to come to my attention was the following.

The Case:

My close and trusted friend, J. A. K. Combs, of Honolulu, who is a fellow student of kahuna lore, and who has given me much invaluable aid, had for a grand-mother-in-law one of the most powerful women kahunas in the Islands. She loved Combs and told him many things about her secret knowledge, her power, and her practices. On the occasion in question, Combs attended a beach party at her country home. Many guests had arrived when a car drove up to the edge of the beach sand and several Hawaiians got out. Among them was a man who was slightly intoxicated. He missed his step from car to soft sand and fell. As he fell, there was the characteristic snapping sound of breaking bones.

Inspection showed a compound fracture of the left leg just above the ankle. The bone ends pressed visibly out against the skin. Combs, who had heard the familiar sound of breaking bones and had himself suffered such a break, realized the seriousness of the injury and proposed that the man be taken at once to Honolulu for treatment, but the elderly kahuna arrived on the scene and took over. Kneeling beside the injured man she straightened the foot and leg, pressing on the place where the ends of the broken bones pushed out the skin, and then began a low chanted prayer for healing. In a short time she fell silent. Those who stood about watching tensely could see nothing until her hands suddenly moved slightly on the man's leg, and she took them away, saying quietly in Hawaiian, "The healing is finished. Stand up. You can walk."

The injured man, now entirely sobered, rose wonderingly to his feet, took a step, and then another. The healing was complete and perfect. The leg showed no indication of the break in any way.

Comment:

The kahuna explanation of instant healing is one which involves (1) a High Self with a superior form of mentality and with ability to do the work. (2) The high voltage of vital force or mana, natural to all High Selves, and used in all miraculous works. And (3) the flesh, bone and blood (technically these are all known as bodily "tissues") of the injured limb (taking the case above as an example), and the aka or shadowy body of the patient, particularly that part of it which duplicated the broken section of the leg.

The shadowy body of the low self is a mold of every cell of the body, also of its general shape, so the kahunas believed. To heal a broken bone, the High Self dissolved the injured bone and other tissues into ectoplasm, this usually being invisible, but not always. As the shadowy body mold is made of invisible (etheric?) substance, it cannot be broken or injured. Thus, with the mold of the normal leg there at hand, the ectoplasmic material of the dissolved parts is resolidified in the mold, with the result that the healing is instant and the limb is restored to its former condition.

This explanation applies equally to all healing in which abnormal conditions of deformity or disease prevail. If there is a cancer, it is changed to ectoplasmic substance and then made into normal tissue to fill the mold of that part of the body as it was before the cancer developed.

While the kahuna explanation is simple to state in general terms, it must be noted that there are certain conditions which must be made right, if they exist, before healing is granted. There must be no complexed doubt or conviction of sin or guilt that has not been cleared away. What has been called "faith" is a condition of freedom from any hindering complex.

The COMPLEX or FIXATION OF IDEAS was referred to by one kahuna as the "thing eating inside." It is a belief or conviction held by the low self. It may or may not be a correct belief. Once it is fixed or lodged in the memory of the low self, it is difficult to find and more difficult to remove.

Modern psychology, fortunately, has explored the subconscious and found the complex, making it unnecessary to go to great lengths to prove that the kahunas were right in believing that such things existed and caused trouble.

One thing, however, which modern psychology has not yet learned, but which the kahunas knew to their profit, is the fact that all efforts to remove a complex will be far more successful if those efforts include a combination of logical appeal to the patient's conscious self, mild suggestion, and the use of a physical stimulus to accompany the administering of suggestion.

The low self is so accustomed to having the middle self think of imaginary things, that anything resembling an imagining is paid scant attention. The low self is best impressed by REAL AND

TANGIBLE THINGS. For instance, the water used in religious ceremonies to "wash away sins" is something tangible, and therefore impressive to the low self. The kahunas have used water in ceremonial washing of the patient while giving the spoken suggestion that all sins are being washed away. They have used many other physical stimuli—for perhaps ten thousand years.

Proof that the broken bone, in the case given above, was dissolved into invisible etheric substance or ectoplasm, and then made solid again as bone in the unbroken mold of the shadowy body— such proof—is difficult to give because nothing is to be seen by the observer.

For this reason it is necessary to call attention to the findings of Spiritualism and Psychical Research, for in these we find visible and tangible bodily tissues and other substances which have been seen to vanish into nothingness and to reappear—a process called "dematerialization" and "materialization."

Little need be said about the verification of these findings. So many cases have been verified by trained investigators that it is no longer possible to deny the actuality of the phenomena touched upon in this part of the study of kahuna beliefs.

Case 21 Proof Through Apports Preliminary Notes:

Because of the inability of Science to explain the phenomena of Spiritualism, it has been customary for the press and schools to ignore them. For this reason the average person knows little or nothing of such phenomena.

Take the matter of apports. There are volumes of detailed reports covering instances in which objects have appeared or disappeared in a way quite contrary to the accepted laws of physics. At Stanford University there are a number of cases filled with apported objects produced as from the void by spirits attending the seances of the famous apport medium, Bailey. And yet, these amazing happenings are kept from the public at large.

An apport is something which is dissolved into invisible form at one spot, is carried to a desired place, and solidified to the original state. Spirits of the dead are usually associated with the process.

It has been said by way of objection, that the spirit of a dead man could not do things a living man cannot do. This objection is logical enough to throw the unsound present theories of Psychical

Research into a turmoil, but not the theories of the kahunas. The kahunas put forth the belief that the spirits of the dead, just as do the spirits of the living, in the body, sometimes gain contact with a High Self and get it to use the high voltage of vital force to dematerialize, and later rematerialize, the substances contained in the shadowy body mold of the apported object. It was believed by the kahunas that all things had a shadow body.

We know that when the voltage of an electric current or discharge is sufficiently high in atom-smashing machines, various elements are transmuted and become other elements. Knowing this, we may agree that the mana or electro-vital force in man, when stepped up to the highest voltage, can be used to change visible matter to the invisible form, and back again to the visible.

In making such changes—so we are told by Science—there would be generated great heat and cold. But, as the High Self is able to control temperature changes in fire-walking, it would have no difficulty in exerting a similar control in causing the apporting of objects and things.

Living creatures have been frequently used as apports, and have ranged from tiny insects through birds, fish, beasts and men. Hot objects have been apported, and remained hot upon their arrival.

The Cases:

(A) Ernesto Bozzano, one of the most famous Psychical Research leaders, reported an apport case which will well illustrate the matters under discussion.

"In March, 1904, in a sitting in the house of Cavaliere Peretti, in which the medium was an intimate friend of ours, gifted with remarkable physical medium-ship, and with whom apports could be obtained at command, I begged the communicating spirit to bring me a small block of pyrites which was lying on my writing table over a mile away. The spirit replied (through the mouth of the entranced medium) that the power was almost exhausted, but that all the same he would make the attempt. Soon after the medium sustained the usual spasmodic twitchings which signified the arrival of an apport, but without hearing the fall of any object on the table or on the floor. We asked for an explanation from the spirit-operator, who informed us that although he had managed to disintegrate a portion of the object desired, and had brought it into the room, there was not enough power for him to be able to reintegrate it. He added, 'Light the light.' We did so, and found, to our great surprise, that the table, the clothes and hair of the sitters, as well as the furniture and carpet of the room, were covered with the thinnest layer of brilliant impalpable pyrites. When I returned home after the sitting I found the little block of pyrites lying on my writing table. Missing from it was a large fragment, about one-third of the whole piece, which had been scooped out."

(B) A medium named Mrs. Guppy, who was a woman of wealth and note in the early days of Spiritualism, gave a sitting with her friends for Henry W. Longfellow in Italy. At the sitting a block of ice over a foot square was brought as an apport and dropped with a crash on the table. At a second sitting, while the famous poet was holding both the medium's hands, several oranges were apported. At still another sitting, in which the spirit spoke through the medium and asked what things were desired, the following items were apported: A banana, two oranges, a bunch of white grapes, a bunch of black grapes, a cluster of filberts, three walnuts, half a dozen damsons, a slice of candied pineapple, an onion, a peach, some almonds, three figs, two apples, four very large grapes, a potato, and several other objects. At still another sitting there were apports of pots of scalding hot tea and sizzling pans of frying eggs. Mrs. Guppy herself was brought as an apport from her own home to that of a friend. The distance was over a mile, and Mrs. Guppy was very stout.

(C) In 1926 at the British College of Psychic Science, Mrs. Barkel, a medium, saw the "shadow" of a bunch of violets near an electric light globe overhead. That evening, in the same room, at a sitting with the apport medium, Heinrich Melzer, a quantity of violets dropped from empty air on to the table.

(D) One of the most famous and most studied mediums of the past century was Mme. d'Esperance. A spirit called "Yolande" frequently appeared, fully materialized as a pretty Arab girl, in good light and produced apports so that the sitters could observe all that was to be seen in the process. On June 28, 1890, she brought as an apport a rare golden lily measuring more than seven feet from roots to top and carrying eleven perfect flowers. Toward the end of the sitting she tried to dematerialize the plant to take it away, but the force was too weak by then and she failed. She asked that it be kept in a dark closet until she could try again. The plant had been borrowed, so she said, and had to be returned. At half after nine on

July 5th, the plant was removed from the dark closet and placed in the center of the circle of sitters. Almost instantly it vanished. Another spirit, not Yolande, explained that the plant, in its invisible form, had been brought into the room at the first sitting fully an hour before it was solidified and became visible.

Comment:

In the above cases may be seen the mention of power or force similar to that suggested by the kahunas. The spirits undoubtedly had access to Beings able to use this power to produce apports, and, as the living cannot produce apports, it is to be concluded that the dead must have aid from some superior Being. The shadowy body of the apported objects has been seen at times, filmy, but having the form of the apport. In some instances the thinly massed cloud of material is seen, suggesting that in its disintegrated condition the substance of the apport may be slightly visible, and, of course, greatly expanded.

There is no injury done plants, insects, animals or people when they are used as apports, even when brought from a distance and passed through sealed doors into the seance room. By comparison, the use of the same processes to heal a broken bone is but a trifling matter.

While the kahunas were not able to give a detailed explanation of how the High Selves use the high voltage of vital force to control temperature or to dematerialize and rematerialize apports, they were very sure that this force was used and that it was nearly always provided by the living. They were also sure that the shadowy body was always an important part of the process.

People who have been used as apports report either a short period of unconsciousness or a similar period in which the senses and mental faculties seem sharpened and quickened to a remarkable degree. However, they report little physical sensation during the course of the changes. This evidence tends to verify the Huna theory that we have in our low shadowy body a duplicate set of all the organs and tissues, and that these function when we are temporarily out of the body as in apporting cases, or after death when we are permanently out of the body.

CHAPTER XII

RAISING THE DEAD, PERMANENTLY AND TEMPORARILY

The dead can be raised. There are two kinds of "raising," however, one a complete restoration to life in the physical body, the other a temporary materialization of a physical body for a departed spirit to use. In both these cases we find proofs of the correctness of the ancient beliefs of the kahunas.

We have accounts of men being permanently raised from the dead in Christian and other religious literature. The kahunas were able, under certain conditions, to demonstrate such feats and also to explain them in a comprehensible fashion.

The temporary raising of a living body for the use of a spirit of the dead was common in Polynesia, and as "Materialization," has been studied and repeatedly verified in Psychical Research.

CASE 22 A Kahuna Raises the Dead Before Dr. Brigham Preliminary Notes:

It takes but a short time in a warm climate like that of Hawaii for a dead body to begin to decay. However, there is a condition of deep trance or coma which so closely resembles death that there is a grave danger of being mistaken for dead if in such a condition, and of being buried alive.

The kahunas believed that decay could not set in until the shadowy body of the low self was entirely withdrawn from the body. The two spirits of the lower man can be out of the physical body in their shadowy bodies, and can travel to a great distance, as is done in "astral travel," but there is always a connecting thread (the "silver cord" of Theosophy) of shadowy material joining the physical body and the low shadowy body. It is only when this thread is broken that decay sets in.

After the connecting thread is broken, it would take an act of the High Self to restore tissues which had begun to decay and make possible the return to life of the one who had died. On the other hand, if the thread is unbroken, as is often the case when death comes without an injury to the tissues, as in drowning, life may be restored if a return to the body is made possible for the spirits.

The shadowy body of the low self, as has already been explained, is an ideal storage place for vital force, and when the spirits leave the physical body, most of the vital force is taken along in the shadowy body. When the dense physical body is left behind, after the removal of the elements of consciousness and vital force from it, unconsciousness and inaction result. Studies made of patients suffering from epilepsy, show that after the characteristic "cry" and fall, there is no action of either the body waves or brain waves, as measured by recording instruments. The indication is that the two selves of the patient, in their shadowy bodies, have been driven out of the body temporarily, or, as an alternate possibility, the two selves have remained in the body but have been robbed of the last vestige of vital force by a spirit of the obsessing type. Consciousness returns to the patient in about the length of time required to rebuild the supply of vital force.

The Case:

Dr. Brigham, during one of his field trips in search of rare indigenous plants in Hawaii, took refuge in a coastal village during a very severe storm. In the storm a native lad of about sixteen was drowned. All efforts to revive him failed, and a kahuna living some distance away was summoned.

The kahuna, an old man, arrived and began work about eight hours after the accident. The boy's body was cold, and, when examined by Dr. Brigham shortly before the arrival of the kahuna, seemed to have begun to stiffen in rigor mortis.

The kahuna sat down near the body and set to work to use his psychic powers to learn what had become of the lad's two spirits. In this work, as he later explained, he had the help of several spirit friends. (The shadowy body cord must still have connected the body to the low self of the lad, although probably stretched to the breaking point.) The boy's selves were found wandering in a confused state, and brought back to the body, being urged to remain there and make every possible effort to reenter it.

The body was warmed, and while the kahuna applied his hands to it, he gave of his own vital force. He also used verbal suggestion to cause the return into the body, using as a physical stimulus a stroking and squeezing, as if the spirits were reentering by way of one of the big toes, and was being squeezed up the leg into the body. The kahuna also invoked "the god" (High Self) asking for aid. After about an hour he announced that the spirits of the boy were entering the body. Gradually the flesh became warmer. The heart began to beat and the boy opened his eyes. The recovery was so rapid that in a short time he was asking for food.

Dr. Brigham, greatly impressed by the demonstration of kahuna magic, asked many questions of the kahuna, learning little beyond the fact that the "god" whose aid had been given was one of the Aumakuas, or parental and greatly trustworthy spirits who have formerly been men living in bodies on earth.

He kept track of the Hawaiian lad for a number of years and there seemed never to have been appreciable after effects from the death by drowning.

Comment:

The aid of spirits who have once been men and women in the flesh, is no new thing. The annals of Spiritualism and Psychical Research are filled with accounts of successful healing of the living through the ministrations of the spirit "dead." The most successful of these spirit healers often speak of their work being done by prayers to higher spirits or the conventional concept of God.

The spirits, like the living, have no way to make direct contact with the level of consciousness one step above, and can only speculate about the High Beings and their form of mentation which enables them to use a mysterious power for magical healing. Many spirits have given their ideas of the mechanisms by which healing is accomplished, but even when they claim to have exact knowledge, no two of them agree.

They are amusingly like the living—each evolving his own explanation and rejecting all others. In the face of the sharp contradictions found in the explanations given by the spirits of the dead, we do well to fall back on the ancient explanations given by the kahunas, for they are correct in all details so far as we are able to check them with our present limited knowledge, and what is more important, THEY WORK as a basis for practical application.

Case 23 Raising the Dead Temporarily. Full Materialization Preliminary Notes:

Nothing in Psychical Research has been so fascinating, so incredible, so violently denied (if futilely), so inexplicable or so deeply significant as "full materialization," or the temporary raising of the dead.

In raising the dead, as the process applies to the spirits of those long since passed over, there is the same need for the various elements which constitute a normal living man. The low and middle spirits of the deceased individual come to a spiritualistic seance. They furnish the element of consciousness. They live in the combined low and middle shadowy bodies, so bring these with them and thus furnish a mold of the physical body which they once had on the earth level. What the High Self lacks is the former physical body and its naturally large charge of vital force. To supply this lack, vital force and physical matter are drawn from the circle of living sitters. The physical matter is changed to the thin ectoplasmic form and then solidified in the mold of the spirit's low shadow body.

This results in a "full materialization" of an actual living, breathing, warm and completely normal physical body with the two spirits resident inside it. Such bodies have repeatedly stood close medical inspection. However, they are not permanent. In from a minute to seldom more than an hour, the ectoplasmic material is returned to the living and the solid form vanishes.

It is conceivable that such a materialized body might be permanent if borrowed physical substance did not have to be returned. The Second Coming of Jesus might thus be accomplished were some devotee willing to step out of the flesh into the life of the departed and give his body to be used in this way to fill the mold of the shadowy body of the great Teacher.

In one of the Pacific islands a few years ago, there was quite a furor caused by a group of Polynesian natives who held secret seances at night and succeeded in getting a dead chief raised by the process of materialization. This chief, who had died a leper, was very wise and much loved. Oddly enough, he materialized and remained in the body for much longer periods than is common in the West. Because the authorities feared that the natives would be stirred to rebellion by the chief, the excuse was made that the materialization might spread leprosy, and the seances were broken up.

The Cases:

(A) THE KAHUNAS AND MASS MATERIALIZATION IN HAWAII. In Hawaii, where the kahunas were the most powerful workers in psychic phenomena, mass materializations have been reported down the years. Usually a native chief with from ten to fifty of his followers (all long dead) materialize at night and march through the countryside. Often they materialize drums and torches. Sometimes they remain invisible but the sound of marching feet and of the drums and voices may be clearly heard. These ghostly processions are well known in Hawaii, have often been well substantiated, and many times described in books and articles about the Islands.

Dr. John Tanner, who studied the kahunas in Hawaii for some time, told me that he was at Waikiki Beach one night when he heard the ghostly marchers in procession moving toward the center of Honolulu. He guessed that they might be following the route described as usual by the older Hawaiians—that from Waikiki to the royal tombs near the old Missionary Church at the center of the city. Taking his car he drove to the old church and waited. In a surprisingly short time the same sounds of marching feet became audible, also soft chanting and low conversation. The sounds seemed to be swallowed up by the tomb of a native king long dead, in the church yard. Dr. Tanner saw nothing.

Dr. Brigham had many first-hand accounts of seeing visible marchers by torchlight and moonlight. The Hawaiians agree that the fully materialized marchers, armed with war clubs and spears, are dangerous to anyone who interferes with them. If such a procession is seen to approach, the wise native gets out of the way, or hides himself and remains very quiet while watching it pass. There are several accounts of men having been killed by such marchers. One Hawaiian of my acquaintance claimed to have run face to face into a small group of such marchers, all armed, and garbed in feather cloaks. One warrior rushed at him with a spear, but he instantly called out that he was a living relative and a friend. He was given time to tell his name and to recite the names of his ancestors. It was almost inevitable that, traced back a few generations, he should come to a family relation with any former citizen of these parts—and he did. He was pardoned for his accidental intrusion into the line of march and sent on his way.

While it is evident that much fiction has been added to the commonly accepted facts concerning the ghostly processions in Hawaii, I have no doubt that the basic facts are true. Legendary lore of the Polynesians is filled with accounts of mass and single materializations. The "gods" help the spirits of the dead to materialize, and it is related that vital force and substance for ectoplasm are borrowed from the living while they sleep, or, on rare occasions, are taken from animal and plant life.

(B) A BISHOP MATERIALIZES AFTER FOUR HUNDRED
YEARS OF DEATH. Carlo Mirabelli, a South American medium
of Italian blood, provided excellent examples of nearly all types of
psychic phenomena.

Dr. Fodor writes: "[Mirabelli's] phenomena of materialization
were astounding. The figures were not only complete, they were not
only photographed, but medical men made minute examinations
which lasted sometimes as long as for fifteen minutes and stated
that the newly constituted human beings had perfect anatomical
structure. After the examination was completed the figure began
to dissolve from the feet upwards, the bust and arms floating in the
air. One of the doctors exclaimed; 'But this is too much,' and rushed
forward and seized the half of the body. The next moment he ut-
tered a shrill cry and sank unconscious to the ground. On returning to consciousness he only remembered that when he had seized
the phantom it had felt as if his fingers were pressing a spongy,
flaccid mass of substance. Then he received a shock and lost consciousness. For thirty-six minutes in broad daylight the materialization of the little daughter of Dr. Souza, who died of influenza,
was visible to all the sitters. She appeared in her grave clothes.
Her pulse was tested. Father and child were photographed. Then
the phantom raised itself and floated in the air....

"In another sitting Mirabelli announced that he saw the body
of Bishop Dr. Jose de Carmago Barros who lost his life in a ship-
wreck. 'A sweet smell as of roses filled the room. The medium went
into trance. A fine mist was seen in the circle [of sitters]. The mist,
glowing as if of gold, parted and the bishop materialized, with all
the robes and insignia of office. He called his own name. Dr. Souza
stepped to him. He palpitated the body, touched his teeth, tested
the saliva, listened to the heart-beat, investigated the working of
the intestines, nails and eyes, without finding anything amiss.
Then the other attending persons convinced themselves of the reality of the apparition. The Bishop bent smilingly over Mirabelli and
looked at him silently. Then he slowly dematerialized.' 'At the sixth
sitting, Mirabelli, tied and sealed, disappeared from the room, and
was found in another room still in trance. All seals on doors and
windows were found in order, as well as the seals on Mirabelli himself.' Once among fourteen investigators his arms dematerialized.
On the photograph only a slight shadow is visible."

(C) YOLANDE AND HER MATERIALIZATIONS. Mme. Eliza-
beth d'Esperance, a famous medium, had, among other spirits who

materialized at her seances an Arab girl of fifteen named Yolande. This girl would appear as a mist and take several minutes to become fully materialized. Then, in good light, she was accustomed to talk with the living and to make objects in the room appear and disappear. She produced apports in great numbers, and caused plants to grow in waterbottles filled with water and sand, a large plant being grown in a few minutes. The medium was found by the investigator Alexander N. Aksakof, on one occasion, to have dematerialized the lower half of her body while visible spirit materializations were in the seance room. The upper half of the medium seemed to be suspended in air. She was not in trance, and was frightened to discover her condition, calling the investigator's attention to the situation. Others present also assured themselves that there was nothing in the collapsed garments of the medium below the waist. Ten years later, Aksakof published a weighty opinion which years of study and observation had forced upon him: the opinion that, in some cases at least, "the body of the medium is entirely absorbed for the production of apparitions...."

(D) ANIMAL MATERIALIZATIONS. The kahuna contention that all things have shadowy bodies which are molds of their microscopic parts as well as of their full form and shape, applies to animals as well as men. (Also insects and inert objects such as rocks.)

Gambier Bolton had a peculiar experience. He had befriended and doctored a wounded seal at a Zoo, but the seal had died. Ten days after its death, at a seance with Mrs. Craddock, and with a number of men of science present, a seal—seemingly the one known to Bolton—materialized and flapped its way across the room, staying close to Bolton for several minutes. The spirits officiating at the seance were asked to explain this. They said, "Their actions (those of animals at seances where they materialize) are altogether independent of us. Whilst we are busily engaged in conducting our experiments with human entities who wish to materialize in your midst, the animals get into the room in some way which we do not understand, and which we cannot prevent; obtain, from somewhere, sufficient matter with which to build up temporary bodies; coming just when they choose, roaming about the room just as they please; and disappearing just when it suits them, and not before; and we have no power to prevent this so long as the affection existing between them and their late owners is so strong as it was in the instances which have come under our notice."

Dr. Fodor points out that the above statement from the medium's spirit controls seems contradicted by the fact that in the famous animal materializations at the Kluski seances, there invariably appeared a human apparition acting as keeper of such animals as appeared. The keepers and animals seldom moved about at the same time, but the keepers, although still, were to be plainly seen. However, there was one animal which appeared with no keeper. It was an ape man spoken of by the investigators as Pithecanthropus. It had coarse shaggy hair, smelled like a cross between a deer and a wet dog, and was frolicsome, evidently of a low level of intelligence, but gentle and ready to obey. Its great strength caused fear at a few of the sittings at which it appeared. It lifted heavy men, seated in their chairs, high above the heads of the others. It picked up a large and very heavy case of books and carried it about the room, also a large sofa. It made only smacking sounds and scratched itself frequently.

Dogs, cats, parrots, bats, weasels and many other dead pets have returned to visit their former owners at seances. Hairs from one small pet animal were left behind in some lace in which its leg had been entangled during the appearance (the lace had been torn four inches). These hairs were placed in a light-tight and damp-proof box and were inspected often. After a few days the hairs dwindled in size, and before long vanished entirely, evidently dematerializing much more slowly than had the little animal itself.

(E) PARTIAL MATERIALIZATIONS OF THE LIVING A number of instances have been reported by investigators in which the living have appeared at seances in partial materializations. Horace Leaf saw the head, shoulders and one arm of a relative alive and living four hundred miles distant. A conversation was carried on in which matters known only to themselves were discussed for several minutes. Alfred Vout Peters, in a seance with Cecil Husk, saw the materialization (apparently almost complete) of a living friend who, it was later learned, had been asleep at his home at the time.

Dr. Nandor Fodor, in his long article on Materialization in his Encyclopaedia of Psychic Science, made a comment which bears strongly on the ancient theories of the kahunas (unknown to Dr. Fodor at the time of writing). "Indeed, one is tempted to speculate whether it would be possible to build up, through the process of dematerialization and materialization a living organism on altered lines. Perhaps some of the miraculous cures in which organic parts of the body had been restored will find an explanation in the future along such speculative lines."

(F) CHANGES IN NORMAL SIZE IN MATERIALIZATION. Many reports have included the appearance of materialized forms which were either larger or smaller than it is to be supposed the living person had been. This is similar to the phenomena of elongation of the living mediums at seances, in which the medium's body has been seen to become longer by as much as two feet. (The kahunas believed that the shadowy body of a thing could be made larger or smaller.)

Mme. Bisson studied a naked female figure not more than eight inches tall which repeatedly materialized, often with a change of hair arrangement, dancing and performing gymnastic exercises. It even stood on Mme. Bisson's hand some of the time, but usually on the hand of the medium, Eva.

In the sittings of Mme. Ignath small heads the size of walnuts and very beautiful materialized in glasses of water. The spirit control, Nona, gave the opinion that they were materialized plastic thought forms.

Partial materializations such as heads and hands have often been seen to be only a fraction of normal size.

(G) MATERIALIZED CLOTHING Very few of the temporarily materialized spirits have come without clothing. Harry Price, most careful and skeptical of the S.P.R. investigators, in a recent book tells of the periodic materialization of a little girl unclothed— in dark seances held by her mother and a few friends, one a good medium. Attending such a seance, Price found the bare little body warm, solid and of normal weight in his hands. The child spoke a few words in answer to a question. The floor of the room had been sprinkled with white powder, the openings sealed, and all precautions taken against fraud. No footprints crossed the powdered floor and no seals were broken, satisfying Price of the genuineness of the materialization.

On the other hand, spirits clothe themselves in materials ranging from misty gray vapors to cloth so solid that pieces of it have repeatedly been cut off by investigators to study after the dematerialization of spirit and garb. A peculiarity of the materialized fabric is that it is nearly always lighter and finer than ordinarily would be the case.

Sylvan J. Muldoon, famous for his practice and reports on astral travel, writes of once seeing clothing forming itself around his astral body when it had left the physical body but a few feet. The clothing was identical to that on his living body which lay recumbent on his bed.

Not only do the bodies of mediums dematerialize partly or completely at materializing seances on occasion, but sometimes their clothing also vanishes for the time being—though at other times it is left behind. Usually the cloth materialized at a seance remains white, even if the vanishing clothing of the medium is black.

Katie King, a spirit who frequently materialized at Miss Florence Cook's seances and was much studied by Sir William Crookes, often allowed the fabric of her ghostly clothing to be examined. Sometimes she cut as many as a dozen pieces from the bottom of her skirt and handed them to sitters to be examined. The holes in the skirt immediately closed up as the sitters watched. Most of this fabric vanished when the phantom dematerialized, but a few pieces were rendered enduring, in which case similar holes were found cut in the skirt of the medium after the seance ended, tending to show that the material of her skirt had been borrowed for materialization purposes, and that it was not returned when pieces were rendered permanent.

In passing it must be noted that the fabric of the ghostly garment was not like that of the skirt in which a hole had been left. It is thus seen that it is possible to transform matter through the process of dematerialization and materialization, changing one thing to another, and rendering the changed part permanent—as must be done in instant healing if the kahuna theory is correct.

Katie King said that in making bits of drapery permanent she was forced to take away permanently some of the medium's vitality (check the kahuna theory that all materializing operations involve the use of vital force of the living) and so weakening her. This material when presented to drapers with the request that it be matched, proved to be like nothing in the market. The drapers expressed the opinion that it might be cloth of Chinese manufacture.

A piece of Yolande's spirit dress was torn off and made permanent at a sitting with Mme. d'Esperance in Christiania. A similar hole, partly torn and partly cut appeared later in the medium's skirt. The piece from the spirit's skirt was several times larger but of exactly the same shape. The fabric was white and much lighter in texture, being almost as thin as gauze, but composed of definitely woven threads.

Some materialized fabric has been found not to be woven. It resembles filmy sheets of material slightly like rubber, often filled with holes to make it appear like lace.

At a sitting with George Spriggs in Cardiff, a piece of the rich, bright red silk girdle of a materialized spirit form was cut off and left behind. It soon faded, but at a later seance, when called to the attention of the same spirit, was restored to its original color and lustre in some unexplained way.

Locks of hair cut from the heads of materialized spirits and left behind as permanent or as slowly vanishing souvenirs, have in almost all cases been found to be softer and finer than the hair of the medium through whose seance the apparition was enabled to materialize.

(H) MATERIALIZATION OF THE "LITTLE PEOPLE." Fairies and other "little people" seem to materialize in visible and even tangible forms at times, most often in the presence of children. Around the year 1915 two young girls in England used their father's camera to get pictures of fairies and gnomes. The pictures were published and quite a stir created. A better camera was provided and more pictures obtained. The charge of the suspicious that the negatives could have been "faked" was never proved.

In Hawaii there is a belief in the gnomes or menehunes, these materializing at times and resembling the brownies of other lands. During my stay in Honolulu the papers were filled with accounts and comments after school children discovered one of the little men on the playground and followed him excitedly until he took fright and escaped from them by diving under a building set a few feet off the ground. He seemed to disappear into thin air under the building. The teacher, hearing the shouts, came on the scene and questioned the children. They all told the same story and described the little man in the same way.

The menehunes were credited with the building of many stone walls to enclose arms of the shallow sea and act as artificial fish ponds. In native folk lore a variety of such "little people" receive mention.

While the evidence of the materialization of elves, fairies, gnomes and their like is poorly verified, it would seem to be a mistake not to mention the possibility of their reality in listing the materials of the study at this point.

Comment:

Several things need to be especially noted in the above cases. The shock which rendered the doctor unconscious when he seized an apparition at one of Mirabelli's seances, indicates the electrical factor involved in materialization. Many investigators have studied the evidence of electrical vital or psychic force at work during materialization and have found it very real, even if its function was not fully understood. Spirits of the dead give contradictory opinions as to the nature and use of the force, some saying it is drawn from the brain of medium or sitters, others saying it comes from their bodies, and still others saying it is present in the atmosphere and has only to be collected.

Modern studies by medical men have proved that, when the electro-vital "body electricity" or "mind electricity" or both, are exhausted in a living person, unconsciousness results. This agrees with the kahuna belief that all consciousness functions only when there is at hand a proper amount of vital force of the necessary voltage. (Remember that they believe that the low self makes the vital force from foods we eat, that the middle self takes this low voltage force and steps up its voltage for its use in "will," and that the High Self takes the force and steps up its voltage to the highest voltage—in which condition it becomes similar to the "atom smashing" voltages known to science.)

The vitality of mediums and sitters at seances has often been depleted by materializations. The famous medium, D. D. Home, was sometimes left lying almost unconscious on the floor after such a seance. One investigator, F. W. H. Meyers, was so depleted after a seance that he went to bed for two days. Mediums frequently have been forced to take long rest periods between sittings.

The kahunas, in their healing practices, watched for the danger of the theft of vital force from the living by the dead. While doctors do not recognize such possibilities at the present time, it is evident, in the light of the long study of the kahuna lore, that some illness is directly caused by such theft of vital force. The doctors do, however, know that when vital force falls below par in the individual, the control of the conscious mind over the subconscious is greatly weakened, causing thought impressions to enter the subconscious without being subjected to the usual process of judgment by reason, causing unreasonable complexes or fixations. We have seen that shock impressions are dangerous when one is very tired or vitality is low because of illness or strain; that if, for some reason the normal supply of vital force continues for some time to fall, depressive states come, and—at more advanced stages—insanity results.

While medical men make no mention of the rest of the usual story, the patient, once insanity becomes pronounced, seems no longer to suffer so greatly from lack of vital force. Often there is violent physical action—indicating that the kahunas were right in thinking that the spirits of the dead often obsess the living, beginning by stealing vital force and ending by pushing out the resident pair of spirits and taking over the body for themselves—thus accomplishing a form of "rising from the dead" for themselves. (Doctors frown on the idea, but when they administer insulin shock or electrical shock to cure the insane, they are doing nothing more or less than the physicians of early times when they made the stay of obsessing spirits so painful in the body of the insane patient that the invaders left, allowing the rightful owners of the body to return.)

The passage of matter through matter in materialization is demonstrated when apports and even bodies of large animals and men are dematerialized and brought through closed and sealed doors to be materialized in the seance room. This indicates the fact that in the dematerialized state physical substance is sufficiently thin to pass through wood and other not-too-dense substances. (Glass seems too dense to allow such passage of thin materials or shadowy body molds through it.)

It is not necessary for the spirit of a dead person to materialize in denser form in order to carry vital force with it. Also, dematerialized physical substances need not be solidified to the visible state to be used as an invisible hand in moving solid objects, providing there is enough vital force lodged in the invisible ectoplasmic substance used by the spirit.

A case illustrating this came under my observation. A young man was to arrive by plane and have dinner with his sweetheart and her mother. The plane crashed and he was killed in the landing. A few minutes later the door bell rang at the house he had intended to visit. The sweetheart answered the bell but found no one there. The bell rang three times, the mother joining the girl in trying to learn who had caused the ringing. Some months later, at a seance, the young man communicated through a medium saying that he had not been aware of his death, and had gone to the home where he had been expected. He rang the bell three times, being greatly surprised and agitated to find that he was not seen or recognized by his friends. He failed after the third ring to be able to press the button (vital force evidently expended) and concluded that something was very wrong.

All the evidence accumulated by the study of hundreds of cases of haunting and poltergeist phenomena indicates that the kahunas were right in believing that the spirits of the dead can store large amounts of vital force in the shadowy body of the low self. At the moment of sudden death the shadowy body is charged with vital force, and seems to remain charged and ready to ring bells and do other kinds of work until the charge is exhausted. The poltergeist, being usually a low self cut off from his middle self after death, and given to childish antics, steals vital force from the living and uses it to move solid objects or make noises. The shadowy body appears to be an excellent storage battery for vital force, and when heavily charged, may become sufficiently solid to be used to move material objects. A small amount of. ectoplasmic material of the invisible and very thin grade may be needed to stiffen the shadowy body— later study may show whether or not this is true.

In cases where animals materialize at seances, one can only conclude that High Selves are present and doing the work. If the spirits of the dead disagree so largely on how materialization is accomplished, so showing that they are ignorant of the part played by the High Selves, it stands to reason that animals would not have sufficient intelligence to cause a materialization for themselves.

One more thing should be kept in mind. The materials of a supposedly living and fleshly nature used in forming ectoplasm with which to materialize animals, birds and insects, cannot be said to come from the medium and sitters. It must be found in other quarters by the High Selves and borrowed for temporary use. In fact, materializations have often been observed when no visible material was drawn from either medium or sitters, although the expenditure of vital force from the circle is very usual.

In the blacker phases of ceremonial magic it is probable that the vital force of sacrificed animals or even humans, was taken and used by spirits, but it is to be concluded that the High Selves would never use vital force or the bodily materials of sacrificial victims. The kahuna name for the High Self was "Entirely Trustworthy Parental Self," and there seems to be no question as to its aversion to cruelty.

With the end of this chapter I finish the work of presenting the basic elements in the theories of Huna, together with some of the proofs derived from comparison with the findings of Psychic Science and the Psychologies, also, to a lesser extent, various religious beliefs.

CHAPTER XIII

THE LIFE-GIVING SECRETS OF LOMILOMI AND LAYING ON OF HANDS

With the basic elements of the ancient Secret, or HUNA, explained, we now take up the practical application of those elements.

In this chapter I wish to discuss the simpler healing methods used by the kahunas, and to point out ways in which we can all profit greatly by their knowledge and experience.

In Hawaii and throughout Polynesia at a very early date, according to the semi-historical legends of the South seas, the healers often made use of physical manipulation as an aid to what might be called "mental" healing.

This manipulation was called lomilomi, and was a combination of massage, bathing and deep manipulation—every action being accompanied by an action of mind to aid healing and relieve pain.

If we modern people would combine Swedish massage, the various baths, chiropractic, osteopathy, the use of suggestion, and the ancient religious practice of "the laying on of hands" (to heal), we should approach the scope of lomilomi as a skilled kahuna might practice it.

Case 24 Lomilomi Preliminary Notes:

Dr. Brigham spent an evening giving me the details of a lomilomi treatment which he observed in the Hilo district in the early days.

The patient was a man of about forty who had returned from a long trip on foot to see the lava overflow the vast pit of Kilauea Volcano. He had come home tired out, feeling ill, and aching in various joints. He was especially pained by what seemed to be lumbago.

The kahuna who treated him was a woman. She claimed no high healing powers, but had the standing in the community which might have been accorded a nurse.

The Case:

When Dr. Brigham heard of the treatment and arrived at the place where it was being given, the first steps had already been taken. The man had been sponged off with a warm tea made by boiling several herbs and leaves in water to which had been added a little salt of the unrefined sort made by evaporating sea water. After the bath the patient was dried and placed in the warm sun clad only in a loin cloth. The woman had recited a form of chant during the bathing, saying all illness was being washed away and all pain was being soothed. With variations in her words, she described the benefits being brought through the touch of her healing hands and the touch of round stones which she raked from a fire, washed off, and used to massage stiff muscles and aching joints.

The use of the hot stones was followed by the use of her hands alone, the small fire being kept burning so that she could often heat her hands before kneading deeply into sore spots.

When the patient's aches and pains had been much relieved, she became more vigorous in her manipulations, twisting and pressing joints, starting with cracking the finger joints and knuckles, and ending by cracking all possible joints in neck and spine, especially where there was the greatest soreness or pain. The lumbago condition seemed to be centered around a very sore spot in the middle of the lower back, and the treatment there was very gentle at first with protracted heating, and at last alarmingly heavy pressure was exerted with the heels of both hands.

As a last part of the treatment, the woman placed her hands on the hands of the man and told him to rest and let the healing power run from her hands into his to make him well and free of pain. This took several minutes, at the end of which time the patient was covered warmly and told to take a nap. His face was shaded from the sun and his wife came to sit beside him and keep away flies with a small switch of green leaves.

Later in the day when Dr. Brigham inquired as to the outcome of the treatment, the man said that he had no more pain and that he felt very well except for a little soreness of the skin of his back where the treatment had been most severe.

Comment:

On the face of it the treatment given above seems very simple. But when we consider it in the light of the Huna lore, and weigh each step in terms of what has been discovered in recent years, it becomes inclusive, greatly significant, and suggestive of steps which Western healers have not yet learned to take separately, to say nothing of combining in one treatment.

Step 1. The use of thermal baths is familiar to all races. The herbal decoction of the Hawaiians was frequently made with the leaves of the ti plant and held a supposed power to drive away any spirit of the low self class which might be trying to steal vital force from a patient. (On this I shall have more to say later.) Natural mineral springs which provide hot water for baths, including hot mud, are known to give relief in many kinds of illness. The Turkish or hot steam bath is a substitute and among the Navahoes and other Indian tribes prolonged steam baths were taken as a means of purification before certain ceremonial rites.

The application of heat, through stones or other mechanisms has been used by healers for centuries. Modern doctors apply heat in various forms, deep electrical, surface, lights and so on. If there is to be a manipulation of joints, heat is used to relax tense muscles and allow easier manipulation.

Step 2. The manipulation of joints, deep massage and rubbing to increase circulation are all part of the ancient practice of lomilomi. While it is certain that the natives who practiced deep massage after heating and relaxing the muscles, did not have a clear understanding that certain spinal joints might be slightly slipped and so pressing on nerves (as demonstrated so thoroughly by osteopaths and chiropractors, and as denied with dogmatic violence by the strictly medical doctors—who have no training in the matter and disdain taking any) they did an excellent job of making adjustments. They pressed or pulled or twisted until a joint "popped," if they were able to make it do so. Most joints, when so manipulated, fall back into their proper alignment if the displacement has not been of too long standing. It will be seen that lomilomi included the basic use of heat for relaxation, followed by manipulation of joints for adjustment, and deep massage and rubbing to increase circulation and soothe the patient. This was followed by a period of rest for the patient—an excellent thing in itself.

Step 3. This is the step which we moderns have still to learn to take. It is the use of vital force in healing. The nearest we have come to it is the application of electrical currents of varying kinds through the use of electrical machines. There is a new school of physicians, stemming from chiropractors, which teaches that each of the organs of the body has an electrical charge of a voltage peculiar to itself. A machine is used to test the voltage of each organ, and when any organ is found to be below the average or standard charge, treatments are given to charge the defective organ directly from the machine. While this form of diagnosis and treatment is still far from general acceptance (and in many cases is possibly mixed with a certain amount of downright ignorance or fraud), the general idea may be said to be our closest approach to the kahuna theory of vital force and its part in life and consciousness.

It is agreed in medical circles that the electrovital force of the body must be up to a certain strength to maintain health. As mentioned when discussing the basic problems of the three voltages of vital force (the mana, manamana and mana loa) the body waves and brain waves have been successfully measured and some progress made in the study of their significance in bodily and mental health and illness.

In the kahuna practices of healing, the knowledge of the vital forces and of the mild forms of hypnotic suggestion went hand in hand. In the West we made a good beginning, in the discovery of mesmerism, toward recovering the ancient Huna practice of giving the patient vital force through the touch of the hands while administering the suggestion of healing. Mesmer, who demonstrated the power of suggestion over a century ago, believed that he was healing by transferring to the patient some of his own "animal magnetism," and that this force did the healing. He touched his patients after making a mental effort to fill himself with this force by holding magnets.

What Mesmer and his followers actually did was to use the transfer of vital force as a healing agent, coupling it (unknowingly) with the use of very potent suggestion. This point is of great importance for all students of healing and for all those who desire to gain more knowledge. Dr. Braid, coming much later than Mesmer, discovered the fact that hypnotic suggestion could be given and made to take effect without physical contact between patient and operator. He announced his discovery and gave to the world a knowledge of hypnotic suggestion, but caused the almost utter loss of the knowledge of the fact that vital force could be made to flow from one person into another with beneficial healing effects. Our doctors who use suggestion in healing and as an adjunct to psychoanalysis and the draining off of fixations, are still lacking a definite and very important part of their healing art.

Some people have a natural ability to lay their hands on another who is weak or ill and cause vital force to flow into them from their own bodies, thus strengthening the patient. This is the simplest form of treatment with shared vital force. Better results are obtained by a slightly more advanced type of healer of religious orders. This healer "lays on hands" and prays to God to do the healing. If the High Self is contacted and acts, a miraculous healing results, otherwise the best that can be expected is that the desire to heal will act as a hypnotic suggestion to cause the vital force of the healer to enter the patient and take with it the suggestion of health. Note well the dual activity here.

Vital force—bodily electricity or low mana (the voltage peculiar to the low self and the body, not the middle self and the will or mind)—has an amazing characteristic which is still unknown to modern researchers. This characteristic is THAT IT RESPONDS TO THE COMMANDS AND DIRECTION OF THE CONSCIOUS- NESS OF SENTIENT BEINGS almost as if it were itself conscious.

This fact will be written large across the text books of the future.

The kahunas have passed on down to us in a vague and tangled form the information that the universe has

I been created by the ACTION OF CONSCIOUSNESS UPON FORCE TO CREATE MATTER. (I believe that is a correct statement of what they believed, but it is possible that there is much more to it of explanatory detail which we shall understand only as we make progress in Physics.)

Science tells us that all matter is made up of an electrical form of force or energy which has been set to moving in certain relations to other units of moving force, and that—seemingly because of the balance between the positive and negative forces in any given combination—we have the various forms of matter.

Huna tells us that the thing which sets this electrical force into fixed motion is CONSCIOUSNESS. The High Self can use its consciousness to cause vital force to become high in voltage and to cause changes in temperature and matter—as in fire-walking and instant healing. Above the level of the High Self are supposed to be still higher levels of consciousness which are entirely beyond human conception, but which can create on a world scale. (We pray to the High Self, asking it to pray in turn to these still higher Beings if such prayer is needed.) (Check the Christian practice of praying to God through the mediation of Jesus, the Son.)

It follows that, while the low self of a man cannot use his lesser form of consciousness to cause his vital force to make changes in matter as does the High Self, his control of the bodily vital force is still remarkable.

Baron Ferson demonstrated the ability of a trained man to fill himself with a surcharge of force. In the light of kahuna lore we conclude that this was vital force. When a surcharge is accumulated and the will is used to direct it, a flow can be sent from the hands into the body of a patient.

The important thing to be learned from the kahunas is the fact that when vital force flows from one person to another it may carry with it various substances, particularly thought forms, or thoughts embodied in their tiny shadowy bodies. .

This secret of the kahunas throws a new light on suggestion— auto suggestion as well as hypnosis. The art of suggestion consists of transferring to someone else some of your low mana or vital force, and on the flow sending the thought forms of the suggestion—be it one of health or of actions to be taken by the recipient of the suggestion.

In giving suggestion the contact may be made by laying the hands on the patient. However, if the patient has once been touched, a thread of shadowy body material thereafter connects the healer to the patient, and when a "willed" command is given to the low self of the healer to reach out along the thread and touch the patient, even at a distance, contact can be made and vital force and the thought forms of suggestion sent, as along a telegraph wire. This is "absent treatment," or treatment by telepathic means. To use this form of treatment takes training and practice.

A still further secret of GREAT IMPORTANCE is to be had from the kahunas. In the West we strive to make our suggestion as potent and hypnotic as we can when putting it to healing use. The kahunas used only mild suggestion, if it may be called that. But they knew that if a physical stimulus was used to accompany mild suggestion, the effect was enhanced to a marvelous degree. A physical stimulus is a material something, or act—a thing real and tangible which impresses the low self of the patient. Take the classical example of the doctor who gives his patient a dough pill and tells him that it will cure his ailment. The dough pill is a physical something which causes the patient to believe that a remedy is being given. The suggested healing on the part of the doctor may be hardly hypnotic at all in its potency, but when reinforced by the actual physical something—the physical stimulus—of the dough pill, the healing suggestion takes magical effect.

"Absent treatment," which must rely on the telepathic communication of vital force and the thought forms of the suggestion of healing, is much less powerful than suggestion given with direct contact, and this is largely because of the lack of a physical stimulus to accompany absent treatment. The practitioner or healer who places his hands on his patient, and who gives healing suggestion, uses a physical stimulus in the very act of touching his patient. His very presence before the patient is a stimulus to make the suggestion take effect. But if something directly associated in the mind of the patient with healing is used, such as a medicine, even if it be useless in itself, the effect is far greater.

The low self is, as we have seen, illogical. It depends largely on two ways of getting information. (1) On learning about a thing through the five senses. If a low self sees a flower, touches it, smells it, tastes a petal and hears a bee bumbling in the flower, it gets a very strong impression of that flower—so strong that it cannot be convinced that it has not seen just that flower in just that way. (2) It gets information from the middle self which may add, in the case of the flower, the information that it is the property of the neighbor across the fence and that it must not be picked.

The low self relies on the evidence of its senses more than on anything else. It is always a little reluctant to accept the information offered by the middle self, for the simple reason that it has learned that this form of information is not always correct. For instance, as a child the middle self may have decided that it would be great fun to roll down hill in a barrel, even if the low self was frightened at the idea. The experiment may have proved very painful, and the resulting deduction (animal-like reasoning power) on the part of the low self may have been that the middle self was not too reliable in its conclusions.

Many ills are caused by fixed ideas held by the low self. These fixations are usually illogical, but they are stubbornly held. It has been said that three-fourths of our ills come from such mental causes. While this may be an exaggerated estimate, the importance of mental causes of illness, accident or trouble is not to be ignored. If we add the fact, learned from the kahunas, that the future of each of us is built by our High Self from the hopes, fears, plans and thoughts of our daily lives, we may say that all our states and conditions can be traced to some mental origin. (To these "origins" the kahunas add the chance of attack by poltergeists or by normal departed spirits composed of combined low and middle selves, and living in combined low and middle shadowy bodies. Such attacks are far more frequent than is supposed.) We must also keep in mind the chance that we may pick up a suggestion which will result in illness or accident, even if the person or circumstance giving the suggestion may be said to have no intention of doing harm.

An example of a circumstance giving us a suggestion of illness may be found in reading any report on the findings of psychoanalysis. A typical case almost always involves a person who became very low in vital force through weariness or illness, then (when the middle self was weakened and unable to give the low self a logical explanation of a physical stimulus in the form of something shocking) some shocking thing took place. The shock may be caused by suddenly seeing a crippled or injured or very ill person, or one maimed, or one just being injured. Or the shock may come from a sudden thought which comes to the weary person and becomes illogically "fixed" in the low self. A woman, when tired after a dance, saw a man with part of his face eaten away. Her low self associated the diseased face with itself illogically but disastrously. The woman became certain that her own face was becoming diseased, and could not be reassured. She went from doctor to doctor until a psychoanalyst got to the bottom of the trouble and brought the incident to light where it could be rationalized and "drained off." In another case a very ill and tired young man slipped on an iron step. Thereafter he was illogically terrified by any iron step and could not use it. Psychoanalysis brought to light the cause of the trouble and cured it.

The low self is accustomed to having the middle self IMAGINE things all day long. Most of our leisure thoughts are about things that are not real and solidly present. Because of this, the low self, when told by suggestion that it is healed of a malady, inclines to consider such a statement just another imagination. It is quite convinced that it is ill and that nothing has been done to heal it. It therefore refuses to accept and react to the thought forms implanted into it by way of the hearing when the healer speaks the healing suggestion. It is the same when we try to pray with full faith and try to tell ourselves that we "have received" that for which we have prayed. It is the same when we try to "hold the thought" that we have a new house or a healed body. The low self does not cooperate. It acts like a naughty boy, sneering and thumbing its nose

at our efforts. IT TAKES NO STOCK IN THINGS IT CANNOT
VERIFY WITH THE SENSES in some way.

If the healer gives the suggestion of healing, and at the same
time administers a dose of medicine with the suggestion that it will
heal, and if the patient will keep mentally relaxed and not tell his
low self that the medicine is no good, the suggestion BECAUSE OF
THIS PHYSICAL STIMULUS in the form of actual, tangible medicine will be accepted and acted upon. In other words, the low self
which has not healed the illness as it should ordinarily have done,
is caused to set to work and bring about the condition of health suggested by the healer and the medical dosage.

If one prays for a house, uses faith, declares that he has already received the house, and gives thanks for the gift of a house,
he may get results only if he uses a physical stimulus to impress
his low self that the house really has been given and is on its way.
A woman I knew who prayed for houses and usually got them, had
in some way divined this secret of the need of a physical stimulus.
She told me that she prayed, then got a board and a nail, set them
before her and proclaimed that they were the beginning of the
house which was being given in answer to the prayer. It worked,
slowly but surely, for her. She accumulated houses until she was
able to live on her rentals.

If suggestion is given at the time that vital force is transferred
through the hands of the healer, and the massage and manipulations act as a physical stimulus, the combination is most perfect.
Lomilomi at its best included all three of these important elements.
In addition, medicine might be administered, as herbal baths and
doses. Kahunas of a special class were expert in the use of native
herbal medicines.

These are Life-Giving secrets indeed. Vital force is life. Without it, consciousness in the form of the low and middle selves cannot function. Without it, the physical body dies.

Restore the vital force and implant suggestion in the mind of
the low self that the force is to be used for healing the body. Use a
physical stimulus to cause this suggestion to be accepted. Do this
while laying on hands, or use absent treatment through the connecting threads of shadowy body material. This is magic. It is low
magic while prayer to the High Self and instant healing is High
Magic.

I knew a man who was bedfast with hardening of the liver and who was in constant pain. A doctor who had stumbled upon the secret of the laying on of hands and had practiced this form of healing, coupled with suggestion, began to treat the sick man. He told him that he could not restore his liver, but that he could remove the pain with suggestion and spinal adjustments. He made slight adjustments and so "laid hands" on his patient. He gave suggestion as he willed to send healing and soothing power into the sick man. After the second treatment the pain left and the man left his bed. He had a weekly treatment and lived without discomfort for three months, dying suddenly, an easy death.

I saw the same doctor take a nurse, aged fifty, who had been sent by her hospital doctors to live with her daughter until she died. They could do nothing for her and gave her a few months to live. No one knew just what was the trouble. She had lost her vitality by degrees and could not walk. She could speak but a few words at a time, always passing into hysteria and sometimes convulsions. This wise doctor undertook her treatment, making slight spinal adjustments while administering suggestions of returning health and strength. After six weekly treatments the woman was in better health than she had been in years. She walked freely and with her head high. There was spring to her step and a glow in her eyes. Although the doctor knew nothing of the kahunas, he had unwittingly learned to use two simple forms of treatment, neither of which is magical or greatly effective by itself, but when combined are the essence of the life-giving lomilomi.

The practice of hypnotic suggestion in the healing of physical and complex conditions is at present uncertain and in disrepute. Doctors do not study the use of suggestion except in rare instances. Only the psychoanalyst and psychiatrists turn to suggestion, and these get feeble results because they do not know the magical secret of using the physical stimulus and of learning to transfer from themselves a flow of vital force to replenish the patient.

Vital force is like the widow's mite—it increases as it is given. I know a man who has made a practice of healing by laying on of hands and willing his healing force to enter and heal his patients. He calls on the spirits of his dead relatives to aid the process, and some of his healing has been remarkable. I asked him whether or not he found that he exhausted himself by giving out the healing force. He replied that, on the contrary, if he did not use it up in healing, he became miserable and had to take violent physical exercise.

Vital force is made from the food we eat. Almost any person could start out and walk twice as far as he expects to walk on a given day. The daily food of each of us would supply vital force enough for much more physical or mental activity. The physiologists tell us that food is turned to blood sugar which is in turn burned up when we begin to exercise and need vital force. When we do not use up all the blood sugar supplied by the food of the day it is thrown off by the liver as waste.

By an effort of the will one can cause the low self to create an excess supply of vital force. Almost anyone can learn to do this in a dozen lessons of twenty minutes each.

When we have more vital force in our bodies than some other person, and lay our hands on that other person with the will to give them vital force through our hands, the flow commences.

The flowing vital force becomes almost human and intelligent in its response to the willed command of the middle self. It will go to the sick part of a patient's body and strengthen it. It will carry the thought forms of suggestion with it when suggestion is given silently. It will do its work better, however, if the suggestion is also given by voice and the low self of the patient made to understand what is being "willed" to happen by way of healing. If the vocal suggestion is made with the aid of a physical stimulus, it will be most powerful. Let that stimulus be manipulation, massage, heat, bathing with some healing fluid, or giving some dosage.

Now that we have learned from the kahunas that suggestion is only the transfer of vital force from one person to another, and the accompanying transfer of thought forms, to which the relaxed recipient reacts, we can see how foolish have been our fears of hypnosis.

The fear of hypnosis and of any form of suggestion has been almost a phobia with us for the century since mesmerism was discovered. We could not understand it and so we feared it. Because the use of suggestion had not been plainly described and advocated in Biblical healing, the Church warned against its use, as it has warned against all psychical research. (And as it has warned against all medical and scientific progress for centuries on end. Religion always becomes rapidly crystallized and resists anything new that threatens to cause it to change its beliefs or practices.)

I have been hypnotized fully as many times as I have hypnotized others in my experimental work. I have suffered no slightest evil from it. I have watched the use of hypnosis and suggestion for thirty years. I have talked repeatedly with operators and their subjects, not once finding any single thing to show that it is harmful.

Each of us is constantly using auto suggestion. If I "will" to rise from my chair and walk into the next room, that is simply a matter of giving the thought form of the desired action to the low self. It has become accustomed to react to such thought forms when presented by the middle self, and it reacts automatically. It causes the body to rise and walk into the next room.

Auto suggestion is less effective than it should be in its general application by those hardy souls who have guessed its value. The trouble is that it lacks a fitting physical stimulus to go with it. For physical ills, auto suggestion takes effect best if given at the same time that medicines are taken, provided the medicine is not one which has been tried before and has become known to the low self as a failure.

A fitting physical stimulus which has been advocated is that of using vocal affirmations. One speaks aloud, affirming that he is healthy, wealthy or wise. The sound of the voice is a physical stimulus, and if used often enough and with the "Will" (coming from the middle self) to accept it, has definite suggestive effects.

Since the development of recording instruments for sound, suggestion has been experimentally given by such an instrument during sleep. The record is set to play softly at some time during the night, and the person receiving the suggestion goes to bed determined to accept and react to the mechanical suggestion. As full relaxation is obtained in deep sleep, and as the logical conscious mind is asleep and does not contradict the suggestion as heard by the subconscious or low self, the suggestion sinks home as intended. In the next few years we may see amazing work done in this way toward rebuilding health and personality, even stimulating latent talents, abilities and genius.

In recent years investigators have been at work trying to find out to what extent we have been suppressing our abilities and talents by accepting auto suggestion or the unmeaning suggestion of our friends, to the effect that "you can't do that." How many of us know whether or not we can paint, write, lecture, invent, promote or organize? Some self-appointed teachers have soberly sold courses telling us that we have been hypnotized by the "You can't do that" suggestions surrounding us, and telling us how to un-hypnotize ourselves and blossom out. The results observed on the part of students have not indicated much success, but the basic idea may have been fairly close to a part of the truth. When a better method of freeing ourselves from our fixations of "you can't do that" are found, the results should be increasingly better.

Meanwhile, it is high time that we who have not crystallized our beliefs, and who can still accept new truths, get to work experimentally to see if the methods which worked so well for the kahunas will work equally well for us.

I am positive that the majority of a group of newly graduated doctors, regardless of the schools from which they come, could be taught to use the magically potent methods of lomilomi in a course covering, say, sixty days. The ability to accumulate and transfer vital force would come quickly, and—with that art once learned—the need of learning to administer deep hypnosis would be entirely obviated.

Almost anyone, man or woman, can learn to use light suggestion. An hour of practice each school day would make expert operators out of the average doctor in the sixty day period. The rest of the class time would be profitably taken up with the business of learning the new psychology which we are recovering from the kahunas. Out of the groups of doctors thus trained, a few might learn to use the kahuna methods of producing instant healing.

CHAPTER XIV

STARTLING NEW AND DIFFERENT IDEAS FROM THE KAHUNAS CONCERNING THE NATURE OF THE COMPLEX AND HEALING

What the doctors and psychologists have failed to see clearly is the rather startling fact that the subconscious or low self is not the only one afflicted with fixations of ideas—the complex.

Freud, Jung, Adler—all of them fixed their attention on the subconscious, not realizing that the conscious self had similar and equally dangerous fixes.

The astounding truth is that almost all persons have CONSCIOUS BELIEFS OR OPINIONS WHICH ARE FULLY AS FIXED AS ARE THOSE OF THE LOW SELF. For instance, take some outstanding examples which will be instantly familiar to all of us. There is the person who is set in some political belief. He has passed beyond all appeals to common sense and logic in his rabid belief that his political party is right and all others are wrong. He will not listen to any argument against his convictions. Any effort to point to parts of his belief that are wrong will be met with anger and loud resentment.

A similar example can be found in any of the millions who have accepted a religion, and who close their minds entirely against any possible change of their opinion. New facts, new findings, or new circumstances make not the slightest impression on these individuals. They have developed a complexed set of beliefs or opinions which are SHARED BY BOTH LOW AND MIDDLE SELF.

Here is another secret from the lore of the kahunas: if you wish to know whether a person has a complexed belief which is shared by his low self, watch to see whether the emotions react to any suggestion that the beliefs might be less than correct.

If you say to a Republican, "I think the Republicans are making a mistake about last week's legislation," and if you are met with an emotional reaction instead of a quiet consideration of the reasons you may go on to give for your opinion, there is a complex behind the political beliefs of the man.

Criticize a man's religion and watch in the same way for the nature of the reaction. The low self is the only one responsible for emotional reactions. The middle self reacts only with logic and reasoning unless it is entangled with the low self in holding complexed views, in which case reason fails to begin to function as emotions flare.

A man's political complexes, fortunately, seldom react on his health. His religious fixations frequently cause endless illness and misfortune.

The kahunas knew what the psychoanalyst has overlooked to a painful extent. It is the fact that when a man has "sinned" and his low and middle self agrees that he has sinned, the low self may have a fixed idea that punishment must be given for sin. If this is the case, the low self may set about punishing the man through illness or accidents.

The point can be illustrated by the case reported by a psychoanalyst, of a young man who had been brought up by an aunt who had given him a very strict religious training. As he finished high school he felt the urge to take up the ministry, but gave up the idea to take a job in a furniture factory. In the factory the paint and varnish fumes sickened him. He was sent to the wood working department, and the sawdust gave him asthma. He got another job and then another. In every case he was made ill by something connected with the job. He chanced to fall into the hands of a doctor who recognized the symptoms as the indications of a deep-seated complex. His original complex had been formed when he had given up the idea of devoting his life to religious service in the ministry. The low self had shared with the middle self a deep sense of guilt for refusing to give his life to the service of God. Because it was painful to think of the refusal, the young man had shut away the memory of it. But that memory had remained in the low self as a part of the fixation of guilt. As he had been taught that all sins and guilts are punished by God, his low self had expected and feared punishment. However, as the middle self refused to think about the sin of refusing to go into the ministry, the low self did what is known as "translating" or changing the externals of the complex. It hid its anxiety to have the man become a minister behind a dislike that amounted to illness for every other occupation.

The doctor, after the usual questioning and observation period, dug out the cause of the trouble, but instead of being able to point out the source of the fixation and so rationalize and drain it off, he met a new obstacle. When the young man was forced to recall his refusal to enter the ministry, he was still convinced that he had been guilty before God of a great sin of omission.

The doctor tried to argue with him and met a blank wall. The patient would not listen to reason. He became angry and insisted on denouncing himself. In the end he was advised to enter the ministry to regain his health. He did as advised and his illnesses vanished.

In this case the complex was not removed. It could not be removed in the ordinary way because it was held by low and middle selves alike. Reason could not get a hearing. The only remedy was to let him act in such a way that he would obey the dictates of the dual fixation.

In his report, the doctor showed his failure to recognize the complex as a part of the conscious mind of the patient. He wrote: "... although the fixation was at last brought to light and submitted to the usual process of rationalization, it became evident that it had not been removed. Upon making a visit to the furniture factory where the first symptoms developed, the smell of paint and of wood sandings sickened him in turn. Recovery came only after the fixation was accepted as immutable and a school for ministers was entered."

The urgency of the need for better understanding of the single and dual complex and the ways to combat them may be realized when one considers the dire fact that one out of every family of six will eventually need treatment on this score. Unfortunately the present methods of treatment are far inferior to those formerly used by the kahunas. The most effective method is "deep analysis," but this takes months of time and mints of money. If a cursory review of the case and a small amount of treatment by suggestion does not bring a cure, the patient has an alarming chance of joining the throngs which crowd the hospitals for the insane.

A complex of simple nature or a dual one shared by both selves, if not allowed to have its way, creates a "house divided against itself" which certainly will fall—into insanity, or chronic invalidism.

Dr. Edward S. Cowles, famous for his "soul clinics," said a few years ago that he was certain that the mental conflicts caused by fixations were the direct cause of the steady lowering of "nerve energy" which, if continued, ended in disaster. He explained that if the usual supply of nerve energy or vital force falls slightly below normal, the individual begins to feel a lack of spirit and cheerfulness. This turns to a feeling of depression. Further depletion results in melancholia, and there come the progressive symptoms as depletion continues: deeper states of depression, hysteria, fear, nervous breakdown, mania, and psychosis. The dismal fringe of insanity is touched. If one continues to sink lower, exhaustion brings helpless insanity in which reason is lost and memory vanishes. In this condition the patient lies inert and must be artificially fed.

It might be added that during the gradual depletion, there is always the danger that a poltergeist type of low self which has been separated from its middle self, may drive out the selves of the ailing body and obsess it. In these cases there is a return of physical energy but, with the original low self deposed, memories are gone, and with the original middle self gone, all reason is lacking.

With violent death so frequent in the two World Wars, it is inevitable that there are more of these ghostly low self spirits of the poltergeist class abroad awaiting a chance to seize a body and obsess it. We continually read articles calling attention to the alarming increase of insanity. At the present rate of increase, some estimate, we shall in a few years have so many insane that there will not be enough sane people to feed and care for them.

In self defense we need to learn what methods were successfully used by the kahunas to combat the complex in its single and dual form, and to treat the unfortunate victims of obsession.

For the moment let us take up the first part of the problem.

Case 25 Kahunas Treat Illness Caused by Dual and Single Complexes Preliminary Notes:

Because modern psychology is so young and so little advanced, it offered little help when I tried to understand the significance of the things the kahunas did in treating patients to remove complexes. Their success proved to me that they had a very superior method, but from a close study of what they did, I was unable to learn what action of mind they used or what force was employed, both of these things being invisible and silent in operation. Only from the externals of treatment and ritual could I draw conclusions. Much later I was able to see what actually took place.

The Cases:

(A) There was a driver of "rent" cars in Hawaii in 1926, a handsome, healthy and charming Hawaiian. He had been brought up by a very religious father and had married a very religious wife. He attended church faithfully.

A few years after his marriage he fell violently in love with another woman, even though he remained devoted to his wife. He was much afflicted by his conscience, and greatly oppressed by a sense of guilt for having sinned. His wife discovered his infidelity but, after a stormy scene, forgave him on his promise that he would not repeat his offense.

However, before a year had passed, he had again fallen by the wayside. This time he was not found out, but his sense of guilt was greater than before.

At this time he happened to catch cold. The cold took on the symptoms of influenza, and despite excellent medical care and nursing, he failed to recover. On the contrary, he gradually became weaker and weaker. He lost interest in his surroundings, refused food, and turned his face resolutely to the wall.

His wife, after hearing the verdict of the doctor that he could not live more than another day or two, called in one of the few remaining kahunas who were at work in Honolulu at that late date.

The old kahuna listened carefully to the wife's account of what the white doctor had said. He asked a few questions, and then began his treatment. He bared the body of the sick man and began to rub him slowly.

From time to time he paused and rubbed his own hands slowly together, then applied them to the sick man's back, chest or head, always telling in a low voice how he was pouring strength into the patient to make him strong.

After a time he began questioning the man, asking what he might have done that had hurt someone—had been a sin. At first he was met by a stubborn refusal to answer, but finally the sin was blurted out. After making his confession the patient asked to be let alone to die in peace.

The kahuna, however, reasoned gently. He called in the wife who had been sent to prepare a hot tea of native ti leaves, and told her very simply that her husband had sinned against her and was dying because he could not face her. The wife was enraged for a moment, but facing the danger of death to her husband, agreed to forgive once more. She kissed him and wept over him, then went back to her kitchen.

The kahuna, following a very ancient ritual, produced from the bundle which he had brought with him, four small white stones. He placed one of these at each corner of the bed, commanding them to act as a wall to keep away any spirit who might come to try to interfere with the treatment. Next he took sea water and a brush of green leaves, sprinkling the room while he ordered all unwelcome spirits to leave the place.

The wife brought the decoction of ti leaves boiled in salted water, and it was diluted with cold water in a calabash bowl. Taking a brush of the green sword-like ti leaves, the kahuna approached the patient, telling him that because his wife, who had been sinned against, had forgiven him, his sins could now be washed away with the water in the bowl. Describing carefully the way the sins were being dissolved in the water and being washed away, he sprinkled the patient's body, then brushed vigorously with the leaves, getting some water back into the bowl. He declared that all the sins had now been washed away and had entered the water remaining in the bowl. He asked the wife to raise the patient's head so he could see with his own eyes that the water carrying the sins was poured on the ground outside the door and so was disposed of forever.

The patient was carefully dried and rubbed, being told that his strength was rapidly returning and that he would soon be very hungry, would eat, and then sleep. Upon awakening he was promised that he would be well on the way to recovery. The man's strength did return, he did eat, and he fell asleep. When he awakened hours later, he sat up and called for more food. His wife brought thick soup and he was sitting up happily talking with her when the white doctor called. He was one long in the Islands and experienced. After a careful examination of his patient he turned to the wife and asked, "You had the other kind of doctor?" She nodded, and he went out shaking his head wonderingly.

(B) A white woman, young and lately married to an officer of the Marines, was my neighbor during part of my years in Honolulu. Before her marriage she was a very staid Methodist, looking upon dancing as a sin and considering drinking a very grave sin indeed. Her husband introduced her into a circle where dancing and drinking were the order of the day. She was laughingly pressed to join the fun, and gradually threw off her reluctance and began to learn to dance, even taking a cocktail. She had learned to dance a little when, during a dance at the home of a friend, she tripped over a rug and twisted her ankle. The twist was slight and she continued dancing. But the next day the ankle remained slightly sprained. It did not get well as she had expected that it would, and in a week or so became worse. She went to a doctor, who examined the ankle and made X-ray pictures, finding nothing to explain the failure to recover. In a short time she could hardly walk. Then there developed a strange, deep running sore below the ankle joint. The doctor called in a consultant. It seemed very puzzling. All treatment failed. It was then that the young woman came to me to ask my opinion as to whether the kahunas—of whom she had heard me speak—might be able to help her. I advised her to try one, and she did.

This kahuna was a younger man and more worldly wise if less expert than older healers might have been. He at once suspected a complex—or, as they say, "something eating inside." He asked what sins she had been committing, and she at once confessed dancing and drinking, telling him of her former church affiliations.

With great patience he set to work to explain to her the kahuna point of view regarding sin of all kinds. The kahunas had a very simple way to tell what was a sin and what was not. One asked oneself whether any act was such that it injured another or hurt another's feelings. If it hurt no one in any way, that act was not a sin. He pointed out to her the logic of the kahuna belief that God was too high and all-powerful for any human being to hurt by any act. Little by little he convinced her that dancing and the taking of a cocktail were not really sins. This done, he performed a ritual of forgiveness of sin, sprinkling her bare arms and face with salt water and declaring that all her guilts of every sort had been forgiven and washed away. He then carefully massaged the bad ankle, telling her over and over that it was now becoming healed. He bound the ankle in a poultice of native herbs and told her to repeat frequently to herself, aloud: "I cannot sin against God. I am too small. I have been forgiven for all my sins. I have hurt no one. My ankle is getting well very fast."

The success of the kahuna's treatment became apparent in a short time. The running sore closed and healed with hardly a scar. The ankle recovered its full strength and flexibility.

Not realizing the fact that the trouble had been caused by a state of mind which had been altered by changing her attitude toward dancing and drinking, the young woman failed to obey the kahuna's orders to continue her affirmation of "No hurt, no sin." Again she danced a little and drank a little. As habits of thought are as easily reestablished as, for instance, habits of smoking or using alcohol to excess, her two selves gradually slipped back to the old beliefs. She found herself worrying for fear the kahuna had been wrong and her religious instructions of childhood right.

One morning, to her dismay, she found that the sore had reopened. Going back to the kahuna, she asked him to heal her anew, but when he had questioned her, he refused. He explained that when an old habit of thought, "an eating inside," had been awakened after once having been removed, it was almost impossible to remove it a second time. In the end the ankle was operated on by doctors, bone cut away, and it is to be supposed, enough pain suffered to convince her low self that she had made amends for her sins. She gave up dancing and cocktails, and the sore did not return.

Comment:

In the two cases given above, the important thing to note and to remember is that the middle self can share a complex with the low self.

In Case "A" the Hawaiian had sinned by being unfaithful to his wife. No form of forgiveness could have convinced him that he had not so sinned. To convince his reasoning middle self that he had been forgiven, his wife had actually to forgive. He had to see her and hear her speak the words of forgiveness—these being physical stimuli which could and did impress the low self which had accepted or brought on illness as a punishment for the sin. While this case does not deal with a deep-seated and hidden complex, it illustrates very well the common cause of illness based on strong fixed beliefs which have their origin in actual facts, and which are shared by both low and middle selves.

The kahunas taught that nothing is a sin if it does not hurt someone. This is a truth which must be shouted from the housetops endlessly if we are to escape the ill effects of the teaching that it is a sin to break dogmatic taboos of various religions. There is no way of knowing how many thousands of cases of illness, insanity and disaster have been caused by complexed religious beliefs developed in childhood, such as the belief of the young woman in Case "B" that dancing and drinking were sins.

The sex urges are the most prolific sources of complexed ideas of sin with which we have to contend, since as children we are taught modesty and are shamed or punished for any display of sex interest. Religious instruction implants the idea that sex urges are sinful and that, therefore, children are born from and in sin.

The kahunas were logical in their approach to sex. If sex acts did not hurt another, they were not considered sins. In any case such acts were not sins against Higher Beings. Sins were only acts that hurt others.

Dr. Emmanuel Freud, discoverer in the West of the subconscious or low self, found that in treating illness by suggestion, the subconscious would not accept suggestion in many cases. His search for the reason for this brought to light the complex of ideas which can be held by the low self. It was found that the low self, which is the one which accepts suggestion, will reject suggestions which are contrary to its fixed beliefs in morals or its complexed belief in some imaginary condition.

Later on it was discovered that the low self, if thwarted in acting in accordance with a complexed belief, would "translate" that complex or change it so that it seemed to have little connection with the first and important complex.

There was the case of the small boy who developed a complexed dislike for attending church. He may have been forced to attend church when ill, weak or otherwise indisposed. (He may have been punished for not wishing to attend church and so given a shock complex.) The boy loved his parents, and when they explained why he must go to church to worship, and begged him to be a good boy and do as he was told, he tried to obey. He tried to love church, as he had been instructed, and seemed properly convinced that it was his religious duty to attend services. However, the low self, which had become complexed with dislike for attending church, showed the animal-like craftiness so well known to psychologists and the kahunas of old. It translated its fixed determination not to go to church into a major dislike for the smell of incense. Upon smelling incense, the boy would invariably be sick and have to be rushed from the church. The situation then became one in which the child was willing enough to go to church, but could not. The low self had its way.

In complexes built upon sex restraints, the low self may translate the externals of the complex several times. The result of such action is that even the long psychoanalytical study of the patient's dreams and thought associations may fail to bring to light the original complex so that it can be talked over and submitted to "rationalization"—being thus "drained off" or brought under the control of the middle self as are normal thoughts and ideas.

Freud decided that all complexes were based on sex frustrations. Later psychologists modified the severity of this decision, but there is still a school of psychologists who hold with Freud and present very telling arguments to support his stand.

Because the complexed low self will refuse to accept suggestion to remove the symptoms of trouble caused by the complex, the healing value of suggestion is greatly lessened. In Case "B" the low self of the young woman would have refused healing suggestion after the complex had been restored in the second breaking out of the ankle sore. Low selves refuse to accept any hypnotic suggestion that is contrary to the subject's moral beliefs. A hypnotist cannot force a subject to perform acts which he considers immoral.

Because the low self creates all of the emotions for us, it is possible in many instances to discover the presence of a complex or fixation by watching for an emotional reaction when such a complex is stirred into action.

We are accustomed to the spectacle of someone "flying into a blind rage" over some trivial happening. It may be only a word. These small things that touch off emotional explosions are the "triggers," so to speak. Once the trigger has been touched, the full force of all former rages connected with the circumstance that created the complex in the first place is released.

On the other hand, there are good complexes and their triggers. One may have many complexes developed in connection with his daily occupations. For example, the alarm clock rings, and even against our desires, we stir and begin to follow our habitual actions of arising.

One of the ways in which the low self forces its wishes on the middle self is through engulfing the middle self with a great wave of emotion—in which it usually is caught and overpowered. Waves of hate or of desire or of distaste are well known, as are those of homesickness and longing. Of all the emotions, love is the most interesting to study. It seems to be the one which the middle self can most nearly share. Basic physical attraction may be added to by elements of parental or filial love, and to these may be added the logical approval and admiration of the middle self. The resultant emotional mixture is one of the driving forces on all levels of consciousness.

CHAPTER XV

THE SECRET KAHUNA METHOD OF TREATING THE COMPLEX

While modern psychoanalysts have never found a simple and effective method of finding the complex and bringing it to light to be rationalized and drained off, there is a method to be learned from the kahuna lore.

The importance of finding such a method cannot be overestimated, for, if we can learn to use it, the healing art will take its greatest single stride forward since the discovery of suggestion.

This method is a violent one. It will seem very strange to the civilized man at first glance, but no stranger than the use of violent insulin shock on insane patients in modern asylums.

Because this secret method is so new and radically different to us, it will bear a step-by-step explanation.

Please recall the fact that the kahunas believed that thoughts were invisible little things—thought forms—and that they were very real and substantial. The thought form (aka) is made when we think. Every thought is made into a permanent thought form. Thought forms come in clusters of associated thoughts, thus linking one idea or thought to the one which came before or after it, and to all similar thoughts.

Recall also the fact that thought form clusters flow on currents of vital force, which in turn flow along tiny threads of shadowy body material connecting two per, sons, as in telepathic communication. In giving suggestion there is a flow of vital force from the operator to the subject, through hands placed on the subject, through shadowy substance threads connecting the two after the first physical contact, or through contact established by the line of sight or even the sound of the voice. (Also through one traveling during sleep in the shadowy body, or by means of contact made through the assistance of the spirits of the dead.)

SUGGESTION IS THE IMPLANTING OF A STRONG THOUGHT FORM IN THE LOW SELF OF THE SUBJECT. The power of the vital force accompanying the implanted thought form plays a part in its effectiveness, but not nearly as large a part as is generally supposed by psychologists. I have seen hypnotists strive to put their "will" into a suggestion to make it effective, their eyes burning, their faces becoming red, and perspiration standing out on their foreheads, and still no results were obtained. The "will" or middle self voltage of vital force is not the hypnotic agent. It only directs its own low self to plant the thought form of the suggestion in the shadowy body of the low self of the subject. The effectiveness of the suggestion depends on the acceptance of the thought form by the low self of the subject.

As already explained, the acceptance of the thought form of a suggestion is greatly hastened by the use of a physical stimulus— something physically real that may be sensed by the low self of the subject and which will make it believe that a real something is behind the suggestion.

Now comes the vital secret of dealing with the complex.

It is not necessary to search for the original complex of the patient as is done through deep analysis in psychoanalysis. It is not necessary to study the patient's dreams for symbols and hints. No matter whether the original complex has been translated from one form to another and to another, it can be treated by suggestion. THE SECRET IS TO MAKE THE LOW SELF OF THE PATIENT ACCEPT A SUGGESTION CONTRARY TO ITS COMPLEX OF BELIEF. This is done by an almost violent use of low voltage vital force.

Recall the kahunas who filled throwing sticks with low voltage vital force by an effort of their wills to accumulate such force and transfer it to the stick—and the almost human way in which the force obeyed instruction to leave the stick and knock the enemy senseless or paralyze him on contact when the stick was thrown.

Recall the American Indian medicine men who accumulated this force (which they called orenda and other names) and discharged it through a touch of a finger into the body of a strong brave, rendering him unconscious.

Remember the case of Dr. Brigham and the death prayer directed at one of his boys while in the mountains of Hawaii on a collecting expedition. The death prayer was a matter of charging low self spirits with great charges of low mana, then sending them to contact the victim and discharge into him the full shock force of the charges. This shock force broke down the resistance of the victim's low self, particularly if it harbored a guilt thought or complex, and forced it to accept the thought form of death sent by the kahuna.

The low self spirits then attached themselves to the victim and drew from him his vital force, storing it in their shadowy bodies, and preparing to take it with them after the death of the victim through exhaustion of vital force. (The suggestion of death causes the victim's low self to stop making enough vital force to sustain life. Most illnesses which do not mend in the normal course, grow worse when for some reason the usual supply of force is not made.)

THE SECRET OF FORCING THE LOW SELF OF A PATIENT TO ACCEPT A THOUGHT FORM OF SUGGESTION LIES IN THE USE OF AN OVERPOWERING SHOCK OF A LARGE CHARGE OF VITAL FORCE—THIS CHARGE ACCOMPANYING THE OFFERING OF THE SUGGESTION.

Dr. Brigham gave me one evening a detailed account of a case of kahuna healing which had long puzzled him, and which puzzled me in my turn until I came to understand the methods outlined above.

A kahuna had been treating a native patient for a fugitive set of symptoms which prevented the patient from crossing the beach to his canoe to go on his daily round of fishing. At first a paralysis of the left leg would appear when he tried to cross the beach. This was treated and seemingly cured, but next there came dizzy spells at the approach to the beach, and next, complete blindness which lasted until the patient left the beach and returned to his home.

The final treatment, which Dr. Brigham did not see, but which was described to him at great length later, consisted of a very impressive use of a physical stimulus accompanying a suggestion in the form of the repeated assertion that the treatment was removing all things that prevented the patient from crossing the beach and going to fish in the usual manner.

The physical stimulus took the form of a large wooden bucket filled with brackish water. The kahuna, in the presence of the patient, worked for a long time over the water to make it potent and ready to cure. He stirred it with green ti leaves, added grated yellow ginger root, and placed the palms of his hands repeatedly on the surface.

When he was satisfied with his preparations he called his patient and instructed him to sit down before the bucket and thrust in his face, holding his breath and drinking as much as he could. The patient was told that the water would enter him and drive out all the things which had been causing the trouble and that they would never return.

The patient did as instructed and began to drink, the kahuna placed his hands on his arms and commanded the illness to leave the body. The patient drank very rapidly for a moment, then sagged and fell over the bucket as if dazed. He was slightly lifted by the kahuna to clear his face from the water, but was left huddled in that position for several minutes, the kahuna quietly repeating his assertion that the ills had vanished never to return.

The man had recovered from his dazed condition and had immediately been taken by the kahuna and ordered to cross the beach. He found that he could do so without a return of the mysterious maladies. He was then told not to think of his trouble—a usual precaution taken by the kahunas to prevent the recurrence of the complex—and the work was done. The trouble did not return.

A review of the case, long after Dr. Brigham described it, and in the light of knowledge gained of the kahuna "Secret," brought out the undoubted fact that the kahuna had filled the water in the bucket with a shocking charge of low mana or vital force. He had used this force literally to break down the resistance of the low self of the patient and make it accept his thought form suggestion of the removal of all ills which prevented the usual crossing of the beach to the canoe. (One is reminded of Mesmer's practice of charging a vat of water from which iron rods protruded to contact his patients and transfer to them the vital force which he called "animal magnetism.")

It is to be noted that the original complex was never located or drained off by recognition and rationalizing. THE COMPLEX WAS REPLACED BY ANOTHER COMPLEX IN THE SHAPE OF A THOUGHT FORM IMPLANTED BY THE SUGGESTION-SHOCK TREATMENT. The thought form of the suggestion was, of course, a cluster of many related thought forms. The suggestion had included rational arguments to show that there was no valid reason why the beach could not be crossed and the fishing done.

Case 26 Direct Physical Reaction to Suggestion Preliminary Notes:

While we do not know the limits of the ability of the low self to act on the body to bring about healing, the evidence accumulates which shows that the power is very great.

The Case:

While I was living in Honolulu, a young white man came to sell me advertising space in a newspaper each week. He became interested in the Hawaiians and often told me of attending their dinner dances given in the open.

One day he came to me much upset. He had become acquainted with a Hawaiian woman at a dinner party, and the woman had admired his girlishly fine skin. She had asked him thoughtfully if he did not find it a great chore to shave daily, and had solemnly told him that she could make his beard stop growing if he wished to be relieved of the shaving chore. She said that many Hawaiian men had so been relieved of the necessity of shaving. In a tolerant mood he pretended to accept her offer gladly, being certain that it was a native superstition of no consequence.

Taking him aside the woman stroked his right cheek with her fingers for a short time, saying that the beard would stop growing on his face and that he would be free of the need of shaving.

He had forgotten the incident when, about two weeks later, he suddenly noticed that there was a place on his cheek the size of a dime upon which no beard grew. To his alarm the spot grew larger day by day. When it became as large as a half dollar, he remembered that I had spoken of the kahunas and came rushing to me to ask my advice. He was almost girlish of face and realized that without a shadow of beard he would be disastrously feminine in appearance.

I advised him to inquire among his Hawaiian friends for the woman who had caused the difficulty, and when he found her, to ask her to reverse her suggestion. He had some trouble finding the woman, but did eventually, and she reluctantly stroked his cheek and gave the suggestion (it was suggestion beyond doubt) that the beard would return to the bare spot. In a little over a week the beard again began to grow in the denuded circle. Where I had found the skin bare, I could see the dark beard stubble reappearing. In a short time the beard was back to normal.

Comment:

Such control is of great interest in as much as it shows how surprisingly the low self can react to suggestion in making changes in bodily functions.

Suggestion may get results for any functional control with the possible exception of invading foreign bodies which normally lie beyond the range of the control of the low self. Most disease germs can be brought under control by the low self in due time. The kahunas believed that contagious diseases were like accidents in that they just happened to come along. If a person had an accidental injury or contracted a contagious disease the low self would set to work to heal the injury or combat the disease. If not afflicted by a complex or weakened in some way, or of advanced age, the chance for recovery was good.

While nothing has so far been learned of the kahuna attitude toward cancer or similar growths which seem to be invasion of foreign cells in the body, it is probable that the low self of the sufferer from these afflictions may have allowed such an invasion because of a complex, but may not be able to expel the intruding tissues by its own efforts even after the complex is removed. For the cure of these things there may be a method of controlling the consciousness behind the invading cells, whatever that consciousness may be. However, the instant healing to be had through the High Self is the positive cure.

The importance of the kahuna methods of dealing with the complex may be better grasped if we realize that in the United States we have about four thousand psychiatrists, and hundreds of thousands of patients needing their help. We have a very few trained psychoanalysts, and only a handful of them have learned to use suggestion to help delve for the complex. None know the method of shock with charges of vital force to cause the patient to accept suggestion to replace the complex.

Out of the young men found otherwise physically fit for war duty in World War II, twelve out of every hundred were unfitted for service because of psycho-neurotic conditions which needed treatment.

The average doctor knows little or nothing of the treatment of these cases, nor will he take the time to learn to use suggestion. The professional hypnotists have been allowed no standing by the medical associations, and practice at their peril where healing is the objective.

CHAPTER XVI

HOW THE KAHUNAS FOUGHT THE HORRID THINGS OF DARKNESS

There are horrid things which belong in the realm of darkness, but which we are powerless to combat because we have become too civilized to realize that they are there. Doctors know nothing of them. Priests and ministers have such a garbled idea of devils that their advice is useless. Spiritualism knows only enough to be afraid, and to warn dabblers to be careful.

All primitive peoples know something of them, but their methods of meeting the threats of the dark ones is of precarious value.

Modern occultists have guessed at a whole train of evil things, writing gravely about "black" magic, spells and enchantments. They draw their magic circles and retreat within them to escape the dark forces, not sure that such forces are present. They go back to the Middle Ages and revive the use of talisman and charm. They cense the air and invoke the protection of God through His seventy-two supposed names.

The practitioners of mental healing religions recognize these forces as "malicious animal magnetism," lit-de understanding their nature, but waging frequent war on them when their activities are suspected.

Among the priceless gifts to the world from the kahunas, is a clear and comprehensive knowledge of the dark forces and the way to fight them.

For years I have studied all available information concerning the dark things. My knowledge is still incomplete. I cannot penetrate the Huna or "Secret" of the kahunas to go into the lowest levels of evil things, nor the highest. However, I believe that I have uncovered the facts vital to normal living on this plane and on the next one after death. (It is vitally important that we gain the right understanding of things here, for when we die and cross into the after-life in the shadowy bodies, the things we have believed here become almost fixations, and may haunt us there.)

The world of invisible spirits is much like our solid world in as much as it has its jungles and wild animals, so to speak. If in this world a man should go into wild country and meet lions, tigers and gorillas, he would have to defend himself. The same applies over there in the world of disembodied things living in their shadowy bodies.

Fortunately for us, the contact with the shadowy world is slight. Only now and then do the dangerous or actively evil things break through to us and endanger our lives or sanity.

I believe I am correct in saying that when any sentient being dies and takes up life in the invisible world in its shadowy body, it makes its own level or gravitates to it through its thinking. If it thinks of familiar surroundings on earth, it makes such surroundings—the kahunas say it makes everything out of the shadowy stuff of dreams. Through these dream scenes and places, however, move real and genuine spirit beings. Thus, a man when he dies enters a world of dream scenery, sharing the dream scenes of his friends and relatives and adding his own touches. The animals of the jungle enter a dream jungle. Savage peoples enter places like those they left, and find there friends and foes.

Seldom do the spirits of the dead, when in contact with the living, report that they have gone to a place unlike the earthly places to which they are accustomed. They find themselves garbed as they were here, and they live in similar houses; the spirits of certain Eskimo tribes report living in the same lands of ice and snow as they did on this side.

The dead who expect to arrive in a Christian heaven report finding one. Those who imagine purgatorial scenes find them. Hell alone seems not to be peopled, perhaps because no one really expects to be judged utterly bad.

An elderly anthropologist promised before her death to report back to me on what she found after death. She did so, through a medium, identifying herself to my entire satisfaction by mentioning things she loved to do, to wear and to say while here-living. She said that she found friends and American villages and scenery. After becoming accustomed to new conditions, she set about hunting for various savage and semi-savage tribes with whom she had lived and whom she had studied here. She found that these tribes had gravitated to their fellow tribesmen on the there-living side, and inhabited the same dwellings in the same scenic surroundings. Her friends recognized her and they had happy reunions. Amongst these tribes were certain head hunting peoples of mountainous Formosa—friends of years past—still imagining that they might do more head hunting when they got around to it, although they had rather neglected the art for some long time. The anthropologist tried to tell them that they were dead and could do no head hunting. She tried to tell them other things, but their ability to grasp new ideas proved far, far less than when they were on this physical level of life.

The fact that on the other side we have very little vital force compared to what we have while in physical bodies, seems to make the difference between swift learning and sluggish inability to grasp unfamiliar ideas. All thought demands the use of vital force. Memories can be recalled and "remembered" with almost no vital force, but to make a new thought form is difficult, especially for the mentally undeveloped. The dead tend to stick tight to the things they believed, hoped for or feared while alive. Those here-living who have tried to teach new things to the there-living will attest the difficulty of teaching the there-living. For this reason it seems of the utmost importance that while here we store the mind with as much knowledge as we can gain from the kahunas, as well as modern psychologists and psychical researchers, and get the straight of things before we go over. I have repeatedly tried to get my spirit friends to find advanced kahunas who have gone across, and usually they fail utterly. The kahunas knew the straight of things while alive, and this knowledge gave them a superior ability to progress to more important things in the shadow world. They do not get entangled in the dream scenes and dream-like vague repetition of acts similar to those they knew on this side.

There is a definite going on for those who know the after-life conditions for what they are and who are thus enabled to escape being caught there and held back. The goal is not that of reincarnation. Only a few come back to inhabit other bodies as the Reincarnationists believe. The low selves come back as the middle selves of individuals being born on this physical level, but the middle selves, at least those from fairly civilized people, eventually go on to the level next higher. Those who know this secret waste little time in the "summerland." They obey the urge to evolve and to go on.

The uninitiated, however, stay on for a very long time in the dream-surroundings, frequently coming back to contact the earth and loved ones here. Only now and then do they make trouble.

The trouble makers are the low selves who get separated from their middle selves after death. They are the poltergeists or noisy ghosts who haunt houses and often molest the living. They are without the ability to reason, having lost contact with their middle selves, and are the spirits which obsess the living and render them insane. (There are many kinds of insane persons. Some are gentle and docile and dull. In asylums they sit all day doing nothing. There are also the wild and dangerous. Between these levels are those who are very like children, anxious to please, or prone to playing pranks and getting into mischief.)

There are also low self spirits who stay near the here-living by choice, and many of them learn to touch the shadowy bodies of the living and steal vital force. If they can steal enough, they can solidify their shadowy bodies (even while leaving them invisible to us) sufficiently to enable them to move solid objects. Because the entire stolen charge of vital force can be used or expended in one action, they can perform feats of amazing strength.

Harry Price of the National Laboratory of Psychical Research studied for three weeks a Roumanian girl, Eleonore Zugan, who was haunted by a spirit of this kind. It was a source of much trouble, moving objects around the room when the girl was in it, marking her skin with peculiar marks and thrusting pins and needles painfully into her flesh.

A young widow in Ohio was haunted by a poltergeist which was studied by the professors at a medical school which she attended. One of its feats of strength was the tearing away of the spindles of a strong banister, spindle by spindle as the young woman mounted the stairs. It threw objects and smashed things in a maliciously destructive way.

Bed covering has been jerked from sleeping individuals very often, this seeming to be a favorite trick. Water has been brought and dumped over haunted persons, and several cases have been studied in which fire has been brought and set to bed or clothing or rooms of the haunted individuals—usually adolescents of a mediumistic nature, ones from whom vital force was easy to steal.

In a few cases the poltergeists have been useful doing chores such as setting tables and washing dishes during the night.

These low selves may be fairly harmless, and seem to be for the most part. On the other hand they are the horrid and darkly evil beings who stalk the living and prey on them, stealing their vital force, often to the point of complete exhaustion and mysterious death, or of seizing their bodies and rendering them obsessionally insane.

Thousands of the living are silently and invisibly haunted in this way, by low selves who appear as secondary or multiple personalities. They are not "split off" parts of the resident selves of a body, as is the popular belief today of our psychologists. They are individuals in their own right.

Not only do the low selves, separated from their middle selves, fasten themselves on the living as foreign "personalities," but middle selves separated from their low selves do the same to a lesser degree, and now and again a normal ghostly spirit composed of both low and middle selves is guilty of taking up its abode in the shadowy body of a living victim.

It is not for nothing that the living have an instinctive fear of ghosts. They have always had good reason to be afraid. Dreadful things are done constantly to the living, with none to recognize the invisibles who are taking their life forces and, even worse, are implanting thought forms as suggestions into their low selves to cause endless erratic behavior, crimes, mischiefs and sometimes utterly vile and evil acts.

The tradition of vampires is an ancient one. The dead were supposed to rise in the night from their graves and attack those who slept, making fine holes in their throats and draining out their blood so that they were left white and weak upon awakening.

Because, through the centuries, people sometimes fell into death-like trance conditions and were buried for dead; and because these people were sometimes taken from the grave and found undecayed and with blood still fluid, the tradition was not unfounded. It was supposed that these people kept alive in the grave by going mysteriously to steal blood from the living. There are weird tales in ancient books telling how the dead and buried were seen and recognized as they sought to steal blood. If they were, they appeared as materialized ghosts, and at most could steal only vital force.

While no proof of the correctness of any of these tales is to be had, they mention with alarming frequency the recognition of the supposed vampire ghost, by means of a dream or actual sight. The lapse of time between burial and disinterment has sometimes been given as a matter of many days, and when the body has been taken up and found not to be decayed, the only conclusion is that life was preserved in some way. In former times the blood was supposed to be the life-giving fluid. Blood found in the coffins of the dead may have been imaginary or caused by injuries to the buried individual when awakening and trying to free himself. However these things may be, there is the long chance that the entranced individuals, long familiar with vampire tales, found themselves trapped in their coffins and endeavored to keep alive by trying to suck blood from the living. They would be far more likely to absorb vital force from them, and if they could get even a little nightly supply, could preserve the scant life in the entranced body for a considerable period.

In the Middle Ages a stake was driven through the heart and into the grave soil of anyone suspected of having vampire possibilities. There were other precautions in the way of spells, incantations and religious rites. Cremation of the dead was considered a very sure way of guaranteeing that they would not molest the living.

There is a poorly defined thread of belief that may have been shared by the kahunas, that there exist beings or dark forces which have never been incarnate in fleshly bodies, even as there are good forces of a similar kind on a higher level—the Beings of Light. Nothing is actually known of either of these types, and even if they exist, their primary purpose could not be that of affecting the living human beings.

A final danger remains to be considered. It is the danger of purposeful attack by a normal there-living person who wishes to punish a here-living person for some injury done a here-living loved one. Or the punishment may be in revenge for injuries done during life to the one who has gone across with heart filled with hatred.

Suggestion plays a much greater part in our lives than most of us suspect. We take and give suggestion in association with our families and friends each day, especially if there is a physical stimulus accompanying a suggestion. The anxious mother who calls her child to her and says, "You don't look right. Do you hurt anywhere?" and then feels of the child's cheeks, may implant a suggestion of illness.

The normal dual low-plus-middle self departed spirit can also use suggestion, especially if it can get from the living a supply of vital force, and often the thought form used as the suggestion is taken from a living person.

A kahuna, in explaining this to me a long time ago in Hawaii, stressed the danger of thinking and voicing any thought which might be used as a suggestion by a normal ghost. (A normal ghost is called kino wailua, or body of two waters, water being the kahuna symbol of vital force. If a ghost had two kinds of vital force it was composed of a low and middle self living in their interblended shadowy bodies.) I was warned never to say, even in fun, "He ought to be shot," or "I hope he chokes," lest this thought be taken and given as a potent suggestion by some spirit enemy.

In Hawaii it was not the kahunas alone who knew of this possibility. The layman also knew of it, and what is more, made use of it when injured and unable to get redress from the one who had caused the injury. The injured one made a mental or telepathic appeal to the spirit of some loved relative who had passed on and did what was called "grumbling"—a rehearsal in detail of just what had been done to injure him (or her).

I will present two instances of this practice.

Case 27 Attacks on the Living by the Dead Preliminary Notes:

As I have explained in telling of the death prayer, a person's low self will usually protect itself against all marauding spirits. It usually has more of a charge of vital force than an attacking spirit (unless a heavily charged one sent by a kahuna), and because of this can repel a less heavily charged spirit. It is the low self in each of us which possesses what we call the psychic sensibilities, and it senses the presence of spirits of which we middle selves are quite unaware.

If, in instances where we have a deep sense of guilt for some real or imaginary sin or where this guilt sense has become a complex, we are attacked by a spirit bent on "punishing" us by implanting a thought form of a punishing illness or accident or condition, our low self may meekly accept the suggestion because of its conviction that it deserves such punishment.

This matter of the guilt complex, especially when we have actually hurt another and have not made restitution and gained forgiveness, and when the middle self is thus aware that it is guilty of a misdeed, is the weak spot in the armor. It has been the secret and greatly important thing known to the kahunas, but only faintly glimpsed and entirely misunderstood by religionists the world around. The Theosophists, borrowing their ideas largely from India, recognize the danger from unseen beings and speak of the great danger of rupturing the astral shell so that spirits can come through to attack.

The idea of rupturing the astral or shadowy body does not explain how mediums can work with the spirits for years and not be obsessed. The idea also lacks inclusion of the part played by the vital force as well as the complex.

The Cases:

(A) In Honolulu I studied a case of spirit attack involving the brother of a Chinese-Hawaiian friend of mine. The young man had for a sweetheart a pretty Hawaiian girl. While he had not proposed to her, it was taken for granted that he would do so as soon as his financial affairs were in such condition that he could marry.

When his new business of salt making was established, his father stepped into the situation and demanded the customary right of a Chinese father to select a bride for his son. The son loved and respected his father and, although much embarrassed by his predicament, agreed to stop courting the Hawaiian girl and give time for a parental choice to be made. He knew that the Hawaiian girl would be deeply hurt when he broke off seeing her, but was so filled with a sense of guilt and shame that he did not try to go to her and explain what had happened. Undoubtedly he developed a guilt complex which lodged in his low self and which was shared by the middle self in its conviction that he had done the girl a wrong.

The girl was heartbroken for a time, then fiercely angry at the treatment accorded her without a word of explanation. Following the tradition of her people she began "grumbling," calling on the spirit of a beloved grandmother to avenge the wrong.

Soon the young man was overtaken by a strange malady. He would faint at unexpected times and without warning. He fainted and fell into a fire, burning himself painfully. He fainted while driving to his salt works and wrecked his car, narrowly escaping severe injury. He fainted and fell on his bed while smoking, setting fire to the bed and again burning himself. Three doctors were consulted, but none of them could diagnose the cause of the trouble. Almost from the first his Hawaiian mother had urged him to go to a kahuna, but the son was very modern and had been taught at school that the kahunas were superstitious impostors and nothing more.

When all treatment failed, however, he did as his mother suggested. The kahuna, then a man well advanced in years, listened to his story, sat for a time in silence with his eyes closed, then raised his head and announced that he had sensed the spirit of an old Hawaiian woman near him, and that from her he had learned that the young man had been guilty of one of the worst sins of all—that of hurting one who loved and trusted him. The spirit of the grandmother had been doing her best to avenge the injury.

The young man was amazed. He admitted his guilt and asked what he should do. The kahuna explained to him the ancient rule of the Hawaiians that no one should hurt another, bodily, or through theft of goods or through injury to feelings. These were the only sins, and for them there was but one remedy. The guilty one had to make amends and get the forgiveness of the injured party.

Taking his leave, the young man went directly to the girl. He was met by anger and disdain, but he persisted doggedly in his effort to make her understand his position in the matter. Scornfully she refused to be pacified. The next day he returned with gifts and more apologies, and the next day and the next. At last his pleas broke down the girl's anger and aroused her sympathy. She forgave him and agreed to go with him to the old kahuna to acknowledge her forgiveness.

The kahuna seemed to be expecting them. He praised the girl for her kindness, called to the spirit of the grandmother to observe that the wrong had been righted and forgiveness obtained. He thanked the spirit for having done so well in forcing justice to be done, and asked her to cease her attack. When she agreed to his request, he took a spray of ti leaves and sea water, sprinkled the girl and the air where the spirit stood, and spoke the words of the kala or forgiveness with suggestive power. Then dismissing the girl and the spirit, he turned to the young man, explaining that the kala (to bring back the "light") or cleansing for him was a more difficult matter.

Because he had been guilty and because his sense of guilt had made it possible for the spirit to place thoughts of fainting in his mind when she pleased, the punishment might even now be continued by his own low self (unihipili) unless it was well cleansed.

For the cleansing or forgiving ceremony he would have to use a very powerful and effective ritual—one which could not fail to cure the fainting forever. He brought an egg, holding it long in both his hands and chanting a little as he commanded healing and forgiving power to enter the egg.

When the work of filling the egg with vital force was finished, he stood the young man before him and ordered him to hold his breath as long as he could. When he could hold it no longer he was to put out his hand. In his hand would be placed a china cup into which the kahuna would have broken the raw egg while the breath was being held. Without drawing breath the young man was to gulp down the egg. At the same time the words of forgiveness would be spoken and, reinforced by the egg and the power in it, would effect the complete cleansing and cure.

The instructions were followed to the letter. The kahuna gave the suggestion of forgiving and of dispelling the guilt and fainting attacks. He continued the suggestions, rubbing the young man's stomach briskly after he had swallowed the egg and begun once more to breathe. The kahuna announced the complete success of the cure, warned the patient to forget the whole affair as soon as possible, and accepted graciously his fee for his work.

I investigated this case and checked all the details of the healing treatment. I also kept in touch with my young friend for several years following. Never once did the fainting attacks return.

(B) Another case which I studied closely was one involving a young married couple, their infant daughter and the husband's mother, all Hawaiians.

The husband, an only son, had promised that his first child, if a girl, should be named for his mother. Some time later, when the baby girl was born, he had forgotten his promise or chosen to neglect it because his wife had already begun calling the child by a name of her selection.

The child's grandmother was much disappointed. Then, as her son and daughter-in-law became engaged in their own affairs and came to see her only at longer and longer intervals, she gradually became hotly resentful. As the neglect continued, she began grumbling to her departed relatives, asking that her son and daughter-in-law be forced to end their neglect.

As the kahuna who eventually handled the tangle later explained, the young couple were not aware that they had hurt the feelings of the husband's mother. They were just very busy. They had no sense of guilt. The spirits in trying to attack and punish them to bring them to time were unable to do so because of the lack of a guilt sense. The baby, however, they found to be vulnerable and each day they took from it some of its vital force. It weakened, became more and more ill, and failed to respond to medical treatment.

The baby, still not two years old, was taken to the Children's Hospital in Honolulu. It grew steadily weaker, and one day they were warned that death was impending.

Greatly alarmed and desperate, the young parents took the child from the hospital and carried her in the early evening to the home of three old Hawaiians, all kahunas of different degrees of ability, and all accustomed to practice together. Of these three two were women, the third a man. He was the most psychic and was called the makaula or "eye."

No time was lost. The old man brought a primitive crystal gazing outfit consisting of a small gourd calabash in which was placed a little water and a smooth, rounded black stone. The water was swished periodically over the stone to give it a dark reflecting surface in which psychic images appeared to the old man as he worked to diagnose the cause of the illness.

The two old women brought a warm decoction of tileaf water and began bathing the baby, taking turns placing their hands on her and making an old chant of restoration. (Such chants are very old and often very beautifully worded and rhymed in the native tongue.) The baby had suffered an attack of convulsions before being taken from the hospital and had been crying weakly. She grew quiet and fell asleep.

The old man finished his work and rose stiffly from the darkened corner where he had been on all fours gazing into the calabash in the traditional manner. He announced that he had "fished" in all directions (the reference to the threads of aka substance running here and there in all directions from the patient, and followed to find those who might be associated with him. These threads were also referred to as "fish lines"). He had seen some spirits who were angry and a very angry old woman in the flesh whom he took to be a grandmother of the baby. He asked a few questions to confirm his finding, and gave it as his decision that the grandmother had been hurt and had grumbled with the result that the baby had been attacked.

The young husband was certain that there must be a mistake and that his mother could not have been guilty of such a bad thing, but was hustled out of the house with impatient commands to go fetch his mother at all costs. He hurried to her and found, to his consternation, that the kahuna was right. She railed at him and was quieted only when he managed to tell her that the baby had suffered punishment, and not himself or his wife. It had not been her wish to have the baby hurt, and—tearfully repentant—she hurried to accompany her son to the home of the kahunas.

The old man, his crystal now set aside, questioned the grandmother, learning of her injured feeling and grumbling. He scolded her roundly, scolded the young couple even more, and called the spirits and inquired what they thought should be done by the young parents to make amends. It was unanimously agreed that the child should be named for the grandmother, and that she no longer be neglected. Amidst Hawaiian tears and laughter forgiveness was asked and given. The old man perfunctorily sprinkled everyone including the spirits, but not the sleeping baby, spoke words of cleansing, and warned that the trouble should not be remembered—but, if remembered by accident, a prayer should immediately be made for forgiveness lest some guilt "get inside" and cause trouble.

The baby made an almost miraculous recovery and soon grew plump and strong. She remained well and fine, as did the young parents until the time I left the Islands and lost touch with them.

Comment:

In these two cases can be seen the use of suggestion and a physical stimulus. The holding of the breath with the swallowing of a raw egg highly charged with vital force, and accompanied by suggestions to remove the complex and cause healing, could hardly be more clearly demonstrated.

In the case of the child, not yet two years old, suggestion could hardly have played a part, so the objection often met in the Islands, that all kahuna magic resulted from suggestion, does not apply. That a baby can be so attacked illustrates the grave nature of the danger of spirit attack. To be safe and to keep children safe, all precautions should be taken not to hurt the feelings of others if at all possible to avoid doing so. If it is imperative that something be done or said that will hurt another, it is equally imperative that the reason for the word or act be fully explained and all reasons given ahead of time. Frequently it is better to be long suffering rather than hurt the feelings of one who is not very capable of reasoning things out.

The Hawaiians of yesterday, reared in the old traditions, took great care to hurt no one. They went out of their way to prevent jealousy or envy. To this end they shared their worldly goods in a most prodigal way. The result was a community noted for kindliness and hospitality.

THE TREATMENT OF THE INSANE falls under two main headings. First, of the obsessionally insane, and second, of the insane whose brain tissues are injured, diseased or abnormal.

If the brain is not normal at birth, the low spirit can function in the child but not the conscious or middle spirit. The low self cannot learn except as an animal learns. It remains unable even to use the low self's deductive reason, and so remains idiotic.

The kahunas believed that the seat of the "mind" of the low self was in the shadowy body of the low self, and that this "mind" was in touch with a similar "mind" belonging to the middle self and seated in the shadowy body of the middle self. Both these minds usually keep in touch when the two spirits of a man leave the body during sleep or trance conditions. After death the two selves in their two interblended shadowy bodies leave the physical body. Earth memories, beliefs, complexes and ideas are stored in the shadowy body of the low self, so are taken along at death.

Normally, the two selves use the body and its organs, the shadowy bodies penetrating and blending with all organic parts, including the brain, the nerve centers, and the nerves. If some of the brain centers or nerve tissues are lacking or become diseased, the selves cannot function through them. This is particularly true in cases in which the brain tissues used by the middle self are injured by sickness or accident. The middle self, finding itself unable to function through its part of the body, becomes an outcast and leaves to wander about in the invisible levels. The low self, however, may be able to continue to live on in the uninjured parts of the body.

The asylums hold many insane persons of this class. The middle self is easily driven out of the body through a temporary or permanent injury to its nervous centers. Toxins from bad teeth or from disease may cause the middle self to leave, but the low self is able to function almost as usual. With teeth pulled or diseases treated, the middle self frequently resumes its residence in the body and sanity returns.

The low and middle selves may both be dislodged from the body by some abnormal condition or accident, and an obsessing spirit may take the body and hold it. Or the obsessing low spirit may gain possession of the body only at intervals, in which case the patient is said to suffer from "split personality."

In obsessional insanity the patient may be considered a victim of complete or reciprocal amnesia if the obsessing is done by a normal spirit made up of combined low and middle selves. When such a spirit drives out the rightful owner of the body and takes possession, it brings with it (stored in its own low shadowy body) the memories of another life in a body, and it brings also its own middle self and its characteristic reasoning powers. These cases are not typical of insanity because the obsessing pair of spirits is quite normal and sane.

The famous case of Anselm Bourne is a good example. This man suddenly changed personalities and memories. He left his home to go to the home he remembered, and, as he thought himself to be a storekeeper and his name Albert John Brown, he eventually arrived at Norristown, Pa., and opened a small store. In a short time the original selves managed to get possession of the body and the man awakened to find himself in strange surroundings of which he knew nothing. He was able to return to his home in Providence, R. I. There he was treated by a pair of famous psychologists. They hypnotized him, and under hypnosis were able to get the obsessing spirit to talk to them through the body, and give in detail all the things it had done while the body was in its possession.

Because the spirits who elect to remain close to some living person and steal a little vital force, if not able to steal the whole body, can often be called to enter the body and speak through hypnotic conditions, it has been thought that such spirits were split off parts of the original personality. When, through the repeated use of hypnotic suggestion, such obsession-bent personalities are forced to obey such suggestions as, "Unite with the main personality," there results a most amazing situation in which each patient is unlike any other. The main result is that the obsessing spirit, if a low entity and not a combined low-middle invader, can be brought under control of the resident middle self. This gradually results in the person having the memories of both low selves. In one case treated by Dr. Prince, a girl who was periodically obsessed by an invading spirit was enabled to recall the memories of what she had done while obsessed, and for this reason it was decided that her personality had been reunited.

When there is obsession by a middle self alone, there is a change in temperament and likes and dislikes, but not of memories. A dull and sluggish girl was so obsessed in the case of Dr. Azam's patient, Felida X. This girl was dull and sickly when normal. When under control of the invading "personality" (undoubtedly a middle self) she was gay, intelligent, energetic and well. The obsessional changes took place every five or six days at first, then the obsessing spirit began to hold the body for longer and longer periods until it finally kept the body all the time. As the change improved the girl in every way, it was welcomed by the parents. Dr. Fodor, in telling of this case, is careful to point out the important fact that in this instance, "the memory in the secondary state was continuous." This tells us that the low self of the girl remained constantly in the body and only the middle self changed.

MODERN TREATMENT of the insane centers around the task of restoring normal health conditions if insanity has been brought on through illness or disease. In the ever increasing percentage of obsessionally insane, classed by the doctors as sufferers from some form of "split off personality" or schizophrenia, the obsessing is done by a low self while the resident middle self is either driven from the body, or unable to control the invading low self. The characteristic thing in these cases is the loss of normal memories, showing that the original low self is displaced. There is another characteristic which points directly to a low self being involved. This is the tendency in this form of insanity to live in a dream or imaginary world, paying little or no heed to physical surroundings. Loved ones are not recognized except in the so-called "lucid" periods when the obsessing spirit may temporarily depart and the normal spirit return.

The treatment by hypnotic suggestion has long been regarded as a failure. The insane will not pay attention and seem to reject all hypnotic suggestion. This is natural for the reason that the low self or obsessing spirit has its own sets of beliefs and wishes, and suggestions contrary to these are rejected.

The insulin and electric shock methods of driving out the obsessing spirit or spirits has been the most successful treatment yet discovered. If the pain produced by shock methods is sufficiently great, the obsessing spirit will leave, and—as it is not logical—it will be unable to understand the treatment and will conclude that the body will always be a painful place in which to reside. With the pain gone, the original spirits of the patient can return.

THE KAHUNA METHOD OF TREATMENT of the obsession-
ally insane made use of the shock method of dislodging obsessing
low entities. The shock was produced by accumulating large quan-
tities of vital force in the body of the healer and transferring it to
that of the insane patient with the willed command that the invader be rendered helpless and thrown out of the stolen body.

The kahunas frequently used their psychic powers to sense
the presence of the normal spirits of the patient and instruct them
to stand by to take over the body once the invader had been put
out. The help of the departed was also frequently asked for and
obtained. A good normal person among the there-living could absorb large charges of vital force from the living and, thus greatly
strengthened in will and in its shadowy bodies, could control the
obsessing spirit once it had been put out of the body. Under control,
it was often worked over to team it up with a middle self which had
lost its companion low self—possibly the middle self with which it
had formerly lived in a body before being separated in some way.
(The rejoining of a low to a middle self in this way was a very good
thing as it removed the danger of further obsessing activities on
the part of the illogical and uncontrolled low self.)

The kahuna shock method in which vital force is used as the
shock-producing agent, has the advantage of forcing the obsessing low self to accept a thought form as a suggestion. The thought
form here is that of withdrawing from the stolen body. Because
of complexed and related fixations held by the obsessing low self,
the powerful suggestion was not always accepted and acted upon,
although the theory was that, given a sufficiently large charge of
shocking force, the suggestion would break down and replace all
contrary thought forms held by the obsessing spirit.

While we have not yet taken up in detail the healing methods
which involve the aid of the High Self, it may be said that it was
believed that no human ill could be beyond the power of the High
Self to heal. The High Self was especially able in handling obsessing low selves. The fact has been a part of religious knowledge the
world around and for many centuries. When evil influences were
sensed near or were suspected, the Christian crossed himself and
prayed through Jesus to the Father. In India the rite took the form
of intoning the sacred "Om," and in other parts of the world similar
ritualistic appeals to Higher Beings was made. Charms and amu-
lets were worn and were clutched while prayers for protection were

made. While imagined dangers grew to outweigh by a thousandfold the real danger, the practice was basically sound in that a High Self was called upon for help and a physical stimulus was used in the form of the ritual crossing or intonation, holding of cross or amulet, etc., to cause the suppliant's low self to carry the prayer to his High Self.

Most of the low selves against whom protective measures need to be taken have fixed fears of the Higher Beings, these fears being carried as memories from their lives in the physical. If they were the low selves of a Christian man or woman, they would believe in God and Jesus, and when confronted with their dark deeds and a prayer and cross, would depart in fear. A man whom I am proud to list among my friends, Bishop James, of London, used the Christian ritual of exorcism very effectively to drive horrid things from haunted houses and palaces throughout Europe.

Some of the horrid things appear to be the low selves of savage men who lived in the physical thousands of years ago. (Such traditions can be found today in any of the older and more crowded countries where for many years human life and civilizations have existed.) Not long ago, in letters from England, I had the story of one such spirit attaching itself to a small boy in the south of that country, at the time that the boy found a peculiar bright pebble on a beach. The lad was sufficiently psychic to see the shadowy body of the dwarfed old savage, and amused himself by playing with him and trying to converse by means of hand signs. In time the spirit grew too bothersome in its constant demand for attention, appearing at any time or place and trying to attract attention, constantly touching the boy with its ghostly hands.

The boy had a friend who also could see the little old man in his tattered skin garment. The friend was given the stone as a gift, and the spirit with it. Soon the second boy was partly obsessed by the spirit, the obsession periods growing longer each time they came. Doctors failed to get to the bottom of the trouble but a clergyman of the Church of England, of exceptional psychological knowledge and with more than a smattering of knowledge of kahuna lore, learned of the case and undertook to drive away the old spirit. The exorcism of the church was only temporarily helpful. He thereupon engaged the help of some psychic friends, and the impression was received that if he would add to the Church ritual of exorcism the determined use of his will to force the spirit into a glass bottle (using everything he knew of self-protection against the spirit, to repel any attempt it might make to obsess him) and then throw the bottle and the pebble back into the sea, the case would be closed.

The clergyman used full ritual of the church to purify his surroundings, the place where he stood, and his own person, and called upon the spirit to leave the stone and approach. The old spirit came in a peculiar way, appearing as a wisp of pale vapor oozing across the floor, to the feet of the clergyman—who felt the typical sensation of crawling chill at its touch. He at once began to give hypnotic suggestion to force the spirit into the bottle he held. The chill rose along the legs and then was felt no longer. A medium who was present said that she could see the spirit obeying all orders, finally disappearing into the bottle. The bottle was sealed and thrown with the pebble into the sea. The treatment was effective, and neither boy was bothered again. At a later time it was reported psychically that the old savage seemed to be in some way tied to the pebble, and that it was through the pebble that it was able to contact and obsess the boys.

It is highly probable that certain objects treasured in life by the living become fixation centers for them after death. (I have heard of many such cases.) It is also probable that when the living handle such objects they vitalize with vital force the ancient threads of shadowy body stuff connecting the object to its former owner and attracting them to the living. It is evident that in handling the pebble the boys made such a contact with the savage and made it possible for him to draw vital force from them. Strengthened by this vital force, and attracted to the levels of the living, he tried to steal a body.

These cases all stress the evidence which points to the fact that low selves on the other side of life are held over great periods of time by their fixed thoughts which have been carried across with them after physical death. If they have been separated from their logical middle selves, they cannot use reason to learn of their condition or to progress. They remain "earth bound" indeed, not understanding the significance of the change death of the body has brought to them, and anxious to get back into a living body to continue the life they knew.

We, as civilized men, face another danger in that the insane are fed and housed, and only infrequently treated by insulin or other shock methods. This forms an open invitation to lingering horrid things out of the great past to obsess the living. It is not like it was in ancient days when "mad men" were stoned to death if violent, or left to starve after being driven out of the communities of the sane. This treatment was inhuman, but it was not an invitation to happy obsession in bodies which are fed, housed and cared for in the modern way.

Of course, we will not return to cruelty in these matters, but will come to a better understanding of the forces with which we have to deal, and learn more adequate methods of treating the insane.

From the foregoing it will be seen again how great a light is thrown on the dark places in our knowledge of ourselves by the lore of the kahunas.

CHAPTER XVII

THE SECRET WITHIN THE SECRET

The Secret within the larger Secret was the fact that there was a third self connected with man and his two lower selves. The nature of this High Self (Aumakua) and the means of gaining its aid also belonged to the inner Secret.

In this the kahunas were very far ahead in their findings. They knew that they could never do more than guess at the fact of, or nature of Beings higher in the scale of consciousness than the High Selves.

Their guess was a traditional one. They guessed that the Higher Beings would be similar to the lower ones which they knew in man. They subscribed to the ancient axiom "As above, so below." They may have originated it, for no other psycho-religionists seemed to have had definite and detailed knowledge of the three separate and independent spirits which compose the man.

The kahunas knew man to be a triune being—one of three spirits—so they guessed that the gods and even the final highest and SUPREME BEING would be triune in nature. This idea may have originated with the kahunas or it may not, but it spread around the world and appears in Christianity and Brahmanism if not in the lore of the Great Spirit of the Amerindians.

Wherever the symbol of the triangle appears, it is safe to say that the secret of the triune nature of man and possibly of the gods was incorporated in the religion of the people. True, the real meaning of the three sides of the triangle representing the three selves of man, may have been lost or misunderstood, but the symbol was retained and revered. In Egypt the pyramids presented to the world four faces of triangular form. In Central America the triangle was known and used in religion.

Another ancient and widespread belief which was common to the kahunas and later religionists was that there had been a descent into physical matter of some of the CONSCIOUSNESS OF HIGHER BEINGS. This accounted for the creation of the earth and lower forms of life and gave rise to various versions of the "FALL" which are met in several religions. As a logical result of a belief in a "fall," there followed the belief that all lower creatures, headed by man, were on their way back up the scale, slowly returning to Ultimate God.

Religions are filled with the intricacies of the descent and as-
cent, but because of his mental limitations, man of the middle self
level can never do more than speculate. The ways of the High Self
are unfathomable in a large part, and the ways of still higher beings are totally unfathomable. The various scriptures which have
been supposed to have been given mankind by divine revelation,
show in the things revealed the inventions of the middle self mind.
No two of the revealed writings agree. THE ONLY THING OF
WHICH WE CAN BE FAIRLY CERTAIN IS THAT THERE IS A
HIGH SELF which can be approached to get aid in the problems
of daily living.

In nearly all religions may be found some of the beliefs of the
kahunas, even if warped to uselessness and stretched to fantastic
lengths.

The kahunas knew that the spirits of man come back at least
once to be born again in physical bodies. The low self comes back to
be born as a middle self in another human body. Some spirits may
return to be born again several times in a physical body, but the
idea of endless incarnations of man as a single spirit in innumerable bodies is an example of stretching an original idea to absurd
lengths. In Christianity and in the teaching of the Jews, Moham-
medans and American Indians the idea of reincarnation is found
only in vague reminders. In the latest of the "revealed" religions,
that based on the new Oahspe Bible, no doctrine of reincarnation
is to be found.

The same may be said in a way about the doctrine of Karma
which has become such a millstone around the necks of religionists
in India. The original idea seems to have been that when we hurt
others we laid ourselves open to spirit attack, or we formed guilt
complexes and because of them were cut off from direct contact
with our own High Selves—resulting in various difficulties.

The Hindu idea of Karma resulted from stretching the simple
original conception, even more than the reincarnation idea. With
some logic it was taught that the "Law of Karma" began to function
in the level of consciousness just below God-the-Unmanifest.

All beings lower than this Supreme had to be governed by the
Law. To complete the logic of this absurd guess at conditions in
such unthinkable levels of consciousness, the "Lords of Karma"
were invented to execute the fine justice. They had to have endless
helpers to watch each sentient being in the lower heavens and on

earth to record his good and bad deeds. The records had to be written, and the writing demanded a book, which was invented in the form of invisible akasha where all records were kept and all things recorded to the last tick of time.

The Lords of Karma, as could be plainly seen, did not punish the wicked in the same incarnation in which the wickedness was performed. The wicked flourished very often as the green bay tree. This flaw in the scheme was covered up by inventing the idea that punishment was administered in some later incarnation.

The same idea of an ideal and absolutely balanced divine form of justice is to be found in the Old Testament, but no attempt was made to cover with reincarnation the flaw of the flourishing wicked man. Punishment in hell was fully as effective and made a fine contrast with the idea of a heaven for the good after death.

In Christianity we find many things which did not come as a direct teaching of Jesus, and the origin of which is lost. The idea of the Lords of Karma is replaced by St. Peter as the keeper of the gate of Heaven, and by the Book of Life in which, in some indefinite manner, the angel recorders keep a record of each life.

Christianity is the nearest to the original kahuna lore of any of the great religions. In the rituals of the Church of Rome—the origin of the rituals being unknown—we find the counterparts of the kahuna rituals used in healing. The kahunas required a confession and used water which had been charged with vital force as a physical stimulus to accompany the spoken word of suggestion to "forgive" a patient or break down a guilt complex after amends for hurts to others had been made. In the Roman Church, after confession, holy water is used in the ritual of forgiveness with the spoken words of forgiveness, but the part played by both complex and suggestion has long since been forgotten. The penance done at the order of the priest before the rite of absolution or forgiveness is, however, quite in line with the older rite as a good physical stimulus, even if there are sins to be forgiven which do not consist of hurt to others.

The kahuna methods of exorcising obsessing or haunting spirits is still to be seen in a way in the rites of exorcism of the Church.

The kahuna belief in the High Self or Aumakua is well preserved in Christianity. Jesus, according to the records as they appear in the New Testament, prayed to his Father in Heaven when

he wished divine aid in performing miracles. That is what the
kahunas did, only with a method of praying in which there was
more ritualistic action because of the various elements involved.
In instructing his disciples, Jesus is reported as saying that they
should also pray to the Divine Father, but stressed the fact that the
prayer should be made in His name. This would be logical only if
Jesus looked upon himself as a High Self. In any event, the matter
is not one that will make the slightest difference in using a form of
prayer to the High Self in obtaining aid in healing. Fire-walking is
performed with the aid of the High Self, and that aid is obtained
by men of a surprising variety of religions—none of whom, oddly
enough, is Christian.

In India there is a hint in the Bhagavad Gita at the fact of the
three spirits of man, but the High Self of the kahunas is confused
with the "spirit of the Supreme," which is of an entirely different
level. (Judge translation, page 57: "Those who rest in me, knowing
me to be the Adhibhûta, the Adhidaivata, and the Adhiyajña, know
me at the time of death.") Because it is considered the duty of each
person to suffer and so live down his bad karma, no prayers are
made by the majority of Hindus to gain aid from the Higher Beings
in the matter of meeting the problems of daily life.

In Christianity there is a curious and almost unique mechanism to be seen in the vicarious atonement for sins. This doctrine
is obscure in its origin, but closely resembles the kahuna belief that
one can be forgiven for sins instead of suffering under a hard and
fast law of karma to repay to the last iota. Jesus made the final
and complete atonement for the sins of the world by his death on
the cross, according to Christian beliefs. These sins of the world
seem to include the sins of the newly born babes who are "born in
sin"—a strange dogma at best. The Christian does not necessarily
have to make restitution or amends in kind. In fact, he could not in
case he had taken the name of God in vain, for his words could not
be recalled. Logically, he would have to suffer in hell after death to
make amends, but, according to the Christian plan of salvation, he
may repent and get forgiveness from a priest or, better yet, by direct prayer appeal to God in the name of the great atoner, Jesus.

The kahunas, to repeat once more, knowing that the Higher
Beings cannot be injured by the living man and so cannot be sinned
against, recognize no such sin as that of using profanity. The one
recognized sin is to hurt a fellow human being. For such a hurt
amends must be made to the one hurt. In no other way can the

evil-doer convince himself that he has balanced his account and is no longer guilty of that standard sin. If not convinced that he is no longer guilty, his guilt fixation held by his low self cannot be removed by the ritual cleansing or kala—forgiveness or restoration of the symbolic Light.

In this matter of forgiving the sin in Christianity and removing the guilt complex in the kahuna system, there is one point of great significance which must not be overlooked. It is the fact that the Christian believes that his sins are against God as well as against man, and that he must get forgiveness from God, even if not from those he has injured. In the kahuna practice, the Higher Being is not asked for forgiveness. It seems to have been taken for granted that the sinner had to make amends and bring about his own forgiveness by appealing to the one he had injured. This is startling in its logic to the average Christian to whom it has never occurred that the one and only place to get forgiven is from the individual sinned against. Under the kahuna system, the rational is seen of the Jewish and karmic demand for exact and full repayment for sins, with no evasion through repentance or vicarious atonement. However, the kahuna system is kept down to the size of the sin itself and is not expanded to include gods whose existence and nature are things at which we can only guess.

It will be seen that the Huna system was definite and detailed, logical, and right to the point. It was simple and satisfactory because of a fuller knowledge of the complex and the low self which harbors the complex.

Another angle of the atonement for sin is to be seen in the part played by sin in preventing normal contact between the low self and the High Self of one guilty of a sin. Since the kahunas held that one cannot injure the High Self in any way, and that the High Self has no part in cutting off the line of contact between itself and the low self, it follows that the low self, because of its sense of guilt which it shares with the middle self, feels shame and is like a naughty child which avoids the presence of its parents because of its sense of guilt and shame.

It is thought that the low self has no sense of right and wrong of its own, being an animal self still. It gets whatever idea it has in such matters from the middle self, whose reasoning power makes it possible for it to know right from wrong. Because the low self is taught to accept blindly the decision of the middle self as to the right and wrong of any and all actions, it tends to develop fixations of guilt in a rather surprising fashion. Once a decision is reached as to the right or wrong of an action by the middle self, and that decision is given as a thought form to the low self for safe keeping, the fixation process is almost automatic. This is because the low self has been present and has sensed the solid physical action which caused the hurt to the one injured. This is a physical stimulus of a solid tangible kind and when it has been observed by the low self, it has the effect of fixing the guilt sense immediately, rendering it a complex of much gravity. To drain off this complex it is necessary to convince the middle self that amends have been made before there can be hope of getting the low self to let go of its fixed belief.

If a Christian or other religionist believes that he can sin against God, and perform harmless acts which he believes to be sins, such as the failure to attend mass or the use of profanity, the fixation is not so important for the reason that it has not been accompanied by such a direct physical stimulus. In such cases a vague and general method of making amends is found in fasting and other forms of self denial. As such things are excellent physical stimuli, they work well indeed in clearing up the lesser guilt fixations caused by the breaking of dogmatic religious commands. It is for a very good and practical reason that fasting and prayer have continued down the years to be the most used rite of all in seeking forgiveness for sins.

The sins of omission are generally the ones treated through fasting and other powerful but indirect physical stimuli by the kahunas. To be less than kind, to neglect one's duty, or to fail in any way which leaves one feeling ashamed, tends to form a guilt complex. Often such guilt complexes are present without our knowing it.

The low self is the "conscience," once it has received from the middle self a training in what is right and wrong. This training is usually received in childhood at the instigation of watchful parents. Spankings do much to fix beliefs in right and wrong in the low self before the age of six. When one is smitten by his conscience, it is an emotional reaction, not a logical one. Of course it may be both, if the middle self agrees that it is doing wrong. This vital fact is well illustrated by the peculiar morality of the savage head hunters. They would consider it a great sin to take the head of a friend, but an act of great virtue to take the head of an enemy. Conscience is NOT a God-given instinctive something. It is simply the natural emotional reaction of a low self which has been taught that certain things are right and others wrong.

Only the middle self can sin. The animals in the jungle eat each other without sinning. The low self is an animal even if associated with a middle self, and it is also incapable of sinning.

As has been explained earlier, the contact between the High Self and the lower man is through the low self and along the connecting cord of invisible shadowy body substance derived from the shadowy body of the low self. If the low self is convinced that the man has been guilty of a wrong act, it feels shame and refuses to contact the High Self in the regular telepathic way across the connecting cord. Thus prayers are not delivered to the High Self. Its aid is not requested—and, under the law that man must be allowed to be a free agent in most things—no aid or guidance is given. The result is that the man blunders and gets into trouble. The kahunas spoke of this as a BLOCKING OF THE PATH. The "path," the "way," and the "light" are all symbol words indicating the connection between the low self and the High Self. The kahuna words la and ala translate into these three words. The same use of these words as symbols is found in India and in Christianity, but with less direct and definite meanings.

Because it is confusing to try to consider the teachings of many religions at the same time and to compare them with the lore of the kahunas, it is better to compare the kahuna beliefs with the basic activities found underlying religions.

The first thing to examine is the basic human urge to look to a "god" of some kind for help, or to try to appease the god if he seems to be angry and visits mankind with plagues and disasters.

A contact with the god must be made, and a spoken prayer or request for attention is made, as "Oh, hear our prayer!" As prayers were either not heard or not given attention, the suppliant resorted to various aids to prayer. The American Indians in our Southwest made elaborate sand paintings to symbolize the thing desired in prayer. Jews and Christians fasted as an adjunct to prayer. There were cleansing rites which were supposed to make man sufficiently spotless to be acceptable before the god in prayer.

This cleansing process grew to be an elaborate ritual in most religions. Dogmas developed to teach that a man guilty of sins could not make his prayers heard unless he was first "forgiven" and ritually cleansed. Because the prayers of the good men got scarcely better answers than those of the wicked, there was a hunt for sins of which a good man might be guilty. The sins of omission, and the "original sins" were invented.

In the process of obtaining forgiveness for all forms of sin, and for the general purpose of pleasing the gods and thus gaining their favors, OFFERINGS were made. Such offerings were common in the dawn of history. Fruits, flowers, foods, sacrificial animals, and even human sacrifices were used. Altars were erected as the place of sacrifice, and priests were appointed to officiate in making both offerings and prayers.

When the gods were appeased and the floods and plagues or individual difficulties ceased, there were thank-offerings, but these played a small part in the general scheme.

At the time of death, and the departure of the (almost universally recognized) soul or souls of the man from the body, prayers and sacrifices were made by the living for the happiness and comfort of the departed in the "other world." The wicked might go to a hell, or the average run of men might go to a place of temporary punishment. A deathbed ritual of prayer was commonly performed by a priest in as widely separated places as the Western seats of Christianity and the inner fastnesses of Tibet.

There nearly always arose a doctrine of a "chosen people" in the course of development of religions. The Jews were such a chosen people. The convert to Christianity became one of the chosen because he accepted Jesus as the focal point of his religious beliefs and depended upon an initiation into the ranks of the chosen through baptism, confirmation and various similar rites, the end being to attain "salvation."

All the "salvations" were more or less alike in religions. All need of being "saved" arose from a dogmatic belief that man in his normal state was lacking in some way or ways. He might have been "born in sin," or he might have been from a tribe which was not of any one "chosen" people. In India where there was no vicarious atonement and resulting salvation through a belief in a "savior," the way of salvation was long and difficult. It led through thousands of incarnations while karma was being lived down.

Nearly all religions eventually developed to the point where there was a dogmatic belief that a special building or place was necessary for proper prayer to the gods. From the altar and shrine grew the church and the temple. While the primary purpose of religion was to appease the gods or gain answers to prayer from them, there was also an idealistic concept frequently present in the belief that praise and worship of the gods was necessary. The primitives danced to entertain the god. They fed the god with burnt offerings and blood sacrifices—blood long being considered a probable source from which the god might derive sustenance (in Christianity the "blood of the Lamb" was necessary to appease God and get Him to allow a vicarious atonement for the sins of the world, etc., etc.).

Dogmas multiplied and priesthoods flourished as each religion grew older. In the eternal search for a means of getting an answer to prayers from a god, most illogical and surprising practices developed. Flagellation, castration, abhorrence of all normal sex relations, circumcision to prevent masturbation—the list is very long. In India the austerities practiced were and are surprising. The teaching of Christianity that one should "sell all and give to the poor, then follow me," has never produced a great effect in individual action except as one became a monk or nun, but in India the beggar's bowl and yellow robes are taken outside the monastery as well as by members of monastic orders.

Here and there may be seen religious dogmas combined with rites of purification which touch on the realm of high magic. In Ceylon a rite of purification depends upon the ability of the individual to pass the stern test of the fire-walk. (I have described this rite as seen by the Englishman in Burma and filmed, and whose motion pictures I saw. Some of the candidates walked the fire successfully, and others failed painfully or fatally.)

The Science of Psychology and the Science of Psychism are not a part of religion. Religion has to do with reverence for gods or with the fear and worship given them. As soon as we ask favors of the gods through prayers and additional rites, we enter the field of magic, which is not pure religion. "Religion," to quote again from Professor Paul Tillich of Columbia University, "is the relation to something ultimate, unconditioned, transcendent. The religious attitude is consciousness of dependence, surrender, acceptance.... Magic is the exercise of immanent power; religion is the subjection to the transcendent power.... And even then, the distinction is permanently endangered from two sides. First, there is the necessity that the transcendent manifests itself concretely, and, thereupon, these concrete manifestations become for the religious imagination magic powers. And secondly, there is the natural desire of man to gain power over the divine, thus making it an object of magical practices."

Huna may be called a science rather than a religion because it has almost nothing of religion (as defined above by a Professor of Philosophical Theology) in it. The High Self is not a god. It is the third spirit or part of the man. It is no more divine than is the low self or the middle self. It is simply a step advanced in

Or mental powers and creative abilities. It is older and wiser and is parental in its attitude. It falls under the science of psychology as certainly as do the low and middle (or subconscious and conscious) selves.

In presenting this report on Huna, I have elected to call Huna a psycho-religious system for the reason that it includes so much that has always been considered a part of religion. However, I consider Huna a science in the strictest sense of the word. The kahunas knew nothing about gods—Beings higher, perhaps, than the High Self. They had no way of sensing such Beings. They admitted freely that it was probable that there were such Beings, but were honest in saying that they were convinced that the human mind would never be able to do more than imagine them—invent them in terms of lower humans.

In other words, the basic urge of older religions to appease gods or gain favors from them (religion plus magic) is replaced in Huna by the purely magical operation of prayer to the High Self for the purpose of gaining favors in the way of healing or bettering our circumstances through a change in the predictable future.

Through the High Self an appeal was made by the kahunas to the spirits able to control wind and weather, also to spirits in control of lower forms of life. (Pacts made in this manner prevented sharks in Hawaiian waters from attacking human beings—or at least that is the claim made by the kahunas of yesterday. In any event, the same breed of sharks that attacks men in other places is harmless in Hawaiian waters.)

Instead of feeding the gods with blood and burnt offerings, the kahunas understood the secret that lay behind the externals of all sacrifice. The High Self, in order to produce results in the physical plane must draw from the physical body of the earthy man sufficient vital force or mana to use in the work.

The custom of building temples or shrines to aid in contacting the gods was not practiced by the genuine kahunas, although the spurious kahunas of later times built temples of stone and offered sacrifices in vain efforts to get magical results.

The true kahunas needed no temples or shrines. They knew how to send the telepathic message to the High Self at will, regardless of place or conditions. They used no altar symbols, no incense or other mechanisms. (These things were reserved for use as physical stimuli to impress the low self when suggestion was being given for various purposes.)

The various rites used in religions to insure the dying a survival in spirit form and a certain amount of happiness as a spirit, were unknown to the kahunas. They had no place in their matter-of-fact science for dogmas which would demand a "salvation." Their teaching was simply that all people should know that the spirits of men survived death and that the memories and complexes of physical life were carried over into the spirit life, making it advisable for the individual to rid himself of guilt complexes before death. (This may have given rise in ancient times to the non-kahuna practices aimed at preparing man for a better life after physical death.)

The kahunas believed that after death there was a continuation of growth and progression, the low self reincarnating as a middle self in due time and the middle self eventually rising to the level of the High Selves, first learning to watch over lesser forms of life, and in the end becoming the "utterly truthworthy parental spirit" or High Self of a low and middle self incarnated in the physical., Not a great deal was known about this process of growth and progression, so little was taught about it except as a part of the speculative doctrines of Huna. The graduation, so to speak, of the low self to the level of a middle self is accomplished after death during a period of inactivity resembling a long sleep. One is reminded of the worm which becomes a pupa, is inactive for a time, and then bursts forth a butterfly.

The most important preparation for death must be done by the individual. He must reduce his guilt complexes to the minimum and free himself of dogmatic religious beliefs which will hinder him after he becomes a spirit. It is not necessary to spend more than a few months on the spirit plane before continuing the growth process, providing one knows the ropes as did the kahunas. Knowing Huna is knowing the ropes.

All we can take with us at the time of death is knowledge, and it should be the first duty of each of us to accumulate the correct "take-withable" knowledge by a careful study of the psycho-religions and the discarding of beliefs which cannot be substantiated.

It should be held in mind that no two inspired or revealed religions agree, and that teachings obtained from the departed through mediums show a similar disagreement. There may be one correct revealed religion and one correct teaching from a spirit or a spirit group, or there may be a partial truth in all such sources of information.

At present we have before us only one basic and practical criterion by which to measure such material, and that is Huna. I say this, because Huna worked. It made fire-walking practical. It made mental healing practical, also instant healing through the aid of the High Self. It made practical the system of gaining the aid of the High Self in changing the circumstances and future of the individual.

CHAPTER XVIII

THE SECRET WHICH ENABLED THE KAHUNAS TO PERFORM THE MIRACLE OF INSTANT HEALING

Instant healing is a miracle in terms of religion, and is something before which we stand in awe, not understanding how such healing is performed, or by what agency or under what determining conditions. We can only say, "God did it."

Most miracles are supposed to come in answer to prayer. To pray effectively, one is thought to need to be "pure," else the prayer will not be answered. However, those we consider purest and most holy, usually get no better answers to their prayers than the worldly.

This state of affairs has plagued theologians and laymen alike for many years. It was evident that something was missing in the philosophy, but no one could decide just what. Even prayers to the saints to request them to pray to God for us, and the practice of all Christians of addressing their prayers to God in the name of Jesus, have resulted in no better scores.

The first glimmer of light on the age-old problem came from the discovery of mesmerism. This would seem very odd at first glance, but not so odd on remembering the way religions tend to crystallize into inflexible dogmas and rebuff any slightest effort to change rituals, beliefs or theories.

Mesmerism was a healing agency of sorts, but soon after its discovery, Mesmer's followers were driven by their many failures to look for other measures to augment treatment by the transfer of vital force alone. In Europe and America they began to experiment. Dr. Freud eventually discovered the secret of the subconscious and of the nature of suggestion, although he was far from understanding, as did the kahunas on the opposite side of the world, that the low self was a separate and independent spirit, and that suggestion was the planting of thought forms in the low self and the causing of them to be accepted and acted upon.

Surprising as it is that Freud came this close to rediscovering the ancient psychological lore, it is even more surprising to find that, some years earlier, an American watchmaker named Phineas Parkhurst Quimby, turned to the use of mesmerism in healing, and discovered the kahunas' High Self and high voltage of vital force. Had the two men lived in the same land and had their studies been combined, they might have reconstructed the basics of miraculous healing. However, they worked apart, and the discoveries of each remained short of the mark.

The story of Freud is fairly well known, but that of Quimby is not. The latter's one authentic history is to be found in Horatio W. Dresser's book, The Quimby Manuscripts.

Quimby learned mesmerism from a traveling Frenchman around the year 1840, in New England. He gave exhibitions here and there, doing healing on the side. His favorite subject was a young man named Lucius Burkman. Lucius, when under mesmeric influenc would announce that he could see the cause of a patient's illness, and would then prescribe a remedy, usually medicinal. The results were uncertain at best.

However, with practice, Lucius improved, or the mesmerist improved, or both. In any event the lad had increasingly frequent moments of strange lucidity. He had long been able to see things at a distance, but now he came to catch glimpses of the future. One day, while mesmerized, he said unexpectedly to Quimby, "I can see your kidneys. They are wasting away, but if you will come here and let me place my hands over them, I can heal you."

Quimby had been suffering for some time from kidney trouble. Willing to try the experiment, he allowed Lucius to place his hands over his kidneys. After a time the hands were removed and the lad declared the cure complete. And, in so far as Quimby could see, it was complete. All pains and symptoms vanished.

This instant healing of his own painful condition greatly impressed Quimby. He became convinced that Lucius had touched some invisible and unknown source of healing, and he argued that what his subject could touch, he should be able to touch. He set about experimenting, displaying fine persistence and a touch of real genius.

From the records of his work it appears that, with considerable expenditure of time and effort, he eventually learned to make contact with the Thing that Lucius had found, and get it to heal, now and again, at his request. He was unable to learn what the Thing was, but sensed a presence at times of contact. The presence did the healing almost miraculously, and impressed him as being the very embodiment of wisdom. Knowing no other name for it, and feeling that it was too personal and close by far to be God, he took to calling it simply "the Wisdom."

His method of contacting the Wisdom was based on a silent call or prayer. It was a method learned after much practice. When contact was made, it was accompanied by a sense of great force or power which was used in healing. This he came to call, "the Power."

Little by little Quimby learned to work better with the Wisdom and its Power. He learned that he could sit beside a patient and silently ask the Wisdom to diagnose the case and do the healing. He was given to know by some inward process of mind what the course of the healing would be. Sometimes the healing was to extend over a period of several days and he was told how the patient would feel from day to day. The patient might be much worse on the morrow, but completely healed on the day after. Often he sensed the message that a patient could not be cured, and it was always a wonder to him that anything should lay beyond the healing power of the Wisdom. He searched his mind for possible reasons, and decided that mesmeric suggestion had possibly been given inadvertently by doctors when they had diagnosed the ills of patients who later came to him uncured.

In an effort to counteract this suspected suggestive influence he taught his patients to believe that the disease itself had been caused by the suggestion of the doctors. While this teaching was blatantly illogical, it seemed to get results, and so was continued. (In this step he seems to have anticipated a trend beginning to appear only now in the post World War II days—the trend toward the practice of giving the patient a fictitious or artificial complex and causing him to believe that it is the source of his ills. This artificial complex is then drained off, and cures often result.)

Not yet satisfied, the inveterate experimenter sought for ways by which he could use the patient's deeply fixed religious beliefs to help along the healing. Noting that logic was not demanded by most of his patients, he soberly propounded to them a doctrine that God, being Himself perfect, could have created no imperfect things in His creation. For this reason, all disease and all troubles and imperfections must be creations of the human mind, and therefore unreal, impermanent and imaginary. It followed that, once one could come to know and believe this great truth, his healing would be bound to follow. The patients were urged to deny the reality of their ills, and were helped in the denials by mesmeric suggestion. (This was a really amazing angle of attack on the fixed beliefs of the low and middle selves. He got around the ordinary guilt or "sin" complexes, even when not fully aware of their nature, by including all of the patient's sins and guilts with the other evil and imaginary things created by the human mind. When all imperfect things were denied actuality during the treatment, the guilt complexes were automatically included and rendered inactive in causing disease.)

The term "telepathy" had not yet been coined, but the phenomenon was known as "rapport." Quimby found that after once contacting a patient, he could follow him by the same means by which he kept touch or rapport with a mesmeric subject. He also found that he could in this way send healing suggestions, obtain reports on the progress of the healing, and even seem to furnish a channel by which the Wisdom could use its Power to heal. This form of healing he dubbed "absent treatment."

As his practice grew, Quimby wrote out his explanations of the perfection of God and the unreality of all imperfections. He elaborated on the explanations from time to time, and had several copies to lend to patients to study and to read over and over until they came to accept the doctrine.

One of his patients was Mrs. Patterson (later Eddy). She was healed, but her old nervous afflictions had a way of returning and the treatment would have to be repeated. She became very familiar with Quimby's methods and his written explanations of his doctrines.

Quimby died in 1865 and Mrs. Patterson's spinal or nervous affliction again returned, but with no healer to whom she could turn. In her efforts to use his system to heal herself she was successful, and, it is to be noted, without benefit of mesmeric suggestion. Seeing that the system would work with only the Quimby doctrines of the unreality of evils as its basis, she began to elaborate the doctrines, to teach others to heal, and to organize a new cult which she called "Christian Science." To the original doctrine of Quimby she added the idea of "malicious animal magnetism," which, because of the lack of a working knowledge of the complex, was forced to cover a multitude of otherwise unexplained healing difficulties. (Under this heading, also, came all the difficulties caused by spirit attacks on the living, even if not recognized as such.)

Quimby's teaching that all disease was the result of bad human thinking was partly right. The resulting denial of all physical matter and existence was most preposterous, but could not be avoided if the first premise was to be made to work in a healing system devoid of a full knowledge of the complex and the methods of dealing with it.

Christian Science, perforce, remained illogical in this respect, but the concept was one that could be readily grasped, and by repeated readings of the instruction books the low self could be brought to accept the belief in the unreality of all things physical. It was a system that worked sufficiently well, in the hands of the practitioners who learned to touch the Wisdom and Power, to attract many followers. Unfortunately, because the system is so incomplete, its failures are as notable as its successes.

To become an accepted practitioner one must develop what amounts to a deep fixation of belief in the doctrine. This makes it all but impossible for new ideas to gain consideration, and while it is probably impossible for practitioners of Christian Science to accept in any slightest way the more complete system of the kahunas, it is to be seen that, as a body, the practitioners have made the nearest approach to the high magic that has been made in the West. Many have learned to make contact with the High Self, call it what they may. Many have learned to make the correct thought form prayer and to "hold the thought" through thick and thin and with fine faith. Without being aware of it, they may furnish the High Self sufficient vital force to use in materializing in the future the healed or financially bettered condition of the patient. Absent treatment has taught many the trick of telepathic connection with patients and so has enabled them to send the patients thought forms of healing. If they could also learn to drain off the guilt and related complexes through the use of rituals and physical stimuli, accompanied with a projected set of thought forms and the proper enforcing charge of vital force as suggestion, their success might be greatly enhanced. As a final touch they might study the methods of countering spirit attack and obsession.

Another cult came into being as a direct result of Quimby's discoveries and teachings. This was New Thought. This loosely organized group had various branches and leaders. Almost at the beginning the illogical doctrine of the unreality of matter was dropped and attention was centered on an idea borrowed from India and promoted largely by Judge Troward. The idea was that if one holds the thought of what is desired, one exerts a form of suggestive influence over a "Universal Subconscious" which is forced to materialize the things or conditions represented in the thought forms. "Affirmations" or positive statements of the "here and now" reality of the desired condition became popular. Few practitioners developed, and it was generally a case of "every man for himself." Results were surprisingly good, considering the small segment of magic which was used.

Theosophy, which had borrowed thought-holding and thought-form theories from India, largely through the agency of Mme. Blavatsky, also borrowed the doctrines of karma and reincarnation, the result being that little attempt was made to heal either body or purse.

It is plain to see that modern religious thought has been leaning toward the assimilation of the discoveries of Psychology, but has been too prone to crystallization to remain sufficiently fluid to keep up with psychological discoveries. Nothing gets hardening of the arteries as fast as a religion, once its book has been written and its dogmas established.

Among the revealed religions of the last century we find Mormonism and Oahspe. Mormonism contains nothing superior in the line of magic to what is to be found in the older Christianity. Oahspe, on the other hand, is tantalizing in its hint of hidden magical meanings and mechanisms buried in what appears on the surface to be a history of all men and all gods—under a Supreme God—since the time of Creation. In many ways the teachings of the Oahspe Bible agree with that of the ancient Huna, and, because of the intricate and as yet not completely understood teachings along several lines of psychological and scientific thought, it has not yet crystallized its dogmas. It is possible that members of this group may yet do yeoman service in running experimental checks on Huna beliefs, theories and practices. If the prophesies contained in the Oahspe Bible are fulfilled, it is certain that men will again learn to cooperate with Higher Beings for healing and other purposes, as well as to receive guidance in many things of personal, national and world importance.

Huna lore throws a great light on the moot subject of FAITH. Christians and other religionists have speculated endlessly on the exact nature of faith. It was taught that faith was necessary if prayer was to be answered. Even a small amount of faith would be enough. On the surface of the matter, faith is complete belief. However, we now learn from the kahunas that belief on the part of the middle self is not enough. That alone is not faith. Only when the low self also believes is there genuine and workable FAITH.

This is simply a different way of saying that if the low self has a fixation or even slightly complexed (stubbornly held) belief which is contrary to the one held at the moment by the middle self, the low self will refuse to obey orders. For instance, if I, the middle self, am convinced that telepathy is a possibility and set out to teach the low self to send and receive telepathic or thought-form messages, I can succeed only if the low self has not, earlier in my life, been taught that telepathy is a figment of superstition.

It is very difficult for the individual to find out whether or not he has a fixed belief of a certain kind lodged in his low self. As we are unaware of such fixations, we naturally conclude that we have none. The test is best applied by watching the results we get after. a period of faithful daily practice. If there are no results at all, hunt for a complex.

In the exercise of telepathic abilities, whether communication is between the High Self, another person, or a departed spirit and a living person, there is one very helpful feature in the fact that flowing vital force causes a tingling sensation. This tingle is a great assistance in determining whether or not the low self has obeyed the order and has made contact for us.

Most people are familiar with the tingle or "raising the hair" that comes when ghostly presences are sensed. It is to be supposed that, when a spectral visitor touches us with its shadowy body, it draws from us some vital force, and that this movement of vital force causes the tingle. Very often I have begun to talk to my friends about spirits of the departed, and have soon felt a tingle, as if thinking about dead friends had called their spirits back to me.

The High Self contacts us of its own accord in our sleep, making use, so the kahunas thought, of the connecting cord of shadowy body material. Our thoughts of the day, with our plans, hopes, fears, loves and hates, are examined, taken, (perhaps as duplicated thought forms—we do not know the exact mechanism used), and at the same time vital force is taken. This vital force is stepped up to the high voltage and is used by the High Self to construct a shadowy body which will materialize as a part of our future. Such thought forms were mentioned by the kahunas as "seeds" and were symbolized as seeds which were vitalized by the High Self and grew into actualities of the future. (See the appendix for such words.)

This contact made during sleep is often to be recognized by a tingling, usually in the region of the sacral plexus, and it comes frequently at the moment of falling asleep, or even before that, if we are relaxed. The High Self not only takes from us vital force, it returns a compensating force. Little is known of this compensating force except that it is vital to our health and well being. I have often settled myself for a nap in the afternoon and have felt the tingle as I dozed off. Immediately after feeling it, I have felt rested and refreshed and ready to rise and go on with the work of the day.

If our low self has a shame or guilt complex and repels the approach of the High Self during sleep, we face disaster. We become "lost souls" without benefit of higher guidance. We lose our vitality and become ill. As the kahunas would say, our "path" is blocked to the High Self. Happily for us, the High Self seems able in due time to force a contact—when sick or in trouble most of us pray and so open the door to help—and we return to normal. If, however, the complex is too strong, the resulting illness, or accident, may end with death. The "path" must be kept open.

Case 28 Instant Healing Without Benefit of Priest or Kahuna Preliminary Notes:

From a number of cases of instant healing, I select the following because it illustrates so well the flow of vital force and the nature of the relation which may be had with the High Self. It is also important as a case because the individuals involved were of no particular religious belief.

The Case:

In Honolulu in the early twenties a large hotel was built. A man from the mainland was sent to put in the elevators. I became acquainted with him and found that he had some most unusual powers. He demonstrated these to me in various ways. One demonstration agreed with the kahuna belief that a man can extend his senses along a connecting thread of shadowy body substance and find the one who is at the other end of it, then learn about him. As I had contact with the man, and, according to Huna, had made a permanent connection by way of an invisible thread or cord, it was possible for this man's trained low self to find me wherever I might be and learn what I was doing or thinking at the moment. (I explain this in terms of kahuna lore, although at that time I had yet to rediscover the mechanism of the aka threads.) For one test I arranged to be in an old house, where I had a photographic darkroom, on various nights. I was not to turn on lights or otherwise make my presence known. The man, on his part, was to visit the house after dinner each evening and use his psychic ability to tell whether or not I was there.

The test was made several times, and it worked. He would come to the door and stand there silently for a moment. If he sensed that I was inside, he would knock, otherwise he would go away. I tried once to fool him by not answering his knock, but he refused to leave, knocking repeatedly and calling out, "Open up, Long, I know you are in there and are trying to fool me, come on and open up."

This man's story is this: He had, at an earlier period in his life, a run of bad luck as an installation engineer for a large elevator manufacturing company. Men working on jobs under him were constantly being injured despite his care. At last the elevator company discharged him. At that time he had an invalid daughter over twenty who had been bedfast for months. His wife had died a few years earlier and his daughter had kept the house. When he lost his job the times were so hard that he could not find other employment. To make matters worse, he lost his health, one ailment after another sending him to the doctor until he was compelled to remain in bed most of his time.

In desperation he tried Christian Science, faithfully reading the works of the founder and trying in all ways to follow the orders given him. Getting no results, he turned to New Thought, Unity and such other religious movements as had literature on healing.

At last, running out of funds, becoming almost completely bedfast, and quite desperate, he concluded that all religious teachings were imperfect, but that there must be a higher intelligence to which man could appeal if he could only make his appeal heard. With this in mind he spent his time and strength day after day in an endeavor to reach out and find the high intelligence.

One day he suddenly sensed the fact that he had at last contacted something. He felt an electric tingling which was sharp and short, unlike anything he had ever before experienced. Immediately he cried out for help, imploring the Something which he sensed as with him to restore his health. He cried out that he must have help at all costs, and that he was leaving his bed to demonstrate his faith by the effort. Little by little he managed to rise from the side of the bed to his feet, praying continuously. He took one uncertain step, then another. To his joy he found that he was growing miraculously stronger. His prayers turned to praise and in a matter of minutes he seemed to be completely cured and his full strength restored.

Triumphant and thrilled at his discovery, he went to his daughter's room and told her what had happened. He urged her to try to contact the new Something. He tried to contact it again, himself, but seemed unable to do so.

Several days passed. He took up his life where he had left off, and tried almost hourly to repeat the mental processes which had enabled him to contact the Something. Soon, and again with great suddenness and with the same electric tingling, the contact was made. Instantly he began to pray frantically to the Something to heal his daughter. He rushed into her room, still praying, caught her by the hands and began pulling her to her feet. "Use your faith! Get up and show that you can!" The daughter responded, praying fervently and exerting herself to the utmost to leave her bed. As in his case, the needed strength was supplied. She rose, took a step, then another. The miracle of instant healing came to her as it had come to him. Voicing her thanks she dressed and entered a new life of health.

A few days later he again made the electric contact. He had been waiting for it and had his prayer learned by heart. Instantly he voiced it. He asked to have his former job back with the elevator construction company. Confident that his prayer would be answered, he went directly to the company office and to the man who had discharged him months before. Making no explanation of any kind, he said quietly, "I am ready for work again. Where do you need me?" The man behind the desk looked at him intently for a moment, then took from his desk a bundle of papers which he held out to him, naming the city in which the installation job was to be done.

That was the beginning of an unbelievable career. He learned by practice to contact the Something almost at will, and never allowed a morning or evening to pass without the contact. He learned to ask to be shown any danger which lay ahead on the job, and would be warned by a strong sense of danger if there was an emergency coming up. Once having received such a warning, he would make his contact on the job and ask for guidance. Nothing came in words, but he felt urges to act in certain ways. He would find the sense of danger growing until it became almost continuous and, as he went to different parts of his jobs, the danger sense intensified around some particular place. He would station himself there, calling his trusted foreman or others to stand with him, and all would watch to prevent trouble. Accident after accident was thus caught in the nick of time and prevented.

I asked the man to let me have all details should such a danger arise and be met while he was on the Honolulu installation job. He promised, and in less than a week dropped in to see me and say that he had received a preliminary warning. The next morning, as he related afterwards, the danger sense had increased. He traced the danger spot to the top of a work elevator shaft on the roof of the new hotel. There, with his foreman and another workman who was long familiar with the warnings, he waited. Meanwhile all workmen on the job had been warned to be extra careful. Contact was made afresh and the danger came so close that he could "almost smell it." A Filipino workman approached the head of the elevator shaft with a wheelbarrow on which had been loaded a coil of very stiff and heavy steel cable. The elevator platform was in place and the man lifted the gate. He returned to push his load onto the platform. At the instant when his barrow wheel touched the elevator platform, someone below, without ringing the warning bell, pulled the control rope and the elevator began to drop. The barrow tipped, throwing the cable coil against a part of the shaft frame and breaking the binding wire so that the cable uncoiled, lashing out like a great snake, and striking the workman from behind. He would have pitched headforemost into the elevator shaft, barrow and all, but the three watchers had already exploded into action, gripping him and his load and dragging them back to safety.

I checked on this account and had the same story from all those involved.

This man had, for a period of several years, been drawing from the company each year a very considerable premium because no men were injured on any job which he supervised. He was given the most difficult and dangerous assignments, and he never failed. His health and that of his daughter had remained excellent.

Comment:

In this case we have an example of instant healing of physical ills, also of financial troubles—healings of body and purse. The part played by the vital force is plain to see, as is the necessity of taking time to train the low self in the work of contacting the High Self. Even more important, if such a thing can be, is the fact proved by this case that daily contact and hourly guidance may be had from the High Self IF ASKED FOR.

The kahuna theory is that we are allowed free will, and that the High Self will not interfere with our doings, no matter how we muddle our lives (except for predetermining certain vital events of life) UNLESS WE ASK IT TO COME TO OUR AID. Asking is "opening the door." The kahuna belief is that the High Self yearns over us as a parent over a wayward child, and longs to help and guide us, but is bound to keep hands off our affairs until we make the astounding discovery that there is a High Self, and that there is a way to gain its help in living.

We cannot know what law restrains the High Self from guiding our every act, but we can judge by what happens, invariably arriving at the conclusion that there must be some such law or restraint on the level of the High Self.

The story of this man who found what he called "Something" and who felt at contact an electric thrill which he called "getting the ting-a-ling," would not be complete if I failed to tell of an incident which showed plainly the part a complex plays in blocking the path of contact between the low self of a man and the High Self.

The elevator engineer became interested in photography while in Honolulu and bought a fine camera, getting instruction in its use from me and from an Australian tile-layer who worked on the building under construction. The Australian had a collection of very fine nude studies. He showed them to the elevator man and offered to give him one. The offer was accepted and a modest enough picture selected. This picture, which was a fine example of photography, lighting, posing and tone, was placed on the dresser in the hotel room where the elevator man lived. He placed it there in the evening, and the next morning was puzzled to find that his usual contact with the Something could not be made. All day long he worried over the puzzling failure, going off alone in the new structure to try repeatedly to make contact, but without success.

That evening, upon his return to his room after a hasty dinner, his eyes chanced to fall upon the picture. He approached it questioningly, taking it up for careful examination. It was not a thing he considered wicked. It was photographic art. The picture was a thing of beauty. However, a deep suspicion grew in his mind that the picture had something to do with his puzzling failure. Taking immediate action, he returned the picture to the Australian with the explanation of what the trouble seemed to be. An hour later he was successful in making contact. He asked to be told if the picture was sinful. He got no impression of any slightest kind in reply.

In telling me of the strange affair, he pointed out that he never knew what the Something might or might not consider a sin. He could chew tobacco, and he used profanity most freely. He considered himself about as "wicked as most decent men," but experience had taught him that certain little things might most unexpectedly and inexplicably prevent his making the contact.

It is evident that in his case there was an old complex, probably from early training in sex ethics or modesty, which remained in his low self. The nude study would have been welcomed in any art exhibition, but it served to touch off the complex even when it had not occurred to the middle self of the man that there was anything in the picture to criticize. The low self reacted to the complex and felt that the man was guilty and should be ashamed. Figuratively speaking, it hid its face like the small boy and refused to venture into the presence of its parents lest it be scolded. With the picture out of the way, the "path" of contact was again open.

Note that the picture was a physical thing. It was impressive. It could be seen and touched. It was a PHYSICAL STIMULUS, and it roused the old complex as a hundred imaginings of similar pictures could not have done. The return of the picture to the Australian was a physical stimulus sufficient to put the complex back on the mental shelf, out of the way again.

Over and over the point must be stressed that IF ONE CANNOT GET RID OF SUCH COMPLEXES AS THESE, HE MUST BOW TO THEM.

The elevator man had to give up his pretty picture. The girl who danced and drank and had the open sore on her ankle could not get rid of the early complexed belief that dancing and cocktails were a sin. She would have been wise, had she understood, to have given up dancing and drinking (for her complex was such that it was dangerously easy to re-establish) before the drastic operation became necessary.

CHAPTER XIX

THE MAGIC OF REBUILDING THE UNWANTED FUTURE
(Healing of Financial and Social Ills)

The High Magic of Instant healing is accomplished through the aid of the High Self. This is also true of the healing of purse and circumstances.

Both of these arts use the same basic mechanisms.

In the Bible we read the story of Jacob, who saw in a dream a ladder reaching from earth to heaven, and angels ascending and descending on it. The Lord stood above it and spoke to Jacob.

Like so many of the tales to be found in religion, there can be drawn a comparative picture in the beliefs of Huna. In Huna the ladder is the connecting cord of shadowy body stuff connecting the low self and the High Self, who is the only "Lord" we can ever contact directly and know something about. The Lord spoke to Jacob. The High Self sends its mystical messages. The angels went up and down, perhaps as messengers. The THOUGHT FORMS of the prayers go up and down on the cord as a ladder, moving on the stream of vital force. The Lord promised Jacob that he would be prospered. The High Self stands ready to help us in the same way—provided we learn how to do our part.

Case 29 Changing the Unwanted Future for the Wanted Preliminary Notes:

I wish to make this mechanism of High Magic as plain as possible for it is vitally important. Most lives are a tangle, and to have those tangles removed would mean everything to us.

In selecting this case from my own experience, I am able to give first hand assurance that each step in the work is fully and correctly described. I can vouch for the results, as they were in my own life—and still are.

Contrary to my usual procedure, I shall stop to point out at each step the reason for the things done, instead of waiting for the end of the case to make comment.

The Case:

In the year 1932, in Honolulu, I owned a camera store which was hard hit by the depression and the lack of tourist trade. Threatened with loss of everything, I went to a kahuna for help.

The kahuna was a Hawaiian woman of about fifty. I had known her for some time and when I told her that I was in trouble, she set to work at once to see what could be done to right my affairs. We went into a small dining room and sat down at the table. While she smoked and listened, I told of my difficulties.

I was faced by the necessity of selling out my business, with the stock and fixtures, or facing bankruptcy. The only person in Honolulu who could buy my store to an advantage was my competitor. He owned a larger and older camera store.

I had gone to him three times to try to get him to buy me out at a very low figure, but could not interest him. I had paid a real estate man a round sum to try to make the sale, and he had failed. It began to look as if I would have to lose everything. My lease had but a few weeks longer to run, and to renew my lease for the five year period at an advance in rent was out of the question.

When I had explained everything and had answered a few questions, the healer asked me to think very hard for a little while and then tell her exactly what I wanted to have come to pass. I thought it all over again, then said that I wanted to sell my business and stock and fixtures to my competitor for eight thousand dollars, which would be a great bargain even in bad times. I wanted to help my competitor amalgamate my business and his own, and after that I wished to return to the Coast and to be able to do some writing. I was quite definite.

The healer asked more questions. She would say, "And if that happens that way, are you sure that it will not make a difference in your plans?" She explained that I must overlook no possible contingency and must weigh each step and consider its probable results. I had to consider all the small details and imagine how each thing would work out and react on some other part of the plan.

The idea was to prepare to make the "Prayer" to the High Self. The thought forms of the prayer had to be unmixed with doubts and uncertainties. They had to stand out clear and sharp and definite. Any overlooked angle of the affair might bob up later to upset the working out of the plan.

The healer told me that in her experience most people sent to the High Self a continuous jumble of conflicting wishes, plans, fears and hopes. Each day and hour they changed their minds about what they wished to do or become or have happen. As the High Self makes for us our futures from our averaged thoughts which it contacts usually during our sleep, our futures become a hit-and-miss jumble of events and contrary events, of accidents and good and bad luck. Only the person who decides what he wants and holds to his decision doggedly, working always in that direction, can present to the High Self the proper thought forms from which to build the future as desired and planned and worked toward.

After an hour of discussion the healer was satisfied. She announced that the next step was to contact the High Self and ask whether or not the plan was such that it could be made to materialize.

Instead of using the crystal gazing arrangement of a black smooth stone swished with water in the bottom of a calabash bowl, she brought out a glass tumbler, filled it with water, grated half a teaspoonful of yellow ginger root into the water to cloud it and to act as a physical stimulus to ward off spirit influence of the poltergeist type, should such be near. The grating was done with a thumbnail from a small piece of fresh ginger root out of the garden that afternoon. It was then evening.

The healer then asked for a silver dollar as a preliminary part of her fee. This acted as a physical stimulus to her low self as it represented a reward for work and service—thus appearing as a good thing to the low self. The dollar was placed under the tumbler. She then shaded her eyes from the overhead light and sat for a short time looking down at the surface of the clouded water.

She soon began to see images and to get messages by some form of inner voice. She would remain in a trance-like state for a moment or two, rouse to speak to me to tell what she saw, or to ask a fresh question. This continued for perhaps seven or eight minutes.

The visions in the crystal were all symbolic, and if the symbols were things she had learned by experience to know as good, she counted the answer favorable to my plans. She said she saw a door being opened, then, a little later, a sheaf of wheat. She asked what these things might mean to me or if I had been thinking about them—wishing to be sure that she was not seeing them in my mind instead of from the High Self via the low self.

When she was satisfied that the answer was favorable, she said, "The god tells me that your prayer can be answered. The door is open. Your path is not badly blocked, even if the door was not open all the way. I will now ask what we must do for our part of the work."

Again she gazed into the water and entered the state in which she could see with psychic senses. She began to see my competitor, who was also a good friend of long standing. She described his appearance and checked with me as to whether she was seeing him accurately or not. She saw his office at the rear of his store and checked that with me. She also saw the man whom I had hired to sell my business and who had failed. When this psychic examination of the matter was finished it was growing late.

"Have you hurt anyone?" the healer asked. "Why is the door not wide open and why is your path a little blocked?"

I could think of no injury I had done anyone, and said so.

"Do you feel that you would cheat if you sold your store for eight thousand dollars?" was the next question.

I assured her that I would consider the deal most fair.

"Then it is the little sin ideas which eat you inside because of your Sunday School or Church training," she decided. "Most of the good people, especially if they are good church people, have things like that. To get rid of the feeling of guilt and clear your path to the god you must fast until one o'clock for three days, and while you fast, you must not smoke. After three days, give a gift to some person in need or to some charity. This gift must be large enough to hurt you a little—almost more than you can afford. This will make you feel deep inside you that you have done enough to balance all your little sins. After you have done these things, come to me again."

The healer was prescribing very excellent physical stimuli to impress the low self in me that it was making amends for such acts as it believed to be sins. I had no way of finding out what those small guilt complexes might be, but that made no difference.

I carried out the orders during the three days, finding them difficult enough to impress my low self not a little, as I have been blessed with a good appetite and at that time loved to smoke. My gift was made to the Salvation Army, this being to my mind a good charity organization.

Again arriving in the evening, I sat with the healer at the round table. She again made use of the tumbler mechanism in the same way, and after a few minutes saw the door again, this time wide open. Announcing that my path was now unblocked, she pushed the tumbler from her and reopened the question of my plans. Had I made any changes in my plans? Was I still sure that I wanted everything to happen just as I had stated?

When assured that my plans were clear and unchanged, she made ready to make the prayer for me to the High Self.

When a kahuna prayed to his or her High Self, asking aid for a client, the prayer automatically went to the High Self of the client as well. This involves a belief that all High Selves are linked together in some way we cannot understand and can hardly imagine. They are "many in one" and "one in many." They are Unity in Separation. They have bonds closer than those of bees in a hive. They have learned to work as a unit, but each does individual works. We cannot grasp this, but, from the results obtained through contact with the High Selves, this seems to be the nearest we can come to understanding the matter.

To make the prayer, the healer rose and walked slowly back and forth, breathing heavily. After a few minutes she paused beside the table, said quietly that she would now make the prayer to the god for me, and then—looking as into a distance—began to speak in Hawaiian, slowly and with great force. She voiced the prayer once, then repeated it, and then repeated it again.

This thrice-spoken prayer was offered word for word and idea for idea as nearly as possible, the full force of the suggestive will being mustered to cause the low self to carry to the High Self the thought forms which were being made by the carefully and firmly repeated prayer.

The High Self was contacted by the low self after a direct command from the middle self of the healer, the tumbler not being used, as at this time no return answer was expected or requested. When the prayer had been thrice spoken, the healer resumed her chair and took a cigarette. She smoked and rested after her effort. She had accumulated extra vital force and had presented the prayer as a set of thought forms on a flow of vital force.

Soon the tumbler was brought into action to see what message could be had from the High Self, and what instructions might be given.

In the water surface in the tumbler appeared (to her) a scene in which I did several things. It was an enactment of what the High Self had caused my future to be. The old future was torn down and a new one had been instantly constructed for me.

The old future had undoubtedly contained all the business failures which seemed inevitable to me and which I feared and so visualized as I worried. This probably would have been my future if I had not had the help of the High Self in changing the bad to the desired good.

We do not know the exact way in which the High Self makes the future for the low and middle selves over which it stands as "guardian, parental spirit." We can only guess that the thoughts we make into thought forms are used in some way in shaping the future. At least, the thought forms tell the High Self what we hope, fear, desire and plan. It seems that our futures are made from these thought forms with all care being taken not to intrude on our FREE WILL. We must be allowed to exert free will, and unless we ask for help, it must not be given lest the free will be cancelled. We cannot say why, but we can understand that such a condition of affairs can be.

Because of our mental limitations we cannot conceive of a future made of invisible material, but still containing all the events and conditions which will materialize from minute to minute and hour to hour and day to day for as far ahead as the invisible outline of the future is "crystallized." Perhaps the future is made like the shadowy bodies of the low and middle selves, and as are the thought forms. Perhaps thought forms are made to grow into events. The kahunas did not know. We cannot know. However, so long as we know that the future is made in some such way and that it can be seen ahead in so far as it has been made, and that IT CAN BE CHANGED, that is all we need to know.

The healer saw the new future in her tumbler of water and described to me the things she saw that I must do, also telling me why. She seemed to get the idea of why things were done in some psychic way connected with the psychic vision. The usual method of the High Self of giving symbols was not used here.

"The god tells me," she would say, or "The god shows me."

She saw me going to my competitor with a paper in my hand. She said that on the paper I had written out my proposition to sell, the price, and all details. She said that the god told her that this man was the kind who liked to see everything written out on paper, otherwise he would say "No" from force of habit.

"You write it all out," she instructed. "Then next Tuesday at a quarter after two you go to see him. He will be in his office sitting at his desk and doing nothing. You put the paper on his desk and say, 'Have a look at these figures, will you? I'll be back in about ten minutes.' Then you go off and in ten minutes you come back. He will be finished reading your paper and will say to you that he will buy your business."

To me this was unbelievably explicit and detailed. I asked how she knew, and she told me that she saw me doing it in my new future, and that the god made her understand why the proposition had to be written out.

I marveled at the instructions and promised to obey them to the letter.

At a quarter after two on the following Tuesday I went into my competitor's place of business with my proposal carefully typed out in full. I found him, as had been foreseen, idly sitting at his desk. I placed the paper before him and asked him to look it over, saying I would be back in ten minutes.

In ten minutes I returned, and he was waiting for me.

"I'll take you up," he said. "I'll give you my check for a hundred dollars to bind the bargain and you can make out the bill of sale."

So, with the help of the healer and the High Self, the deal was closed. The price stipulated in the prayer was paid me. I stayed on to help get my business amalgamated with that of my friendly competitor.

With the deal completed, I reported back to the kahuna, paying her all she would allow, which was little enough considering the great service she had rendered me.

Some time later, when I was about to finish up my business affairs and leave for California, the healer ran a check on my future for me to see about the part of the plan I had made which included a desire to do some writing.

She made a fresh prayer asking that I be allowed to write, and then inspected the future with the aid of the High Self via the low self, to see what instructions were given for me. As she had done in the case of the sale of the business, she now did for the writing.

"You will write eight books," she said after a long look into her improvised gazing crystal. "That is as far ahead as the god shows me. Eight books." She sighed. "But you will have to be very patient. It will be a long time from the first book to the eighth. Many things will happen and it will not be easy, although the last four books will be easier than the first four and come faster."

That glimpse of the future which the healer got for me dates back to 1932. Now, in 1947, the first four books are water under the bridge.

Additional Comment:

The psycho-religious system of the "Secret" (Huna) is, first, last and above all, a WORKABLE system. It makes no pretense of understanding or explaining those things which have to do with an Ultimate God which our lower mental ability will not allow us to understand.

This is common sense and practicality. It is the true scientific approach. It gives us a system free from the dogmatic and impractical.

CHAPTER XX

THE HIGH SELF AND THE HEALING IN PSYCHIC SCIENCE

Much healing has been done by the spirits of the dead. Many have been doctors in physical life and, with the aid of mediums, have diagnosed and prescribed much as they did in life.

Spirits have often taken over the body of mediums and have healed by laying on of hands. From many accounts, it is evident that use of the low voltage of vital force is made even while its nature is not well understood.

Mesmerists have made passes over diseased parts of the patient's body for the purpose of healing. The spirits have done likewise. Healing has often been remarkable.

The kahunas, however, seem to be the only ones who knew of the three voltages of vital force and of the fact that vital force could be transferred through the hands from healer to patient, carrying along thought forms of healing to implement the vital force and set it to doing the desired work of restoration.

It is generally agreed that children of less than five years of age do not readily respond to suggestion or hypnosis. Despite this fact, they respond to treatment in which a flow of vital force is made to enter their bodies while the healer creates the thought forms of healing. Liebault, in trying to prove that suggestion was not responsible for all healing in mesmeric practice, laid hands on many children, making many cures. Some of the children were under three. In later times Ochorowitz had similar success healing children under two. Animals have also been healed in this way. Plants have been stimulated thus to outstrip their untreated fellows.

All the evidence indicates that the kahunas were right in their belief that the vital force of the healer was a potent healing agent, whether the healer is living in the flesh or has died and become a spirit.

The spirits of the deceased have often showed fine powers of psychic diagnosis of the ills of the living. A friend of mine had a son who developed a strange illness while in college. Doctors failed to discover the cause, and mother and son went as a last resort to have a sitting with a famous medium by the name of Cayce. (See the book, There Is a River.) This medium was used by a spirit doctor who was responsible for many amazing cures. He made a psychic examination of the young man and said that the illness was caused by some fractured sections of the spinal column, going on to say that the injury had occurred in a canoe accident. The patient had forgotten the accident, but he recalled it at once as very painful at the time. The spirit doctor said that an operation was needed to repair the broken vertebrae, but that the only man skilled in that type of operation in the United States, was in Europe, although he would be at home in Boston soon. The doctor's name was given, but not his address.

After the sitting the mother and son had an X-ray picture made of the spine and a doctor who was not familiar with the case pointed out the breaks. As the spirit doctor had been correct that far, a long distance call was made from New York to Boston, and it was found that there was a doctor of the name given who had just returned from abroad, and who was the ranking specialist in surgery of the kind needed to repair the spinal injuries. He was engaged, and his operation brought the young man back to normal health.

Spirits frequently practice absent healing of a peculiar kind. When the medium through which they work is given a lock of hair of a distant patient (or some other thing formerly in contact with the patient), a fine demonstration of psychometry often follows. The ills of the distant patient are diagnosed and remedies indicated, or treatment by mental or "spiritual" means is undertaken from a distance. Here again we see the threads of shadowy body stuff used as a means of contacting distant things and people, also as a means of getting information, and as a means of sending back healing forces and thought forms.

In all the foregoing healing practices the spirits work much as do the living, provided the latter are psychic enough to make a proper diagnosis, and provided the spirits can accumulate enough vital force to do the healing. In still another matter there is a close parallel. We pray to Higher Beings and so do the spirits of the dead.

Many a medium, controlled by a spirit healer, has been seen to pray in order to call down healing. The spirits have spoken endlessly of the High Self, calling it all manner of names, according to their religious training during life.

And, somewhat like the kahunas, a few of the spirits have had sufficient understanding to enable them to call for and get the aid of the High Self for healing the living. (The instant healings thus brought about are very rare, perhaps because so few of the spirits are familiar with the technique of instant healing, and because the patient is not cleansed of guilt complexes and otherwise made ready to accept such healing. On the other hand, spirits make use of the help of the High Self in the production of physical phenomena such as apporting, materialization, the making of ectoplasm and so on.)

Spirits have sometimes appeared to the living in visions, as did the "Lady" to Bernadette Soubirous at the grotto near Lourdes, and have in some way been instrumental in causing miraculous healing.

In some cases no vision of a spirit has been seen, but the presence of a spirit healing agent has been discovered in one way and another. The records of the Church of Rome are filled with instances in which healing has taken place at the tombs of men and women who had lived saintly lives. A conclave of twenty-two archbishops and bishops wrote to Pope Clement XI: "We are witnesses that before the tomb of Father John Francis Regis the blind see, the lame walk, the deaf hear, the dumb speak."

In 1731 and for as long as twenty-five years afterward there was an invisible and unidentified healing agency at work at the tomb of Abbé Paris, a Jansenist.

Many cases were studied, among them a famous one in which a woman, Mlle. Coirin, had been miraculously healed of a cancer which had entirely destroyed her left breast. Her doctors had given up all hope for her. The breast was restored to its original form, even to the nipple, and not a scar could be seen. The case was vouched for by several physicians who made depositions before notaries at the time, and even the royal physician, M. Gaulard, investigated, was satisfied as to the authenticity of the healing miracle and so reported to the king.

In Hawaii some years ago, two large and oddly shaped stones, supposedly connected in early centuries with kahuna rites, were seen in a dream by a Hawaiian. He later found the stones and had them hauled to a place beside a modern cemetery, and stood on end. A little later the report circulated that a healing agency was to be contacted at the stones. People flocked from all parts of Hawaii to visit them, pray before them, and make offerings of flowers, food, money or whatever their particular religious beliefs dictated. Some veritable cases of healing resulted. The authorities had difficulty handling the crowds for a time, and then the healing power seemed to vanish. One can only speculate as to the coming and going of the invisible beings responsible for healing in these ways and places. While a High Self might possibly undertake such healing work of its own accord, the kahuna theory is that a lower and middle self must make the request before the High Self will take a direct hand in the affairs of the lesser selves, be they in the flesh or spirits surviving physical death. If we are to credit tales of saintly or sainted persons appearing as spirits at the healing centers, we can conclude that these have learned to call down the aid of the High Self for the healing of the scattered few suppliants who are free of guilt complexes and so are able to accept healing ministrations.

If, on the other hand, shrines and sacred relics act as physical stimuli to aid the suppliants in making a workable prayer for healing, that may be the major answer to the mystery of such miraculous healing. The High Self of any who come to pray for healing might be caused to take action. (The kahunas considered the individual High Self the proper source of all healing. Spirits of a level above the High Self were thought to have less personal things to do than heal earthlings. The kahunas recognized no saints in their lists of High Selves.)

The question of the supply of vital force needed by the High Self for healing at shrines can be answered easily. If poltergeists can steal vital force from the living for their noisy activities, it is to be taken for granted that a High Self can draw vital force from those in its care.

The true picture of a healing at a holy shrine should be something like this: One or more normal departed spirits (each having its low and middle selves united to make them normal) elect to remain at the shrine and do all they can to help heal those who come asking for healing. These normal spirits will have learned to call on their High Selves and get them to heal instantly or in a matter of a few hours or as long as three days (as recorded at Lourdes). Many come to pray, making what may be considered a "circle" of value similar to gatherings at spiritualistic seances. The normal spirits are supplied with vital force by the living, so also are the High Selves. When anyone who is free of guilt fixations and who has faith, is able to make a good thought form picture of the desired condition (healing), and is also able to make telepathic contact with the normal spirits and/or (1) through them with a High Self, or (2) without their aid contact their own High Selves directly, the miracle of healing results.

Ectoplasm, as known in the seance room is, as we have seen, bodily substances changed to their invisible form through the use of the high voltage of vital force by the High Self. In instant healing, the physical substance of the broken bone, the cancerous breast, the blind eye, the crooked spine, and similar structures is, according to Huna, dissolved into ectoplasmic form, then solidified as healthy substances filling the part of the patient's shadowy body which corresponds to the injured part. It must be remembered that the shadowy body is a mold of each cell, of all tissues, including blood and other fluids of the body. This shadowy body belonging to the low self is not breakable or subject to disease or injury. Theoretically, a leg that has been amputated for years could be restored were there a source from which to draw ectoplasm which would not need to be returned. If the shadowy body of the low self could be injured, heaven would be filled with cripples instead of restored and happy spirit people who have died to find that they have left behind all their physical abnormalities.

There is another peculiar thing about such healing as is under discussion. It has been pointed out by doctors who have made a study of those healed at Lourdes that often those who have come to pray for the healing of others, have themselves been healed. Mary Austin, the writer, developed cancer. She was given about a year to live, and chose to go to Rome to spend that year studying early documents of Christianity. She became so absorbed in her studies that she was able to forget the cancer. One day, so she wrote in her account of the matter, she came to the sudden realization that the cancer was gone. She had not prayed for healing. But, with her mind on the things of religion, healing came.

The point to this peculiar phase of healing is that it indicates that, if the door is once opened by prayer-requests to the High Self so that it can take a hand in the affairs of the low and middle self person, it may act of its own accord and bring healing when not directly asked. This possibility would account for the help given us, even if not explicitly asked. Nearly everyone can recall some narrow escape from disaster which seems to have been brought about by the guardian angel, or High Self.

The close and constant cooperation and contact between the lower pair of selves and their High Self, is well demonstrated in the case of the strange cult of religionists in Japan whose members walk, or roll with bare backs, on broken glass, cutting themselves, but having their cuts healed instantly and without a scar through a word spoken by the master of ceremonies.

I talked to a woman who had been a member of such a group, although she was a blond American. She had gradually learned to contact the Being responsible for the healing, and later, to get the aid of that Being in keeping her feet from being cut in her hourly performance of walking up a ladder of naked sword blades.

While suggestion may be used as auto-suggestion to prevent bleeding from small wounds, the instant healing of very considerable cuts from broken glass would demand the instant healing action of the High Self.

Unfortunately, when a missionary group of this Japanese cult came to America to convert us (to them we were the heathen), their work was classed with stage magic or circus trickery. After a few demonstrations they gave up, washed their hands of us, and returned to Japan, all of which is very strange when we consider the anxiety shown by so many to learn the truth about God and religion. Here was a chance to study both from a new angle, but we are so crystallized in our beliefs, taking us as a whole, that we overlook such striking opportunities when they come.

CHAPTER XXI

HOW THE KAHUNAS CONTROLLED WINDS, WEATHER AND THE SHARKS BY MAGIC

Hawaiian legendary history tells the story of how the ancestors of the Hawaiians traveled from the original homeland in great double canoes which were driven through the water by the power of magic.

This was the same magic which had enabled the leader, Hawaii Loa, to see half way around the globe and find the island group which was to be their new home. With this same magic the winds and waves were controlled so that the frail crafts of the migratory fleet were not lost.

Still another use for this form of magic lay in the control exerted over sharks and other creatures of the sea.

This work was based on the theory that when the middle self graduates to become a High Self, it serves an apprenticeship acting as a guardian (or as called in Theosophy a "nature spirit") over massive parts of the lower creation. These spirits are the seat of higher consciousness which can be seen at work in crystals, plants, insects, birds, fish and animals. They are the source of the instinctive knowledge which enables the bee to build its honey cell and the bird its intricate nest.

As all High Selves are closely in touch, an appeal for weather control can be made through one's own High Self, who, supposedly, passes it on to the High Self in charge of weather in that vicinity.

However, there was a system of direct introduction to the weather control spirits. A kahuna who knew such a spirit and so had a connecting shadowy thread running to it to be used in sending a prayer, could introduce a student kahuna and so help him to set up a line of connection through a shadowy thread.

Case 30 White Man Learns to Control the Winds Preliminary Notes:

In the following case it will be seen that weather control can be exerted without the use of physical stimuli such as are seen in the ritual snake and other rain dances of our Indians in the South-west.

The Case:

N. S. Emerson, now some time passed over, was a surveyor in Hawaii for many years. His work took him to isolated parts where kahunas were still at work, and he won the friendship of more than one healer. One kahuna, who was adept in the high magic of weather control, undertook to teach Mr. Emerson the art. He "introduced" him several times to the invisible "god" (Aumakua) who controlled the weather, and taught him to recite a ritual prayer to cause the winds to increase or decrease.

The kahunas demonstrated the workability of the magic repeatedly, so giving him faith in it. Under their guidance he made the prayer and watched its answer take form. In the end he came to be able to think of the "god" and recite the prayer, getting results the same as his teacher.

The prayer is a simple one which embodies definite mental pictures or thought forms of the condition wanted. It is repeated aloud, and forms a physical stimulus to cause the low self to make contact and carry the telepathic request of the prayer. The prayer calls on the "Winds of Hilo" and either asks that the little winds be put back in the wind calabash and the large winds released to blow, or that the large winds be put into the wind calabash and the little ones let out to blow. Nothing in the prayer indicates the nature of its power or the mechanism of its magic. It is not so much what is said as it is what goes on in the low self that counts in magic.

Mr. Emerson retained his contact with the High Self of this level all the rest of his life. Repeatedly his friends came to him to get his help in quieting the weather when they wished to go by ship between the islands. On the annual kite day at Kamehameha School for Boys, he was invariably asked to be present, and to make the prayer for the large winds to be let out of the wind calabash (symbolic, of course) so that the big kites could go up. I have talked with a number of people who have witnessed the blowing up of a good strong breeze within ten minutes after the making of the prayer, although I was never fortunate enough to see this myself. If he ever failed the boys and their kites, I have heard nothing of the failure.

Comment:

Rain making was not a usual part of the activities of the kahunas who worked to get weather control for the reason that Hawaii
was blessed with much rain in the inhabited sections.

While it is hard to imagine clouds and rain being manufactured
out of nothing by the High Selves in response to ritual prayers, one
can easily imagine a control by which distant rain clouds could be
brought to empty themselves at the desired place.

Case 31 Control of Sharks and Turtles Preliminary Notes:

While I lived in the Hawaiian Islands I did not hear of a single case in which sharks had attacked and eaten a live person,
although the bodies of those drowned were eaten. The sharks are
supposed to have their High Selves in each group of the islands
in the Pacific, and these are thought to have the ability to take
shark form at will. Many tales are told of the intimate relations established between human beings and individual sharks. Families
were often intimately associated with the various creatures, and
made magical pacts with their Guardian High Selves. This gave
rise to a form of totemism in which certain rites were observed, and
the totem beast of the family was not eaten by that family.

Children and the High Selves who watch over the lower creatures seem to have a strong affinity. Children frequently show
natural psychic ability and see the "little people." In Hawaii there
is a strong belief that human baby spirits may, under certain circumstances, be born into the bodies of small sharks and thus keep
up the totem relations between sharks and the shark-families of
humans.

(Speaking of the awareness of children—as well as primitives—
to the High Self, I am reminded of Mary Austin's story as related
in her autobiography Earth's Horizons. As a very small girl she
came to know the superconscious and called it "I Mary" in contrast
to herself, who was just "Mary." She was able to obtain help from
this spirit in even such small things as crossing a log over a creek
which she could not cross without help. In later life she found that
the Piute Indians knew the same High Self and called it Wakanda
or "The Friend of the Soul of Man." All her life she prayed to this "I
Mary" when in difficulty, and seldom failed to get help.)

In Samoa there was, at least up to 1934, a rite by which children repeated simple chants and, so it seems, made contact with

the High Selves in control of sharks and turtles in those regions.

The Case:

In the Geographic News Bulletin, issue of December 10, 1934, (National Geographic Society) Mr. George H. Hutchinson gave an eye witness account of the ritual of "Calling the Shark and the Turtle" at the village of Vai Togi, Samoa.

The native children and adults gathered for the ceremony, then the children were sent alone to a point of land jutting over the sea. There they recited an old legend telling how a prince and princess had been changed to a shark and turtle respectively. As they chanted they beckoned. In about five minutes a small shark four or five feet long appeared in the clear water beyond the breaking waves, swam around in plain sight for about a minute, and then departed. Soon a turtle appeared in a like manner, remained for a short time, and swam back to deep water.

Comment:

The training of the young to become kahunas began early. By the age of nine or ten it was intensified. It may well be that such training helped the low self of the child to easier and more automatic contact with the High Self or Aumakua, and we moderns may some day begin such training at a similarly early time.

In Christianity there is a hint at such a procedure in the words of Jesus: "Suffer little children to come unto me and forbid them not."

Of significance is the fact that the kahunas were "introduced" to the High Selves of weather and nature control for the purpose of establishing a connecting thread of shadowy substance between these High Selves and the student kahuna.

This may have been an ancient mechanism from which sprang the idea in various religions that new priests had to be ordained. Ordination was accomplished through the aid of an already ordained (or introduced) priest, and once the link was established between the priest and the High Being, he was ready to begin his ministry.

In India there still is a rite by which this form of introduction or thread-connecting is accomplished. The teacher acts to cause the contact, even while not knowing its mechanisms, and suddenly the pupil finds himself able to touch the High Self and becomes "illumined." This rite usually included a physical contact between teacher and pupil, sometimes a slap or even a kick, and it may be that in this act a thread of contact is established through the teacher's shadowy body to that of his High Self.

While these matters are still less than fully understood, the fact that a connecting thread is needed stands out clearly at all times. Various ways seem to be effective to remove complexed blockings and open the path of telepathic communication.

In due time, when we come to experiment on a larger scale to learn to duplicate the works of the kahunas, we may find a way to become "introduced" to those High Selves presiding over the lower forms of life, among which are the parasitic growths which afflict man. Through these Selves we may cause the cancers and tumors to leave. Germs may be handled in a like manner. Only recently I read an account of a person who spoke aloud to the ants in and around her home, promising them the run of the garden unmolested if they would keep out of the house. The pact was effective and continued up to the time of writing the report.

CHAPTER XXII

THE PRACTICAL USE OF THE MAGIC OF THE MIRACLE

The first stage, that of investigating the ancient Huna system is nearing its close. Little more can be done to further our knowledge of it and to check conclusions already tentatively reached until news of the investigation has spread and interest has been aroused so that experimental groups can begin work.

Individuals may begin work by themselves and develop the ability to accumulate high charges of low voltage vital force, then transfer it with thought forms of healing to those to be healed. Almost anyone can learn to use this low magic.

To learn to use the High Magic one has to get rid of hindering complexes, and this is difficult to do for one's self. This difficulty will be best met by group work in which one person assists another to unlock the path of contact with the High Self.

Of course, one can skirt around his own sin or guilt complexes and try for contact. Or, and this is a way open to all, the decision may be made as to just what is wanted, the prayer formulated, and then repeated frequently with the command held over the low self to give the prayer and low mana to the High Self when automatic contact is made during sleep. It is a slow method, but better than the blind prayer offered without an understanding of its mechanism or of the High Self.

Unfortunately there are no kahunas left to whom we can turn at this late date for healing. We will have to develop our own healers, and this will take organization and the selection of those naturally gifted for the work of experimenting. Whether we act swiftly or tardily, depends on ourselves. There are many who cannot wait too long for healers to become trained, and love and mercy urge speed.

For these, however, there is hope, and for their use I offer here, in ending my report of the ancient Science of Huna, these suggestions:

If one aspires to daily practice to learn to contact the High Self, there are several things which will be of great help.

The first of these is the daily reading of writings which will bring before one the desirability of the undertaking and its complete possibility of success. We must never forget that we are creatures of massive mental habits. We get into the habit of thinking certain things in certain ways, and have to pull ourselves up by the bootstraps to prevent the habits from making us give up the practice before the first week is out.

Read each day the accounts given in my report if you wish to keep the original urge to practice polished and to the fore. The Christian Scientists understand this better than any group I know. The person who desires healing of body or purse is set to a daily reading of the writings which make the philosophy appear before the mind clearly and impressively. The low self is impressed by the printed page. It is a PHYSICAL STIMULUS, and if the middle self believes the printed teachings to be correct or even workable, though illogical, the low self will gradually fall into line and accept the ideas. On the other hand, if we do not reread the material frequently, the low self will forget it. It will replace the urge to practice with the old lazy urges to do less strenuous things. Read. Reread. Read and read and read. This will help form a new habit of thought. Thought habits are not all bad or obstructive. If a good Christian has developed habits of mentation which make for faith and trust in the Christian concept of God, this provides a bridge over which the healing practices can pass swiftly. Quimby tied his teachings to the already habituated beliefs of his patients. They believed that God could not be anything but good. They had the complexed belief gained in childhood that God was perfect, that He was good, and that He was all-powerful. Building on these fixed and complexed habits of belief, lodged in the low self and shared by the middle self, Quimby found it easy to cause the patient to believe in his theory that illness and all bad conditions could not exist because they were not of God, who was perfect.

Our complexed beliefs can be a help as well as a hindrance. It is, however, necessary for us to pull ourselves together mentally at daily intervals and make a close and critical examination of our many pertinent beliefs. We may have to dwell daily on the great Huna truth which is for us the epitome of liberation—the truth that we cannot sin against Higher Beings, and that there is no sin other than hurting another human being. NO HURT, NO SIN! Shout it from the housetops each hour for a year if needs be. At all costs GAIN THE SALVATION OF LIBERATION FROM FALSE DOGMAS OF SIN. Or, if you fail in that, humor your complexed low self and cease to do the things it stubbornly and blindly insists on considering sinful.

In any event, READ. The literature of Huna is still scant, but one can read Unity's "Daily Word" or similar publications, with their lessons and affirmations to be repeated day by day. One who knows the secret lore of the kahunas can translate all such readings into terms of Huna. God becomes the High Self—for that is as high as we can ever reach—and we can be very certain that any contact with the still higher Beings will be made for us by the High Self.

The kahunas did not hesitate to use anything that came to hand so long as it furthered their work. They welcomed doctors and enjoyed churches. To them Huna was a thing alive and growing. They welcomed the early missionaries, hoping that they would bring fresh and advanced knowledge and better healing methods. They, like the Polynesian race as a whole, showed the most surprising open-mindedness. They were eager for all things new and good if they proved practical.

Huna is not crystallized and set and dead. It is a living, practical system which holds fast to the proven while reaching out eagerly to inspect anything new and promising. But those who aspire to benefit by the ancient discoveries which compose the heart of the Secret, must also be open and ready for change.

Read this report over and over, if you would break your old habits of belief and profit by the new. At your first reading you will catch the gleam. A week later you will try to recall what you read and find it confused in your memory. That is because the new ideas have clashed with the old ones you have had for years. If you reread the report the gleam will return and stay longer. If you do not, the confusion will increase and in a month you will forget that you ever caught the gleam at all. The low self is the custodian of all our memories and habits of thought and belief. It stores all our memories and thoughts in its low shadowy body, and presides over them stubbornly and illogically. It takes time and practice, reading and rereading, to bring it into line and keep it there—ready to make contact with the High Self.

While the experimental work carried on by individuals will be of great importance, and while almost anyone may discover that he has unsuspected talents in the use of both high and low magic, it is through the groups that the best general advance on the pioneer fringe of the recovered psycho-religious system of Huna will be made.

For instance, those who begin experimenting with the low magic, and use the Baron Ferson method, or a variation of it, to build up an increased charge of vital force in their bodies will need others upon whom to use the force. The force will attract like a magnet if the hands are laid on the shoulders of one less highly charged, then slowly withdrawn. The force will leave one and enter another, carrying thoughts of healing, and the transfer of the force itself will make response to the healing thought more effective.

The individual who has studied my report with care, will be able to plan his own steps, and set himself a daily practice. As prayer is based on telepathic ability (except during natural contact with the High Self during sleep) the practice of telepathy is important. But in this work a partner is absolutely necessary, and, in a group, tests can be made to find out which people work best together. One person may concentrate on a symbol, a picture, a word, etc., and the others in the group may remain receptive and wait to see if they get impressions of a telepathic nature from the sender.

A regularly formed group offers a stimulation of interest and the chance to share one's findings. Organization and team work under an appointed leader, with definite projects and meeting times, is far better than unorganized work.

As experimentation goes forward, and individuals of proper talent begin to get results in healing with low magic or healing with high magic, with fire-immunity, changing the future, etc., it would be well to have a central organization through which findings may be cleared from group to group, and through which information concerning the newly developed healers can be given to those desiring it. Bulletins giving the results of group and individual experiments would be in order, and special instructions should be issued covering specific needs as they arise.

Indications that we are entering a new period in our progress toward world civilization is to be seen in the step from the age-long secrecy of Huna to an open knowledge available to all. The cult of secrecy fostered priesthoods, and priesthoods fostered special privileges and usually ended in imposition, the victims being the laymen.

While there will be those who possess certain natural talents which will enable them to learn to use the kahuna methods and thus to become healers, there will be no longer a blind of secrecy and mystery about the methods used. The layman, while perhaps not aspiring to become a professional healer of body or purse, will be able to read the literature and know the principles of the new psycho-religious system.

This system, while based on ancient fundamentals, will undoubtedly move ahead very rapidly when modern discoveries and laboratory methods are brought into use. For instance, we can now measure and graph on paper the electro-vital impulses which move through the brain at an average speed of about ten to the second (as done by Prof. George L. Keezer of Cornell with an electro-encephalograph) and in no long time we should know more about the mana of the kahunas than they ever knew. This is a machine age, and it is safe to predict that our recovery of the knack of using Huna will be tied up with machines in various ways as we improve steadily on the ancient practices.

The effect of a general knowledge of Huna on world social structures will be fascinating to watch. Because we have had no sufficiently detailed and workable psycho-religious knowledge, we have had no way of unifying our ideas on these subjects. With Huna acting as a criterion and catalytic agent, the chaos of ideas in these fields can be reduced to order. A large part of our social ills has come because, while we have come to know almost everything else, the lost science of Psychology (with its much smaller element of religion) was not recovered after the Dark Ages as was the knowledge of mathematics, physics and astronomy. These early beginnings made possible the swift building of a machine civilization, but left a painful void where there should have been a workable knowledge of man and his elemental parts, powers and associations in physical life, and after physical death. Without the science of psycho-religion, we have lived as animals in a way, prating about high ideals, and brotherhood, but unable to do anything about it because we could not understand ourselves. We have not known what we were, why we were here, or where we were going. In other words, this department of life has been, and is, disorganized and jumbled. We hurt each other, and unite in groups and nations to make war on other groups and nations—a pretty spectacle for intelligent beings in our stage of development.

If we can settle the basics in this field of knowledge, we shall be on the road to apply that knowledge to the betterment of humanity, as we now apply what we know to agriculture and animal husbandry. By freeing ourselves from the blindly resisting dogmas of outmoded religions, we will be able to take sensible and practical steps in a forward direction, replacing the disorganized growth under the dispensation of the animal-like low self by the dispensation of the middle self aided by the High Self. It is as if our civilization had long been allowed to grow as a form of wild life, creating tangled forest and jungle growths, fields choked with weeds, and with the ever-present danger of fire wiping all away. The "wild growth" can be replaced with planned and ordered fields and forests, so to speak, with firebreaks protecting the cultivated sections from those still left wild.

While there will always be those die-hard individuals to whom a new idea contrary to their fixed and dogmatic beliefs will act as a red rag to a bull, and cause furious protests, it is plain that the average man or woman, thanks to the public school system, is capable of approaching new things with a fairly open mind. These, who form the great majority, need only to organize and begin to work together to bring back the lost science which is needed to complete and perfect the civilization which we have all known for some time was mysteriously defective.

That we will organize and press forward may be taken for granted. In every other line we have been swiftly progressive. The disaster of World War II has made us more than eager to find some way in which to turn for betterment, some answer to the shocking failure in the management of human affairs. Disorganized, we remain a jungle growth. Organized, we can move a world to order, let only each individual do his small part.

Union is strength, prosperity and safety. The High Beings ruling the ants and bees demonstrate this. Rugged individualism and disunion, as demonstrated by preying animals who eat other animals, and are in constant danger of being eaten, represent the stage of growth in which the hard lessons of life under Free Will must be learned. Following that stage comes the one which we have been missing so long; the stage in which the man returns to united and cooperative effort, still possessing his free will, but using it in the right relation to his fellows and their free will. And, above all, in the right relation to the High Selves from whence come both help and guidance.

We are at the turning of the road at last, and the prospect which lies ahead, even when seen mistily through a time veil as yet, appears to be very bright indeed.

THE END

BOOK II

Thought Vibration

by

William Walker Atkinson

Table of Contents

The Law of Attraction in the Thought World

THE Universe is governed by Law - one great Law. Its manifestations are multiform, but viewed from the Ultimate there is but one Law. We are familiar with some of its manifestations, but are almost totally ignorant of certain others. Still we are learning a little more every day - the veil is being gradually lifted.

We speak learnedly of the Law of Gravitation, but ignore that equally wonderful manifestation, THE LAW OF AT-TRACTION IN THE THOUGHT WORLD. We are familiar with that wonderful manifestation of Law which draws and holds together the atoms of which matter is composed - we recognize the power of the law that attracts bodies to the earth, that holds the circling worlds in their places, but we close our eyes to the mighty law that draws to us the things we desire or fear, that makes or mars our lives.

When we come to see that Thought is a force - a manifestation of energy - having a magnet-like power of attraction, we will begin to understand the why and wherefore of many things that have heretofore seemed dark to us. There is no study that will so well repay the student for his time and trouble as the study of the workings of this mighty law of the world of Thought - the Law of Attraction.

When we think we send out vibrations of a fine ethereal substance, which are as real as the vibrations manifesting light, heat, electricity, magnetism. That these vibrations are not evident to our five senses is no proof that they do not exist. A powerful magnet will send out vibrations and exert a force sufficient to attract to itself a piece of steel weighing a hundred pounds, but we can neither see, taste, smell, hear nor feel the mighty force. These thought vibrations, likewise, cannot be seen, tasted, smelled, heard nor felt in the ordinary way; although it is true there are on record cases of persons peculiarly sensitive to psychic impressions who have perceived powerful thought-waves, and very many of us can testify that we have distinctly felt the thought vibrations of others, both whilst in the presence of the sender and at a distance. Telepathy and its kindred phenomena are not idle dreams.

Light and heat are manifested by vibrations of a far lower intensity than those of Thought, but the difference is solely in the rate of vibration. The annals of science throw an interesting light upon this question. Prof. Elisha Gray, an eminent scientist, says in his little book, "The Miracles of Nature":

"There is much food for speculation in the thought that there exist sound-waves that no human ear can hear, and color-waves of light that no eye can see. The long, dark, soundless space between 40,000 and 400,000,000,000,000 vibrations per second, and the infinity of range beyond 700,000,000,000,000 vibrations per second, where light ceases, in the universe of motion, makes it possible to indulge in speculation."

M. M. Williams, in his work entitled "Short Chapters in Science," says:

"There is no gradation between the most rapid undulations or tremblings that produce our sensation of sound, and the slowest of those which give rise to our sensations of gentlest warmth. There is a huge gap between them, wide enough to include another world of motion, all lying between our world of sound and our world of heat and light; and there is no good reason whatever for supposing that matter is incapable of such intermediate activity, or that such activity may not give rise to intermediate sensations, provided there are organs for taking up and sensifying their movements."

I cite the above authorities merely to give you food for thought, not to attempt to demonstrate to you the fact that thought vibrations exist. The last-named fact has been fully established to the satisfaction of numerous investigators of the subject, and a little reflection will show you that it coincides with your own experiences.

We often hear repeated the well-known Mental Science

statement, "Thoughts are Things," and we say these words over without consciously realizing just what is the meaning of the statement. If we fully comprehended the truth of the statement and the natural consequences of the truth back of it, we should understand many things which have appeared dark to us, and would be able to use the wonderful power, Thought Force, just as we use any other manifestation of Energy.

As I have said, when we think we set into motion vibrations of a very high degree, but just as real as the vibrations of light, heat, sound, electricity. And when we understand the laws governing the production and transmission of these vibrations we will be able to use them in our daily life, just as we do the better known forms of energy. That we cannot see, hear, weigh or measure these vibrations is no proof that they do not exist. There exist waves of sound which no human ear can hear, although some of these are undoubtedly registered by the ear of some of the insects, and others are caught by delicate scientific instruments invented by man; yet there is a great gap between the sounds registered by the most delicate instrument and the limit which man's mind, reasoning by analogy, knows to be the boundary line between sound waves and some other forms of vibration. And there are light waves which the eye of man does not register, some of which may be detected by more delicate instruments, and many more so fine that the instrument has not yet been invented which will detect them, although improvements are being made every year and the unexplored field gradually lessened.

As new instruments are invented, new vibrations are registered by them - and yet the vibrations were just as real before the invention of the instrument as afterward. Supposing that we had no instruments to register magnetism - one might be justified in denying the existence of that mighty force, because it could not be tasted, felt, smelt, heard, seen, weighted or measured. And yet the mighty magnet would still send out waves of force sufficient to draw to it pieces of steel weighing hundreds of pounds.

Each form of vibration requires its own form of instrument for registration. At present the human brain seems to be the only instrument capable of registering thought waves, although occultists say that in this century scientists will invent apparatus sufficiently delicate to catch and register such impressions. And from present indications it looks as if the invention named might be expected at any time. The demand exists and undoubtedly will be soon supplied. But to those who have experimented along the lines of practical telepathy no further proof is required than the results of their own experiments.

We are sending out thoughts of greater or less intensity all the time, and we are reaping the results of such thoughts. Not only do our thought waves influence ourselves and others, but they have a drawing power - they attract to us the thoughts of others, things, circumstances, people, "luck," in accord with the character of the thought uppermost in our minds. Thoughts of Love will attract to us the Love of others; circumstances and surroundings in accord with the thought; people who are of like thought. Thoughts of Anger, Hate, Envy, Malice and Jealousy will draw to us the foul brood of kindred thoughts emanating from the minds of others; circumstances in which we will be called upon to manifest these vile thoughts and will receive them in turn from others; people who will manifest inharmony; and so on. A strong thought or a thought long continued, will make us the center of attraction for the corresponding thought waves of others. Like attracts like in the Thought World - as ye sow so shall ye reap. Birds of a feather flock together in the Thought World - curses like chickens come home to roost, and bringing their friends with them.

The man or woman who is filled with Love sees Love on all sides and attracts the Love of others. The man with hate in his heart gets all the Hate he can stand. The man who thinks Fight generally runs up against all the Fight he wants before he gets through. And so it goes, each gets what he calls for over the wireless telegraphy of the Mind. The man who rises in the morning feeling "grumpy" usually manages to have the whole family in the same mood before the breakfast is over. The "nagging" woman generally finds enough to gratify her "nagging" propensity during the day.

This matter of Thought Attraction is a serious one. When you stop to think of it you will see that a man really makes his own surroundings, although he blames others for it. I have known people who understood this law to hold a positive, calm thought and be absolutely unaffected by the inharmony surrounding them. They were like the vessel from which the oil had been poured on the troubled waters - they rested safely and calmly whilst the tempest raged around them. One is not at the mercy of the fitful storms of Thought after he has learned the workings of the Law.

We have passed through the age of physical force on to the age of intellectual supremacy, and are now entering a new and almost unknown field, that of psychic power. This field has its established laws and we should acquaint ourselves with them or we will be crowded to the wall as are the ignorant on the planes of effort. I will endeavor to make plain to you the great underlying principles of this new field of energy which is opening up before us, that you may be able to make use of this great power and apply it for legitimate and worthy purposes, just as men are using steam, electricity and other forms of energy today.

Thought Waves and their Process of Reproduction

LIKE a stone thrown into the water, thought produces ripples and waves which spread out over the great ocean of thought. There is this difference, however: the waves on the water move only on a level plane in all directions, whereas thought waves move in all directions from a common center, just as do the rays from the sun.

Just as we here on earth are surrounded by a great sea of air, so are we surrounded by a great sea of Mind. Our thought waves move through this vast mental ether, extending, however, in all directions, as I have explained, becoming somewhat lessened in intensity according to the distance traversed, because of the friction occasioned by the waves coming in contact with the great body of Mind surrounding us on all sides.

These thought waves have other qualities differing from the waves on the water. They have the property of reproducing themselves; in this respect they resemble sound waves rather than waves upon the water. Just as a note of the violin will cause the thin glass to vibrate and "sing," so will a strong thought tend to awaken similar vibrations in minds attuned to receive it. Many of the "stray thoughts" which come to us are but reflections or answering vibrations to some strong thought sent out by another. But unless our minds are attuned to receive it, the thought will not likely affect us. If we are thinking high and great thoughts, our minds acquire a certain keynote corresponding to the character of the thoughts we have been thinking. And, this keynote once established, we will be apt to catch the vibrations of other minds keyed to the same thought. On the other hand, let us get into the habit of thinking thoughts of an opposite character, and we will soon be echoing the low order of thought emanating from the minds of the thousands thinking along the same lines.

We are largely what we have thought ourselves into being,

the balance being represented by the character of the suggestions and thought of others, which have reached us either directly by verbal suggestions or telepathically by means of such thought waves. Our general mental attitude, however, determines the character of the thought waves received from others as well as the thoughts emanating from ourselves. We receive only such thoughts as are in harmony with the general mental attitude held by ourselves; the thoughts not in harmony affecting us very little, as they awaken no response in us.

The man who believes thoroughly in himself and maintains a positive strong mental attitude of Confidence and Determination is not likely to be affected by the adverse and negative thoughts of Discouragement and Failure emanating from the minds of other persons in whom these last qualities predominate. At the same time these negative thoughts, if they reach one whose mental attitude is pitched on a low key, deepen his negative state and add fuel to the fire which is consuming his strength, or, if you prefer this figure, serve to further smother the fire of his energy and activity.

We attract to us the thoughts of others of the same order of thought. The man who thinks success will be apt to get into tune with the minds of others thinking likewise, and they will help him, and he them. The man who allows his mind to dwell constantly upon thoughts of failure brings himself into close touch with the minds of other "failure" people, and each will tend to pull the other down still more. The man who thinks that all is evil is apt to see much evil, and will be brought into contact with others who will seem to prove his theory. And the man who looks for good in everything and everybody will be likely to attract to himself the things and people corresponding to his thought. We generally see that for which we look.

You will be able to carry this idea more clearly if you will think of the Marconi wireless instruments, which receive the vibrations only from the sending instrument which has been attuned to the same key, while other telegrams are passing through the air in near vicinity without affecting the instrument. The same law applies to the operations of thought. We receive only that which corresponds to our mental attunement. If we have been discouraged, we may rest assured that we have dropped into a negative key, and have been affected not only by our own thoughts but have also received the added depressing thoughts of similar character which are constantly being sent out from the minds of other unfortunates who have not yet learned the law of attraction in the thought world. And if we occasionally rise to heights of enthusiasm and energy, how quickly we feel the inflow of the courageous, daring, energetic, positive thoughts being sent out by the live men and women of the world. We recognize this without much trouble when we come in personal contact with people and feel their vibrations, depressing or invigorating, as the case may be. But the same law operates when we are not in their presence, although less strongly.

The mind has many degrees of pitch, ranging from the highest positive note to the lowest negative note, with many notes in between, varying in pitch according to their respective distance from the positive or negative extreme.

When your mind is operating along positive lines you feel strong, buoyant, bright, cheerful, happy, confident and courageous, and are enabled to do your work well, to carry out your intentions, and progress on your roads to Success. You send out strong positive thought, which affects others and causes them to co-operate with you or to follow your lead, according to their own mental keynote.

When you are playing on the extreme negative end of the mental keyboard you feel depressed, week, passive, dull, fearful, cowardly. And you find yourself unable to make progress or to succeed. And your effect upon others is practically nil. You are led by, rather than leading others, and are used as a human doormat or football by more positive persons.

In some persons the positive element seems to predominate, and in others the negative quality seems to be more in evidence. There are, of course, widely varying degrees of positiveness and negativeness, and B may be negative to

A, while positive to C. When two people first meet there is generally a silent mental conflict in which their respective minds test their quality of positiveness, and fix their relative position toward each other. This process may be unconscious in many cases, but it occurs nevertheless. The adjustment is often automatic, but occasionally the struggle is so sharp - the opponents being so well matched - that the matter forces itself into the consciousness of the two people. Sometimes both parties are so much alike in their degrees of positiveness that they fail to come to terms, mentally; they never really are able to get along with each other, and they are either mutually repelled and separate or else stay together amid constant broils and wrangling.

We are positive or negative to everyone with whom we have relations. We may be positive to our children, our employees and dependents, but we are at the same time negative to others to whom we occupy inferior positions, or whom we have allowed to assert themselves over us.

Of course, something may occur and we will suddenly become more positive than the man or woman to whom we have heretofore been negative. We frequently see cases of this kind. And as the knowledge of these mental laws becomes more general we will see many more instances of persons asserting themselves and making use of their newfound power.

But remember you possess the power to raise the keynote of your mind to a positive pitch by an effort of the will. And, of course, it is equally true that you may allow yourself to drop into a low, negative note by carelessness or a weak will.

There are more people on the negative plane of thought than on the positive plane, and consequently there are more negative thought vibrations in operation in our mental atmosphere. But, happily for us, this is counterbalanced by the fact that a positive thought is infinitely more powerful than a negative one, and if by force of will we raise ourselves to a higher mental key we can shut out the depressing thoughts and may take up the vibrations corresponding with our changed mental attitude. This is one of the secrets of the affirmations and autosuggestions used by the several schools of Mental Science and other New Thought cults. There is no particular merit in affirmations of themselves, but they serve a twofold purpose: (1) They tend to establish new mental attitudes within us and act wonderfully in the direction of character- building - the science of making ourselves over. (2) They tend to raise the mental keynote so that we may get the benefit of the positive thought waves of others on the same plane of thought.

Whether or not we believe in them, we are constantly making affirmations. The man who asserts that he can and will do a thing - and asserts it earnestly - develops in himself the qualities conducive to the well doing of that thing, and at the same time places his mind in the proper key to receive all the thought waves likely to help him in the doing. If, on the other hand, one says and feels that he is going to fail, he will choke and smother the thoughts coming from his own subconscious mentality which are intended to help him, and at the same time will place himself in tune with the Failure-thought of the world - and there is plenty of the latter kind of thought around, I can tell you.

Do not allow yourselves to be affected by the adverse and negative thoughts of those around you. Rise to the upper chambers of your mental dwelling, and key yourself up to a strong pitch, away above the vibrations on the lower planes of thought. Then you will not only be immune to their negative vibrations but will be in touch with the great body of strong positive thought coming from those of your own plane of development. My aim will be to direct and train you in the proper use of thought and will, that you may have yourself well in hand and may be able to strike the positive key at any moment you may feel it necessary. It is not necessary to strike the extreme note on all occasions. The better plan is to keep yourself in a comfortable key, without much strain, and to have the means at command whereby you can raise the pitch at once when occasion demands. By this knowledge you will not be at the mercy of the old automatic action of the mind, but may have it well under your own control.

Development of the will is very much like the development of a muscle - a matter of practice and gradual improvement. At first it is apt to be tiresome, but at each trial one grows stronger until the new strength becomes real and permanent. Many of us have made ourselves positive under sudden calls or emergencies. We are in the habit of "bracing up" when occasion demands. But by intelligent practice you will be so much strengthened that your habitual state will be equal to your "bracing up" stage now, and then when you find it necessary to apply the spur you will be able to reach a stage not dreamed of at present.

Do not understand me as advocating a high tension continuously. This is not at all desirable, not only because it is apt to be too much of a strain upon you but also because you will find it desirable to relieve the tension at times and become receptive that you may absorb impressions. It is well to be able to relax and assume a certain degree of receptiveness, knowing that you are always able to spring back to the more positive state at will. The habitually strongly positive man loses much enjoyment and recreation. Positive, you give out expressions; receptive, you take in impressions. Positive, you are a teacher; receptive, a pupil. It is not only a good thing to be a good teacher, but it is also very important to be a good listener at times.

A Talk About The Mind

MAN has but one mind, but he has many mental faculties, each faculty being capable of functioning along two different lines of mental effort. There are no distinct dividing lines separating the two several functions of a faculty, but they shade into each other as do the colors of the spectrum.

An Active effort of any faculty of the mind is the result of a direct impulse imparted at the time of the effort. A Passive effort of any faculty of the mind is the result of either a preceding Active effort of the same mind; an Active effort of another along the lines of suggestion; Thought Vibrations from the mind of another; Thought impulses from an ancestor, transmitted by the laws of heredity (including impulses transmitted from generation to generation from the time of the original vibratory impulse imparted by the Primal Cause - which impulses gradually unfold, and unsheath, when the proper state of evolutionary development is reached).

The Active effort is new-born - fresh from the mint, whilst the Passive effort is of less recent creation, and, in fact, is often the result of vibratory impulses imparted in ages long past. The Active effort makes its own way, brushing aside the impeding vines and kicking from its path the obstructing stones. The Passive effort travels along the beaten path.

A thought-impulse, or motion-impulse, originally caused by an Active effort of faculty, may become by continued repetition, or habit, strictly automatic, the impulse given it by the repeated Active effort developing a strong momentum, which carries it on, along Passive lines, until stopped by another Active effort or its direction changed by the same cause.

On the other hand, thought-impulses, or motion-impulses, continued along Passive lines may be terminated or corrected by an Active effort. The Active function creates, changes or destroys. The Passive function carries on the work given it by the Active function and obeys orders and suggestions.

The Active function produces the thought-habit, or motion-habit, and imparts to it the vibrations, which carry it on along the Passive lines thereafter. The Active function also has the power to send forth vibrations which neutralize the momentum of the thought-habit, or motion-habit; it also is able to launch a new thought-habit, or motion-habit, with stronger vibrations, which overcomes and absorbs the first thought, or motion, and substitutes the new one.

All thought-impulses, or motion-impulses, once started on their errands, continue to vibrate along passive lines until corrected or terminated by subsequent impulses imparted by the Active function, or other controlling power. The continuance of the original impulse adds momentum and force to it, and renders its correction or termination more difficult. This explains that which is called "the force of habit." I think that this will be readily understood by those who have struggled to overcome a habit which had been easily acquired. The Law applies to good habits as well as bad. The moral is obvious.

Several of the faculties of the mind often combine to produce a single manifestation. A task to be performed may call for the combined exercise of several faculties, some of which may manifest by Active effort and others by Passive effort.

The meeting of new conditions - new problems - calls for the exercise of Active effort; whilst a familiar problem, or task, can be easily handled by the Passive effort without the assistance of his more enterprising brother.

There is in Nature an instinctive tendency of living organisms to perform certain actions, the tendency of an organized body to seek that which satisfies the wants of its organism. This tendency is sometimes called Appetency. It is really a Passive mental impulse, originating with the impetus imparted by the Primal Cause, and transmitted along the lines of evolutionary development, gaining strength and power as it progresses. The impulse of the Primal Cause is assisted by the powerful upward attraction exerted by THE ABSOLUTE.

In plant life this tendency is plainly discernible, ranging form the lesser exhibitions in the lower types to the greater in the higher types. It is that which is generally spoken of as the "life-force" in plants. It is, however, a manifestation of rudimentary mentation, functioning along the lines of Passive effort. In some of the higher forms of plant life there appears a faint color of independent "life action" - a faint indication of choice of volition. Writers on plant life relate many remarkable instances of this phenomenon. It is, undoubtedly, an exhibition of rudimentary Active mentation.

In the lower animal kingdom a very high degree of Passive mental effort is found. And, varying in degree in the several families and species, a considerable amount of Active mentation is apparent. The lower animal undoubtedly possesses Reason only in a lesser degree than man, and, in fact, the display of volitional mentation exhibited by an intelligent animal is often nearly as high as that shown by the lower types of man or by a young child.

As a child, before birth, shows in its body the stages of the physical evolution of man, so does a child, before and after birth - until maturity - manifest the stages of the mental evolution of man.

Man, the highest type of life yet produced, at least upon this planet, shows the highest form of Passive mentation, and also a much higher development of Active mentation than is seen in the lower animals, and yet the degrees of that power vary widely among the different races of men. Even among men of our race the different degrees of Active mentation are plainly noticeable; these degrees not depending by any means upon the amount of "culture," social position or educational advantages possessed by the individual: Mental Culture and Mental Development are two very different things.

You have but to look around you to see the different stages of the development of Active mentation in man. The reasoning of many men is scarcely more than Passive mentation, exhibiting but little of the qualities of volitional thought.

They prefer to let other men think for them. Active mentation tires them and they find the instinctive, automatic, Passive mental process much easier. Their minds work along the lines of least resistance. They are but little more than human sheep,

Among the lower animals and the lower types of men Active mentation is largely confined to the grosser faculties - the more material plane; the higher mental faculties working along the instinctive, automatic lines of the Passive function.

As the lower forms of life progressed in the evolutionary scale, they developed new faculties which were latent within them. These faculties always manifested in the form of rudimentary Passive functioning, and afterwards worked up through higher Passive forms, until the Active functions were brought into play. The evolutionary process still continues, the invariable tendency being toward the goal of highly developed Active mentation. This evolutionary progress is caused by the vibratory impulse imparted by the Primal Cause, aided by the uplifting attraction of THE ABSOLUTE.

This law of evolution is still in progress, and man is beginning to develop new powers of mind, which, of course, are first manifesting themselves along the lines of Passive effort. Some men have developed these new faculties to a considerable degree, and it is possible that before long Man will be able to exercise them along the line of their Active functions. In fact, this power has already been attained by a few. This is the secret of the Oriental occultists, and of some of their Occidental brethren.

The amenability of the mind to the will can be increased by properly directed practice. That which we are in the habit of referring to as the "strengthening of the Will" is in reality the training of the mind to recognize and absorb the Power Within. The Will is strong enough, it does not need strengthening, but the mind needs to be trained to receive and act upon the suggestions of the Will. The Will is the outward manifestation of the I AM. The Will current is flowing in full strength along the spiritual wires; but you must learn how to raise the trolley-pole to touch it before the mental car will move. This is a somewhat different idea from that which you have been in the habit of receiving from writers on the subject of Will Power, but it is correct, as you will demonstrate to your own satisfaction if you will follow up the subject by experiments along the proper lines.

The attraction of THE ABSOLUTE is drawing man upward, and the vibratory force of the Primal Impulse has not yet exhausted itself. The time of evolutionary development has come when man can help himself. The man who understands the Law can accomplish wonders by means of the development of the powers of the mind; whilst the man who turns his back upon the truth will suffer from his lack of knowledge of the Law.

He who understands the laws of his mental being, develops his latent powers and uses them intelligently. He does not despise his Passive mental functions, but makes good use of them also, charges them with the duties for which they are best fitted, and is able to obtain wonderful results from their work, having mastered them and trained them to do the bidding of the Higher Self. When they fail to do their work properly he regulates them, and his knowledge prevents him from meddling with them unintelligently, and thereby doing himself harm. He develops the faculties and powers latent within him and learns how to manifest them along the line of Active mentation as well as Passive. He knows that the real man within him is the master to whom both Active and Passive functions are but tools. He has banished Fear, and enjoys Freedom. He has found himself. HE HAS LEARNED THE SECRET OF THE I AM.

Mind Building

MAN can build up his mind and make it what he wills. In fact, we are mind-building every hour of our lives, either consciously or unconsciously. The majority of us are doing the work unconsciously, but those who have seen a little below the surface of things have taken the matter in hand and have become conscious creators of their own mentality. They are no longer subject to the suggestions and influences of others but have become masters of themselves. They assert the "I," and compel obedience from the subordinate mental faculties. The "I" is the sovereign of the mind, and what we call WILL is the instrument of the "I." Of course, there is something back of this, and the Universal Will is higher than the Will of the Individual, but the latter is in much closer touch with the Universal Will than is generally supposed, and when one conquers the lower self, and asserts the "I," he becomes in close touch with the Universal Will and partakes largely of its wonderful power. The moment one asserts the "I," and "finds himself," he establishes a close connection between the Individual Will and the Universal Will. But before he is able to avail himself of the mighty power at his command, he must first effect the Mastery of the lower self.

Think of the absurdity of Man claiming to manifest powers, when he is the slave of the lower parts of his mental being, which should be subordinate. Think of a man being the slave of his moods, passions, animal appetites and lower faculties, and at the same time trying to claim the benefits of the Will. Now, I am not preaching asceticism, which seems to me to be a confession of weakness. I am speaking of Self-Mastery - the assertion of the "I" over the subordinate parts of oneself. In the higher view of the subject, this "I" is the only real Self, and the rest is the non-self; but our space does not permit the discussion of this point, and we will use the word "self" as meaning the entire man. Before a man can assert the "I" in its full strength he must obtain the complete mastery of the subordinate parts of the self. All things are good when we learn to master them, but no thing is good when it masters us. Just so long as we allow the lower portions of the self to give us orders, we are slaves. It is only when the "I" mounts his throne and lifts the scepter, that order is established and things assume their proper relation to each other.

We are finding no fault with those who are swayed by their lower selves - they are in a lower grade of evolution, and will work up in time. But we are calling the attention of those who are ready, to the fact that the Sovereign must assert his will, and that the subjects must obey. Orders must be given and carried out. Rebellion must be put down, and the rightful authority insisted upon. And the time to do it is Now.

You have been allowing your rebellious subjects to keep the King from his throne. You have been allowing the mental kingdom to be misgoverned by irresponsible faculties. You have been the slaves of Appetite, Unworthy Thoughts, Passion and Negativeness. The Will has been set aside and Low Desire has usurped the throne. It is time to re-establish order in the mental kingdom. You are able to assert the mastery over any emotion, appetite, passion or class of thoughts by the assertion of the Will. You can order Fear to go to the rear; Jealousy to leave your presence; Hate to depart from your sight; Anger to hide itself; Worry to cease troubling you; Uncontrolled Appetite and Passion to bow in submission and to become humble slaves instead of masters - all by the assertion of the "I." You may surround yourself with the glorious company of Courage, Love and Self-Control, by the same means. You may put down the rebellion and secure peace and order in your mental kingdom if you will but utter the mandate and insist upon its execution. Before you march forth to empire, you must establish the proper internal condition - must show your ability to govern you own kingdom. The first battle is the conquest of the lesser self by the Real Self.

AFFIRMATION

I AM Asserting the Mastery of My Real Self

Repeat these words earnestly and positively during the

day at least once an hour, and particularly when you are confronted with conditions which tempt you to act on the lines of the lesser self instead of following the course dictated by the Real Self. In the moment of doubt and hesitation say these words earnestly, and your way will be made clear to you. Repeat them several times after you retire and settle yourself to sleep. But be sure to back up the words with the thought inspiring them, and do not merely repeat them parrot-like. Form the mental image of the Real Self asserting its mastery over the lower planes of your mind - see the King on his Throne. You will become conscious of an influx of new thought, and things which have seemed hard for you will suddenly become much easier. You will feel that you have yourself well in hand, and that YOU are the master and not the slave. The thought you are holding will manifest itself in action, and you will steadily grow to become that which you have in mind.

EXERCISE

Fix the mind firmly on the higher Self and draw inspiration from it when you feel led to yield to the promptings of the lower part of your nature. When you are tempted to burst into Anger - assert the "I," and your voice will drop. Anger is unworthy of the developed Self. When you feel vexed and cross, remember what you are, and rise above your feeling. When you feel Fearful, remember that the Real Self fears nothing, and assert Courage. When you feel Jealousy inciting, think of your higher nature, and laugh. And so on, asserting the Real Self and not allowing the things on the lower plane of mentality to disturb you. They are unworthy of you, and must be taught to keep their places. Do not allow these things to master you - they should be your subjects, not your masters. You must get away from this plane, and the only way to do so is to cut loose from these phases of thought which have been "running things" to suit themselves. You may have trouble at the start, but keep at it and you will have that satisfaction which comes only from conquering the lower parts of our nature. You have been a slave long enough

- now is the time to free yourselves. If you will follow these exercises faithfully you will be a different being by the end of the year, and will look back with a pitying smile to your former condition. But it takes work. This is not child's play but a task for earnest men and women, Will YOU make the effort?

The Secret of The Will

WHILE psychologists may differ in their theories regarding the nature of the Will, none deny its existence, nor question its power. All persons recognize the power of strong Will - all see how it may be used to overcome the greatest obstacles. But few realize that the Will may be developed and strengthened by intelligent practice. They feel that they could accomplish wonders if they had a strong Will, but instead of attempting to develop it, they content themselves with vain regrets. They sigh, but do nothing.

Those who have investigated the subject closely know that Will Power, with all its latent possibilities and mighty powers, may be developed, disciplined, controlled and directed, just as may be any other of Nature's forces. It does not matter what theory you may entertain about the nature of the Will, you will obtain the results if you practice intelligently.

Personally, I have a somewhat odd theory about the Will. I believe that every man has, potentially, a strong Will, and that all he has to do is to train his mind to make use of it. I think that in the higher regions of the mind of every man is a great store of Will Power awaiting his use. The Will current is running along the psychic wires, and all that it is necessary to do is to raise the mental trolley-pole and bring down the power for your use. And the supply is unlimited, for your little storage battery is connected with the great powerhouse of the Universal Will Power, and the power is inexhaustible. Your Will does not need training - but your Mind does. The mind is the instrument and the supply of Will Power is proportionate to the fineness of the instrument through which it manifests. But you needn't accept this theory if you don't like it. This lesson will fit your theory as well as mine.

He who has developed his mind so that it will allow the Will Power to manifest through it, has opened up wonderful possibilities for himself. Not only has he found a great power at his command, but he is able to bring into play, and use, faculties, talents and abilities of whose existence he has not dreamed. This secret of the Will is the magic key which opens all doors.

The late Donald G. Mitchell once wrote: "Resolve is what makes a man manifest; not puny resolve, but crude determination; not errant purpose - but that strong and indefatigable will which treads down difficulties and danger, as a boy treads down the heaving frost-lands of winter; which kindles his eye and brain with a proud pulse-beat toward the unattainable. Will makes men giants."

Many of us feel that if we would but exert our Will, we might accomplish wonders. But somehow we do not seem to want to take the trouble - at any rate; we do not get to the actual willing point. We put it off from time to time, and talk vaguely of "some day," but that some day never comes.

We instinctively feel the power of the Will, but we haven't enough energy to exercise it, and so drift along with the tide, unless perhaps some friendly difficulty arises, some helpful obstacle appears in our path, or some kindly pain stirs us into action, in either of which cases we are compelled to assert our Will and thus begin to accomplish something.

The trouble with us is that we do not want to do the thing enough to make us exert our Will Power. We don't want to hard enough. We are mentally lazy and of weak Desire. If you do not like the word Desire substitute for it the word "Aspiration." (Some people call the lower impulses Desires, and the higher, Aspirations - it's all a matter of words, take you choice.) That is the trouble. Let a man be in danger of losing his life - let a woman be in danger of losing a great love - and you will witness a startling exhibition of Will Power from an unexpected source. Let a woman's child be threatened with danger, and she will manifest a degree of Courage and Will that sweeps all before it. And yet the same woman will quail before a domineering husband, and will lack the Will to perform a simple task. A boy will do all sorts of work if he but considers it play, and yet he can scarcely force himself to cut a little firewood. Strong Will follows strong Desire. If you really want to do a thing very much, you can usually develop the Will Power to accomplish it.

The trouble is that you have not really wanted to do these things, and yet you blame your Will. You say that you do want to do it, but if you stop to think you will see that you really want to do something else more than the thing in question. You are not willing to pay the price of attainment. Stop a moment and analyze this statement and apply it in your own case,

You are mentally lazy - that's the trouble. Don't talk to me about not having enough Will. You have a great storehouse of Will awaiting your use, but you are too lazy to use it. Now, if you are really in earnest about this matter, get to work and first find out what you really want to do - then start to work and do it. Never mind about the Will Power - you'll find a full supply of that whenever you need it. The thing to do is to get to the point where you will resolve to do. That the real test - the resolving. Think of these things a little, and make up your mind whether or not you really want to be a Willer sufficiently hard to get to work.

Many excellent essays and books have been written on this subject, all of which agree regarding the greatness of Will Power, the most enthusiastic terms being used; but few have anything to say about how this power may be acquired by those who have it not, or who possess it in but a limited degree. Some have given exercises designed to "strengthen" the Will, which exercises really strengthen the Mind so that it is able to draw upon its store of power. But they have generally overlooked the fact that in autosuggestion is to be found the secret of the development of the mind so that it may become the efficient instrument of the Will.

AUTOSUGGESTION

I AM Using My Will Power

Say these words several times earnestly and positively, immediately after finishing this article. Then repeat them frequently during the day, at least once an hour, and particularly when you meet something that calls for the exercise of Will Power. Also repeat them several times after you retire and settle yourself for sleep. Now, there is nothing in the words unless you back them up with the thought. In fact, the thought is "the whole thing," and the words only pegs upon which to hang the thought. So think of what you are saying, and mean what you say. You must use Faith at the start, and use the words with a confident expectation of the result. Hold the steady thought that you are drawing on your storehouse of Will Power, and before long you will find that thought is taking form in action, and that your Will Power is manifesting itself. You will feel an influx of strength with each repetition of the words. You will find yourself overcoming difficulties and bad habits, and will be surprised at how things are being smoothed out for you.

EXERCISE

Perform at least one disagreeable task each day during the month.. If there is any especially disagreeable task which you would like to shirk, that is the one for you to perform. This is not given to you in order to make you self-sacrificing or meek, or anything of that sort - it is given you to exercise your Will. Anyone can do a pleasant thing cheerfully, but it takes Will to do the unpleasant thing cheerfully; and that is how you must do the work. It will prove a most valuable discipline to you. Try it for a month and you will see where "it comes in." If you shirk this exercise you had better stop right here and acknowledge that you do not want Will Power, and are content to stay where you are and remain a weakling.

How to Become Immune to Injurious

Thought Attraction

THE first thing to do is to begin to "cut out" Fear and Worry. Fear-thought is the cause of much unhappiness and many failures. You have been told this thing over and over again, but it will bear repeating. Fear is a habit of mind which has been fastened upon us by negative race-thought, but from which we may free ourselves by individual effort and perseverance.

Strong expectancy is a powerful magnet. He of the strong, confident desire attracts to him the things best calculated to aid him - persons, things circumstances, surroundings; if he desires them hopefully, trustfully, confidently, calmly. And, equally true, he who Fears a thing generally manages to start into operation forces which will cause the thing he feared to come upon him. Don't you see, the man who Fears really expects the feared thing, and the eyes of the Law is the same as if he really had wished for or desired it? The Law is operative in both cases - the principle is the same.

The best way to overcome the habit of Fear is to assume the mental attitude of Courage, just as the best way to get rid of darkness is to let in the light. It is a waste of time to fight a negative thought-habit by recognizing its force and trying to deny it out of existence by mighty efforts. The best, surest, easiest and quickest method is to assume the existence of the positive thought desired in its place; and by constantly dwelling upon the positive thought, manifest it into objective reality.

Therefore, instead of repeating, "I'm not afraid," say boldly, "I am full of Courage," "I am Courageous." You must assert, "There's nothing to fear," which, although in the nature of a denial, simply denies the reality of the object causing fear rather than admitting the fear itself and then denying it.

To overcome fear, one should hold firmly to the mental attitude of Courage. He should think Courage, say Courage, act Courage. He should keep the mental picture of Courage before him all the time, until it becomes his normal mental attitude. Hold the ideal firmly before you and you will gradually grow to its attainment - the ideal will become manifest.

Let the word "Courage" sink deeply into your mind, and then hold it firmly there until the mind fastens it in place. Think of yourself as being Courageous - see yourself as acting with Courage in trying situations. Realize that there is nothing to Fear - that Worry and Fear never helped anyone, and never will. Realize that Fear paralyzes effort, and that Courage promotes activity.

The confident, fearless, expectant, "I Can and I Will" man is a mighty magnet. He attracts to himself just what is needed for his success. Things seem to come his way, and people say he is "lucky." Nonsense! "Luck" has nothing to do with it. It's all in the Mental Attitude. And the Mental Attitude of the "I Can't" or the "I'm Afraid" man also determines his measure of success. There's no mystery whatsoever about it. You have but to look about you to realize the truth of what I have said. Did you ever know a successful man who did not have the "I Can and I will" thought strong within him? Why, he will walk all around the "I Can't" man, who has perhaps even more ability. The first mental attitude brought to the surface latent qualities, as well as attracted help from outside; whilst the second mental attitude not only attracted "I Can't" people and things, but also kept the man's own powers from manifesting themselves. I have demonstrated the correctness of these views, and so have many others, and the number of people who know these things is growing every day.

Don't waste your Thought-Force, but use it to advantage. Stop attracting to yourself failure, unhappiness, inharmony, sorrow - begin now and send out a current of bright, positive, happy thought. Let your prevailing thought be "I Can and I Will;" think "I Can and I Will;" dream "I Can and I Will;" say "I Can and I Will;" and act "I Can and I Will". Live on the "I Can and I and Will" plane, and before you are aware of it, you will feel the new vibrations manifesting themselves in action; will see them bring results; will be conscious of the new point of view; will realize that your own is coming to you. You will feel better, act better, see better, BE better in every way, after you join the "I Can and I Will" brigade.

Fear is the parent of Worry, Hate, Jealousy, Malice, Anger, Discontent, Failure and all the rest. The man who rids himself of Fear will find that the rest of the brood has disappeared. The only way to be Free is to get rid of Fear. Tear it out by the roots. I regard the conquest of Fear as the first important step to be taken by those who wish to master the application of Thought Force. So long as Fear masters you, you are in no condition to make progress in the realm of Thought, and I must insist that you start to work at once to get rid of this obstruction. You CAN do it - if you only go about it in earnest. And when you have ridded yourself of the vile thing, life will seem entirely different to you - you will feel happier, freer, stronger, more positive, and will be more successful in every undertaking of Life.

Start it today, make up your mind that this intruder must GO - do not compromise matters with him, but insist upon an absolute surrender on his part. You will find the task difficult at first, but each time you oppose him he will grow weaker, and you will be stronger. Shut off his nourishment - starve him to death - he cannot live in a thought atmosphere of Fearlessness. So, start to fill your mind with good, strong, Fearless thoughts - keep yourself busy thinking Fearlessness, and Fear will die of his own accord. Fearlessness is positive - Fear is negative, and you may be sure that the positive will prevail.

So long as Fear is around with his "but," "if," "suppose," "I'm afraid," "I can't," "what if," and all the rest of his cowardly suggestions, you will not be able to use your Thought Force to the best advantage. Once get him out of the way, you will have clear sailing, and every inch of thought- sail will catch the wind. He is a Jonah. Overboard with him! (The whale that swallows him will have my sympathy.)

I advise that you start in to do some of the things which you feel you could do if you were not afraid to try. Start to work to do these things, affirming Courage all the way through, and you will be surprised to see how the changed mental attitude will clear away obstacles from your path, and will make things very much easier than you had anticipated. Exercises of this kind will develop you wonderfully, and you will be much gratified at the result of a little practice along these lines.

There are many things before you awaiting accomplishment, which you can master if you will only throw aside the yoke of Fear - if you will only refuse to accept the race suggestion, and will boldly assert the "I" and its power. And the best way to vanquish Fear is to assert "Courage" and stop thinking of Fear. By this plan you will train the mind into new habits of thought, thus eradicating the old negative thoughts which have been pulling you down, and holding you back. Take the word "Courage" with you as your watchword and manifest it in action.

Remember, the only thing to fear is Fear, and - well, don't even fear Fear, for he's a cowardly chap at the best, who will run if you show a brave front.

The Transmutation of Negative Thought

WORRY is the child of Fear - if you kill out Fear, Worry will die for want of nourishment. This advice is very old, and yet it is always worthy of repetition, for it is a lesson of which we are greatly in need. Some people think that if we kill out Fear and Worry we will never be able to accomplish anything. I have read editorials in the great journals in which the writers held that without Worry one can never accomplish any of the great tasks of life, because Worry is necessary to stimulate interest and work. This is nonsense, no matter who utters it. Worry never helped one to accomplish anything; on the contrary, it stands in the way of accomplishment and attainment.

The motive underlying action and "doing things" is Desire and Interest. If one earnestly desires a thing, he naturally becomes very much interested in its accomplishment, and is quick to seize upon anything likely to help him to gain the thing he wants. More than that, his mind starts up a work on the subconscious plane that brings into the field of consciousness many ideas of value and importance. Desire and Interest are the causes that result in success. Worry is not Desire. It is true that if one's surroundings and environments become intolerable, he is driven in desperation to some efforts that will result in throwing off the undesirable conditions and in the acquiring of those more in harmony with his desire. But this is only another form of Desire - the man desires something different from what he has; and when his desire becomes strong enough his entire interest is given to the task, he makes a mighty effort, and the change is accomplished. But it wasn't Worry that caused the effort. Worry could content itself with wringing its hands and moaning, "Woe is me," and wearing its nerves to a frazzle, and accomplishing nothing. Desire acts differently. It grows stronger as the man's conditions become intolerable, and finally when he feels the hurt so strongly that he can't stand it any longer, he says, "I won't stand this any longer - l will make a change," and lo! Then Desire springs into action.

The man keeps on "wanting" a change the worst way (which is the best way) and his Interest and Attention being given to the task of deliverance, he begins to make things move. Worry never accomplished anything. Worry is negative and death producing. Desire and Ambition are positive and life producing. A man may worry himself to death and yet nothing will be accomplished, but let that man transmute his worry and discontent into Desire and Interest, coupled with a belief that he is able to make the change - the "I Can and I Will" idea - then something happens.

Yes, Fear and Worry must go before we can do much. One must proceed to cast out these negative intruders, and replace them with Confidence and Hope. Transmute Worry into keen Desire. Then you will find that Interest is awakened, and you will begin to think things of interest to you. Thoughts will come to you from the great reserve stock in your mind and you will start to manifest them in action. Moreover you will be placing yourself in harmony with similar thoughts of others, and will draw to you aid and assistance from the great volume of thought waves with which the world is filled. One draws to himself thought waves corresponding in character with the nature of the prevailing thoughts in his won mind - his mental attitude. Then again he begins to set into motion the great Law of Attraction, whereby he draws to him others likely to help him, and is, in turn, attracted to others who can aid him. This Law of Attraction is no joke, no metaphysical absurdity, but is a great live working principle of Nature, as anyone may learn by experimenting and observing.

To succeed in anything you must want it very much - Desire must be in evidence in order to attract. The man of weak desires attracts very little to himself. The stronger the Desire the greater the force set into motion. You must want a thing hard enough before you can get it. You must want it more than you do the things around you, and you must be prepared to pay the price for it. The price is the throwing overboard of certain lesser desires that stand in the way of the accomplishment of the greater one. Comfort, ease, leisure, amusements, and many other things may have to go (not always, though). It all depends on what you want. As a rule, the greater the thing desired, the greater the price to be paid for it. Nature believes in adequate compensation. But if you really Desire a thing in earnest, you will pay the price without question; for the Desire will dwarf the importance of the other things.

You say that you want a thing very much, and are doing everything possible toward its attainment? Pshaw! You are only playing Desire. Do you want the thing as much as a prisoner wants freedom - as much as a dying man wants life? Look at the almost miraculous things accomplished by prisoners desiring freedom. Look how they work through steel plates and stonewalls with a bit of stone. Is your desire as strong as that? Do you work for the desired thing as if your life depended upon it? Nonsense! You don't know what Desire is. I tell you if a man wants a thing as much as the prisoner wants freedom, or as much as a strongly vital man wants life, then that man will be able to sweep away obstacles and impediments apparently immovable. The key to attainment is Desire, Confidence, and Will. This key will open many doors.

Fear paralyzes Desire - it scares the life out of it. You must get rid of Fear. There have been times in my life when Fear would get hold of me and take a good, firm grip on my vitals, and I would lose all hope; all interest; all ambition; all desire. But, thank the Lord, I have always managed to throw off the grip of the monster and face my difficulty like a man; and lo! Things would seem to be straightened out for me somehow. Either the difficulty would melt away or I would be given means to overcome, or get around, or under or over it. It is strange how this works. No matter how great is the difficulty, when we finally face it with courage and confidence in ourselves, we seem to pull through somehow, and then we begin to wonder what we were scared about. This is not a mere fancy, it is the working of a mighty law, which we do not as yet fully understand, but which we may prove at any time.

People often ask: "it's all very well for you New Thought

people to say 'Don't worry,' but what's a person to do when he thinks of all the possible things ahead of him, which might upset him and his plans? Well, all that I can say is that the man is foolish to bother about thinking of troubles to come at some time in the future. The majority of things that we worry about don't come to pass at all; a large proportion of the others come in a milder form than we had anticipated, and there are always other things which come at the same time which help us to overcome the trouble. The future holds in store for us not only difficulties to be overcome, but also agents to help us in overcoming the difficulties. Things adjust themselves. We are prepared for any trouble which may come upon us, and when the time comes we somehow find ourselves able to meet it. God not only tempers the wind to the shorn lamb, but He also tempers the shorn lamb to the wind. The winds and the shearing do not come together; there is usually enough time for the lamb to get seasoned, and then he generally grows new wool before the cold blast comes.

It has been well said that nine-tenths of the worries are over things which never comes to pass, and that the other tenth is over things of little or no account. So what's the use in using up all your reserve force in fretting over future troubles, if this be so? Better wait until your troubles really come before you worry. You will find that by this storing up of energy you will be able to meet about any sort of trouble that comes your way.

What is it that uses up all the energy in the average man or woman, anyway? Is it the real overcoming of difficulties, or the worrying about impending troubles? It's always "Tomorrow, tomorrow," and yet tomorrow never comes just as we feared it would. Tomorrow is all right; it carries in its grip good things as well as troubles. Bless my soul, when I sit down and think over the things which I once feared might possibly descend upon me, I laugh! Where are those feared things now? I don't know - have almost forgotten that I ever feared them.

You do not need fight Worry - that isn't the way to overcome the habit. Just practice concentration, and then learn to concentrate upon something right before you, and you will find that the worry thought has vanished. The mind can think of but one thing at a time, and if you concentrate upon a bright thing, the other thing will fade away. There are better ways of overcoming objectionable thoughts than by fighting them. Learn to concentrate upon thoughts of an opposite character, and you will have solved the problem.

When the mind is full of worry thoughts, it cannot find time to work out plans to benefit you. But when you have concentrated upon bright, helpful thoughts, you will discover that it will start to work subconsciously; and when the time comes you will find all sorts of plans and methods by which you will be able to meet the demands upon you. Keep your mental attitude right, and all things will be added unto you. There's no sense in worrying; nothing has ever been gained by it, and nothing ever will be. Bright, cheerful and happy thoughts attract bright, cheerful and happy things to us - worry drives them away. Cultivate the right mental attitude.

The Law of Mental Control

YOUR thoughts are either faithful servants or tyrannical masters - just as you allow them to be. You have the say about it; take your choice. They will either go about your work under direction of the firm will, doing it the best they know how, not only in your waking hours, but when you are asleep - some of our best mental work being performed for us when our conscious mentality is at rest, as is evidenced by the fact that when the morning comes we find troublesome problems have been worked out for us during the night, after we had dismissed them from our minds - apparently; or they will ride all over us and make us their slaves if we are foolish enough to allow them to do so. More than half the people of the world are slaves of every vagrant thought which may see fit to torment them.

Your mind is given you for your good and for your own use - not to use you. There are very few people who seem to realize this and who understand the art of managing the mind. The key to the mystery is Concentration. A little practice will develop within every man the power to use the mental machine properly. When you have some mental work to do concentrate upon it to the exclusion of everything else, and you will find that the mind will get right down to business - to the work at hand - and matters will be cleared up in no time. There is an absence of friction, and all waste motion or lost power is obviated. Every pound of energy is put to use, and every revolution of the mental driving wheel counts for something. It pays to be able to be a competent mental engineer.

And the man who understands how to run his mental engine knows that one of the important things is to be able to stop it when the work has been done. He does not keep putting coal in the furnace, and maintaining a high pressure after the work is finished, or when the day's portion of the work has been done, and the fires should be banked until the next day. Some people act as if the engine should be kept running whether there was any work to be done or not, and then they complain if it gets worn out and wobbles and needs repairing. These mental engines are fine machines, and need intelligent care.

To those who are acquainted with the laws of mental control it seems absurd for one to lie awake at night fretting about the problems of the day, or more often, of the morrow. It is just as easy to slow down the mind as it is to slow down an engine, and thousands of people are learning to do this in these days of New Thought. The best way to do it is to think of something else - as far different from the obtruding thought as possible. There is no use fighting an objectionable thought with the purpose of "downing" it - that is a great waste of energy, and the more you keep on saying, "I won't think of this thing!" the more it keeps on coming into your mind, for you are holding it there for the purpose of hitting it. Let it go; don't give it another thought; fix the mind on something entirely different, and keep the attention there by an effort of the will. A little practice will do much for you in this direction. There is only room for one thing at a time in the focus of attention; so put all your attention upon one thought, and the others will sneak off. Try it for yourself.

Asserting the Life-Force

I have spoken to you of the advantage of getting rid of Fear. Now I wish to put LIFE into you. Many of you have been going along as if you were dead - no ambition - no energy - no vitality - no interest - no life. This will never do. You are stagnating. Wake up and display a few signs of life! This is not the place in which you can stalk around like a living corpse - this is the place for wide-awake, active, live people, and a good general awakening is what is needed; although it would take nothing less than a blast from Gabriel's trumpet to awaken some of the people who are stalking around thinking that they are alive, but who are really dead to all that makes life worthwhile.

We must let Life flow through us, and allow it to express itself naturally. Do not let the little worries of life, or the big ones either, depress you and cause you to lose your vitality. Assert the Life Force within you, and manifest it in every thought, act and deed, and before long you will be exhilarated and fairly bubbling over with vitality and energy.

Put a little life into your work - into your pleasures - into yourself. Stop doing things in a half-headed way, and begin to take an interest in what you are doing, saying and thinking. It is astonishing how much interest we may find in the ordinary things of life if we will only wake up. There are interesting things all around us - interesting events occurring every moment - but we will not be aware of them unless we assert our life force and begin to actually live instead of merely existing.

No man or woman ever amounted to anything unless he or she put life into the tasks of everyday life - the acts - the thoughts. What the world needs is live men and women. Just look into the eyes of the people whom you meet, and see how few of them are really alive. The most of them lack that expression of conscious life which distinguishes the man who lives from the one who simply exists.

I want you to acquire this sense of conscious life so that you may manifest it in your life and show what Mental Science has done for you. I want you to get to work today and begin to make yourselves over according to the latest pattern. You can do this if you will only take the proper interest in the task.

AFFIRMATION AND EXERCISE

Fix in your mind the thought that the "I" within you is very much alive and that you are manifesting life fully, mentally and physically. And keep this though there, aiding yourself with constant repetitions of the watchword. Don't let the thought escape you, but keep pushing it back into the mind. Keep it before the mental vision as much as possible. Repeat the watchword when you awaken in the morning - say it when you retire at night. And say it at meal times, and whenever else you can during the day - at least once an hour. Form the mental picture of yourself as filled with Life and Energy. Live up to it as far as possible. When you start in to perform a task say "I AM Alive" and mix up as much life as possible in the task. If you find yourself feeling depressed, say "I AM Alive," and then take a few deep breaths, and with each inhalation let the mind hold the thought that you are breathing in Strength and Life, and as you exhale, hold the thought that you are breathing out all the old, dead, negative conditions and are glad to get rid of them. Then finish up with an earnest, vigorous affirmation: "I AM Alive," and mean it when you say it too.

And let your thoughts take form in action. Don't rest content with merely saying that you are alive, but prove it with your acts. Take an interest in doing things, and don't go around "mooning" or daydreaming. Get down to business, and LIVE.

Training the Habit-Mind

PROFESSOR William James, the well-known teacher of, and writer upon Psychology very truly says: "The great thing in all education is to make our nervous system our ally instead of our enemy. For this we must make automatic and habitual, as early as possible, as many useful actions as we can and as carefully guard against growing into ways that are likely to be disadvantageous. In the acquisition of a new habit, or the leaving off of an old one we must take care to launch ourselves with as strong and decided initiative as possible. Never suffer an exception to occur until the new habit is securely rooted in your life. Seize the very first possible opportunity to act on every resolution you make and on every emotional prompting you may experience, in the direction of the habits you aspire to gain."

This advice is along the lines familiar to all students of Mental Science, but it states the matter more plainly than the majority of us have done. It impresses upon us the importance of passing on to the subconscious mind the proper impulses, so that they will become automatic and "second nature." Our subconscious mentality is a great storehouse for all sorts of suggestions from ourselves and others and, as it is the "habit-mind," we must be careful to send it the proper material from which it may make habits. If we get into the habit of doing certain things, we may be sure that the subconscious mentality will make it easier for us to do just the same thing over and over again, easier each time, until finally we are firmly bound with the ropes and chains of the habit, and find it more or less difficult, sometimes almost impossible, to free ourselves from the hateful thing.

We should cultivate good habits against the hour of need. The time will come when we will be required to put forth our best efforts, and it rests with us today whether that hour of need shall find us doing the proper thing automatically and almost without thought, or struggling to do it bound down and hindered with the chains of things opposed to that which we desire at that moment.

We must be on guard at all times to prevent the forming of undesirable habits. There may be no special harm in doing a certain thing today, or perhaps again tomorrow, but there may be much harm in setting up the habit of of doing that particular thing. If you are confronted with the question: "Which of these two things should I do?" the best answer is: "I will do that which I would like to become a habit with me."

In forming a new habit, or in breaking an old one, we should throw ourselves into the task with as much enthusiasm as possible, in order to gain the most ground before the energy expends itself when it meets with friction from the opposing habits already formed. We should start in by making as strong an impression as possible upon the subconscious mentality. Then we should be constantly on guard against temptations to break the new resolution "just this once." This "just once" idea kills off more good resolutions than any other one cause. The moment you yield "just this once, you introduce the thin edge of the wedge that will, in the end, split your resolution into pieces.

Equally important is the fact that each time you resist temptation the stronger does your resolution become. Act upon your resolution as early and as often as possible, as with every manifestation of thought in action, the stronger does it become. You are adding to the strength of your original resolution every time you back it up with action.

The mind has been likened to a piece of paper that has been folded. Ever afterwards it has a tendency to fold in the same crease - unless we make a new crease or fold, when it will follow the last lines. And the creases are habits - every time we make one it is so much easier for the mind to fold along the same crease afterward. Let us make our mental creases in the right direction.

The Psychology of Emotion

ONE is apt to think of the emotions as independent from habit. We easily may think of one acquiring habits of action, and even of thinking, but we are apt to regard the emotions as something connected with "feeling" and quite divorced from intellectual effort. Yet, not withstanding the distinction between the two, both are dependent largely upon habit, and one may repress, increase, develop, and change one's emotions, just as one may regulate habits of action and lines of thought.

It is an axiom of psychology that "Emotions deepen by repetition." If a person allows a state of feeling to thoroughly take possession of him, he will find it easier to yield to the same emotion the second time, and so on, until the particular emotion or feeling becomes second nature to him. If an undesirable emotion shows itself inclined to take up a permanent abode with you, you had better start to work to get rid of it, or at least to master it. And the best time to do this is at the start; for each repetition renders the habit more firmly entrenched, and the task of dislodging it more difficult.

Were you ever jealous? If so, you will remember how insidious was its first approach; how subtly it whispered hateful suggestions into your willing ear, and how gradually it followed up such suggestions, until, finally you began to see green. (Jealousy has an effect upon the bile, and causes it to poison the blood. This is why the idea of green is always associated with it.) Then you will remember how the thing seemed to grow, taking possession of you until you scarcely could shake it off. You found it much easier to become jealous the next time. It seemed to bring before you all sorts of objects apparently justifying your suspicions and feeling. Everything began to look green - the green-eyed monster waxed fat.

And so it is with every feeling or emotion. If you give way to a fit of rage, you will find it easier to become angry the

next time, on less provocation. The habit of feeling and acting "mean" does not take long to firmly settle itself in its
new home if encouraged. Worry is a great habit for growing
and waxing fat. People start by worrying about big things,
and then begin to worry and fret about some smaller thing.
And then the merest trifle worries and distresses them. They
imagine that all sorts of evil things are about to befall them.
If they start on a journey they are certain there is going to
be a wreck. If a telegram comes, it is sure to contain some
dreadful tidings. If a child seems a little quiet, the worrying
mother is positive it is going to fall ill and die. If the husband seems thoughtful, as he revolves some business plan
in his mind, then the good wife is convinced that he is beginning to cease to love her, and indulges in a crying spell. And
so it goes - worry, worry, worry - each indulgence making
the habit more at home. After a while the continued thought
shows itself in action. Not only is the mind poisoned by the
blue thoughts, but the forehead shows deep lines between
the eyebrows, and the voice takes on that whining, rasping
tone so common among worry-burdened people.

The condition of mind known as "fault-finding" is another
emotion that grows fat with exercise. First, fault is found
with this thing, then with that, and finally with everything.
The person becomes a chronic "nagger" - a burden to friends
and relatives, and a thing to be avoided by outsiders. Women
make the greatest naggers. Not because men are any better, but simply because a man nagger apt to have the habit
knocked out of him by other men who will not stand his nonsense - he find that he is making things too hot for himself
and he reforms; while a woman has more of a chance to indulge in the habit. But this nagging is all a matter of habit.
It grows from small beginnings, and each time it is indulged
in it throws out another root, branch, or tendril, and fastens
itself the closer to the one who has given it soil in which to
grow.

Envy, uncharitableness, gossip scandal-mongering, are
all habits of this kind. The seeds are in every human breast,
and only need good soil and a little watering to become lusty

and strong.

Each time you give way to one of these negative emotions, the easier do you make it for a recurrence of the same thing, or similar ones. Sometimes by encouraging one unworthy emotion, you find that you have given room for the growth of a whole family of these mental weeds.

Now, this is not a good old orthodox preachment against the sin of bad thoughts. It is merely a calling of your attention to the law underlying the psychology of emotion. Nothing new about it - old as the hills - so old that many of us have forgotten all about it.

If you wish to manifest these constantly disagreeable and unpleasant traits, and to suffer the unhappiness that comes from them, by all means do so - that is your own business, and privilege. It's none of mine, and I am not preaching at you - it keeps me busy minding my own business and keeping an eye on my own undesirable habits and actions. I am merely telling you the law regarding the matter, and you may do the rest. If you wish to choke out these habits, there are two ways open to you. First, whenever you find yourself indulging in a negative thought or feeling, take right hold of it and say to it firmly, and vigorously, "Get out!" It won't like this at first, and will bridle up, curve its back and snarl like an offended cat. But never mind - just say, "Scat" to it. The next time it will not be so confident and aggressive - it will have manifested a little of the fear-habit. Each time you repress and choke out a tendency of this kind, the weaker it will become, and the stronger will your will be.

Professor James says: "Refuse to express a passion, and it dies. Count ten before venting your anger, and its occasion seems ridiculous. Whistling to keep up courage is no mere figure of speech. On the other hand, sit all day in a moping posture, sigh, and reply to everything with a dismal voice, and your melancholy lingers. There is no more valuable precept in moral education than this, as all who have experience know: if we wish to conquer emotional tendencies in ourselves, we must assiduously, and in the first instance, cold-bloodedly, go through the outward movements of those contrary dispositions we prefer to cultivate.

Smooth the brow, brighten the eye, contract the dorsal rather than the ventral aspect of the frame, and speak in a major key, pass the genial compliment, and your heart must be frigid indeed if it does not gradually thaw.

Developing New Brain Cells

I have spoken of the plan of getting rid of undesirable states of feeling by driving them out. But a far better way is to cultivate the feeling or emotion directly opposed to the one you wish to eradicate.

We are very apt to regard ourselves as the creatures of our emotions and feelings, and to fancy that these feelings and emotions are "we." But such is far from being the truth. It is true that the majority of the race are slaves of their emotions and feelings, and are governed by them to a great degree. They think that feelings are things that rule one and from which one cannot free himself, and so they cease to rebel. They yield to the feeling without question, although they may know that the emotion or mental trait is calculated to injure them, and to bring unhappiness and failure instead of happiness and success. They say, "We are made that way," and let it go at that.

The new Psychology is teaching the people better things. It tells them that they are masters of their emotions and feelings, instead of being their slaves. It tells them that brain-cells may be developed that will manifest along desirable lines, and that the old brain-cells that have been manifesting so unpleasantly may be placed on the retired list, and allowed to atrophy from want of use. People may make themselves over, and change their entire natures. This is not mere idle theory, but is a working fact which has been demonstrated by thousands of people, and which is coming more and more before the attention of the race.

No matter what theory of mind we entertain, we must admit that the brain is the organ and instrument of the mind, in our present state of existence, at least, and that the brain must be considered in this matter. The brain is like a wonderful musical instrument, having millions of keys, upon which we may play innumerable combinations of sounds. We come into the world with certain tendencies, temperaments, and pre-dispositions, We may account for these tendencies by heredity, or we may account for them upon theories of pre-existence, but the facts remain the same. Certain keys seem to respond to our touch more easily than others. Certain notes seem to sound forth as the current of circumstances sweeps over the strings. And certain other notes are less easily vibrated. But we find that if we but make an effort of the will to restrain the utterance of some of these easily sounded strings, they will grow more difficult to sound, and less liable to be stirred by the passing breeze. And if we will pay attention to some of the other strings that have not been giving forth a clear tone, we will soon get them in good working order; their notes will chime forth clear and vibrant, and will drown the less pleasant sounds.

We have millions of unused brain-cells awaiting our cultivation. We are using but a few of them, and some of these we are working to death. We are able to give some of these cells a rest, by using other cells. The brain may be trained and cultivated in a manner incredible to one who has not looked into the subject. Mental attitudes may be acquired and cultivated, changed and discarded, at will. There is no longer any excuse for people manifesting unpleasant and harmful mental states. We have the remedy in our own hands.

We acquire habits of thought, feeling, and action, repeated use. We may be born with a tendency in a certain direction, or we may acquire tendencies by suggestions from other; such as the examples of those around us, suggestions from reading, listening to teachers. We are a bundle of mental habits. Each time we indulge in an undesirable thought or habit, the easier does it become for us to repeat that thought or action.

Mental scientists are in the habit of speaking of desirable thoughts or mental attitudes as "positive," and of the undesirable ones as "negative." There is a good reason for this. The mind instinctively recognizes certain things as good for the individual to which it belongs, and it clears the path for such thoughts, and interposes the least resistance to them. They have a much greater effect than an undesirable thought possesses, and one positive thought will counteract a number of negative thoughts. The best way to overcome undesirable or negative thoughts and feelings is to cultivate the positive ones. The positive thought is the strongest plant, and will in time starve out the negative one by withdrawing from it the nourishment necessary for its existence.

Of course the negative thought will set up a vigorous resistance at first, for it is a fight for life with it. In the slang words of the time, it "sees its finish" if the positive thought is allowed to grow and develop; and, consequently it makes things unpleasant for the individual until he has started well into the work of starving it out. Brain cells do not like to be laid on the shelf any more than does any other form of living energy, and they rebel and struggle until they become too weak to do so. The best way is to pay as little attention as possible to these weeds of the mind, but put in as much time as possible watering, caring for and attending to the new and beautiful plants in the garden of the mind.

For instance, if you are apt to hate people, you can best overcome the negative thought by cultivating Love in its place. Think Love, and act it out, as often as possible. Cultivate thoughts of kindness, and act as kindly as you can to everyone with whom you come in contact. You will have trouble at the start, but gradually Love will master Hate, and the latter will begin to droop and wither. If you have a tendency toward the "blues" cultivate a smile, and a cheerful view of things. Insist upon your mouth wearing upturned corners, and make an effort of the will to look upon the bright side of things. The "blue-devils" will set up a fight, of course, but pay no attention to them - just go on cultivating optimism and cheerfulness. Let "Bright, Cheerful and Happy" be your watchword, and try to live it out.

These recipes may seem very old and timeworn, but they are psychological truths and may be used by you to advantage. If you once comprehend the nature of the thing, the affirmations and autosuggestions of the several schools may be understood and taken advantage of. You may make yourself energetic instead of slothful, active instead of lazy, by this method. It is all a matter of practice and steady work. New Thought people often have much to say about "holding the thought;" and, indeed, it is necessary to "hold the thought" in order to accomplish results. But something more is needed. You must "act out" the thought until it becomes a fixed habit with you. Thoughts take form in action; and in turn actions influence thought. So by "acting out" certain lines of thought, the actions react upon the mind, and increase the development of the part of the mind having close relation to the act. Each time the mind entertains a thought, the easier becomes the resulting action - and each time an act is performed, the easier becomes the corresponding thought. So you see the thing works both ways - action and reaction. If you feel cheerful and happy, it is very natural for you to laugh. And if you will laugh a little, you will begin to feel bright and cheerful. Do you see what I am trying to get at? Here it is, in a nutshell: if you wish to cultivate a certain habit of action, begin by cultivating the mental attitude corresponding to it. And as a means of cultivating that mental attitude, start in to "act-out " or go through, the motions of the act corresponding to the thought. Now, see if you cannot apply this rule. Take up something that you really feel should be done, but which you do not feel like doing. Cultivate the thought leading up to it - say to yourself: "I like to do so and so," and then go through the motions (cheerfully, remember!) and act out the thought that you like to do the thing. Take an interest in the doing - study out the best way to do it - put brains into it - take a pride in it - and you will find yourself doing the thing with a considerable amount of pleasure and interest - you will have cultivated a new habit.

If you prefer trying it on some mental trait of which you wish to be rid, it will work the same way. Start in to cultivate the opposite trait, and think it out and act it out for all you are worth. Then watch the change that will come over you. Don't be discouraged at the resistance you will encounter at first, but sing gaily: "I Can and I Will," and get to work in earnest. The important thing in this work is to keep cheerful and interested. If you manage to do this, the rest will be easy.

The Attractive Power - Desire Force

WE have discussed the necessity of getting rid of fear, that your desire may have full strength with which to work. Supposing that you have mastered this part of the task, or at least started on the road to mastery, I will now call your attention to another important branch of the subject. I allude to the subject of mental leaks. No, I don't mean the leakage arising from your failure to keep your own secrets - that is also important, but forms another story. The leakage I am now referring to is that occasioned by the habit of having the attention attracted to and distracted by every passing fancy.

In order to attain a thing it is necessary that the mind should fall in love with it, and be conscious of its existence, almost to the exclusion of everything else. You must get in love with the thing you wish to attain, just as much as you would if you were to meet the girl or man you wished to marry. I do not mean that you should become a monomaniac upon the subject, and should lose all interest in everything else in the world - that won't do, for the mind must have recreation and change. But, I do mean that you must be so "set" upon the desired thing that all else will seem of secondary importance. A man in love may be pleasant to everyone else, and may go through the duties and pleasures of life with good spirit, but underneath it all he is humming to himself "Just One Girl;" and every one of his actions is bent toward getting that girl, and making a comfortable home for her. Do you see what I mean? You must get in love with the thing you want, and you must get in love with it in earnest - none of this latter-day flirting, "on-today and off-tomorrow" sort of love, but the good old-fashioned kind, that used to make it impossible for a young man to get to sleep unless he took a walk around his best girl's house, just to be sure it was still there. That's the real kind!

And the man or woman in search of success must make of that desired thing his ruling passion - he must keep his mind on the main chance. Success is jealous - that's why we speak of her as feminine. She demands a man's whole affection, and if he begins flirting with other fair charmers, she soon turns her back upon him. If a man allows his strong interest in the main chance to be sidetracked, he will be the loser. Mental Force operates best when it is concentrated. You must give to the desired thing your best and most earnest thought. Just as the man who is thoroughly in love will think out plans and schemes whereby he may please the fair one, so will the man who is in love with his work or business give it his best thought, and the result will be that a hundred and one plans will come into his field of consciousness, many of which are very important. The mind works on the subconscious plane, remember, and almost always along the lines of the ruling passion or desire. It will fix up things, and patch together plans and schemes, and when you need them the most it will pop them into your consciousness, and you will feel like hurrahing, just as if you had received some valuable aid from outside.

But if you scatter your thought-force, the subconscious mind will not know just how to please you, and the result is that you are apt to be put off from this source of aid and assistance. Beside this, you will miss the powerful result of concentrated thought in the conscious working out of the details of your plans. And then again the man whose mind is full of a dozen interests fails to exert the attracting power that is manifested by the man of the one ruling passion, and he fails to draw to him persons, things, and results that will aid in the working out of his plans, and will also fail to place himself in the current of attraction whereby he is brought into contact with those who will be glad to help him because of harmonious interests.

I have noticed, in my own affairs, that when I would allow myself to be side-tracked by anything outside of my regular line of work, it would be only a short time before my receipts dropped off, and my business showed signs of a lack of vitality. Now, many may say that this was because I left undone some things that I would have done if my mind had been centered on the business. This is true; but I have noticed like results in cases where there was nothing to be done - cases in which the seed was sown, and the crop was awaited. And in just such cases, as soon as I directed my thought to the matter the seed began to sprout. I do not man that I had to send out great mental waves with the idea of affecting people - not a bit of it. I simply began to realize what a good thing I had, and how much people wanted it, and how glad they would be to know of it and all that sort of thing, and lo! My thought seemed to vitalize the work, and the seed began to sprout. This is no mere fancy, for I have experienced it on several occasions; I have spoken to many others on the subject, and I find that our experiences tally perfectly. So don't get into the habit of permitting these mental leaks. Keep your Desire fresh and active, and let it get in its work without interference from conflicting desires. Keep in love with the thing you wish to attain - feed your fancy with it - see it as accomplished already, but don't lose your interest. Keep your eye on the main chance, and keep your one ruling passion strong and vigorous. Don't be a mental polygamist - one mental love is all that a man needs - that is, one at a time.

Some scientists have claimed that something that might as well be called "Love" is at the bottom of the whole of life. They claim that the love of the plant for water causes it to send forth its roots until the loved thing is found. They say that the love of the flower for the sun causes it to grow away from the dark places, so that it may receive the light. The so-called "chemical affinities" are really a form of love. And Desire is a manifestation of this Universal Life Love. So I am not using a mere figure of speech when I tell you that you must love the thing you wish to attain. Nothing but intense love will enable you to surmount the many obstacles placed in your path. Nothing but that love will enable you to bear the burdens of the task. The more Desire you have for a thing, the more you Love it; and the more you Love it, the greater will be the attractive force exerted toward its attainment - both within yourself, and outside of you. So love but one thing at a time - don't be a mental Mormon.

The Great Dynamic Forces

YOU have noticed the difference between the success-ful and strong men in any walk of life, and the unsuccessful weak men around them. You are conscious of the widely dif-fering characteristics of the two classes, but somehow find it difficult to express just in what the difference lies. Let us take a look at the matter.

Burton said: "The longer I live, the more certain I am that the great difference between men, the feeble and the powerful, the great and the insignificant, is energy and in-vincible determination - a purpose once fixed and then Death or Victory. That quality will do anything that can be done in this world - and no talents, no circumstances, no opportuni-ties will make a two-legged creature a man without it." I do not see how the idea could be more clearly expressed than Burton has spoken. He has put his finger right in the center of the subject - his eye has seen into the heart of it.

Energy and invincible determination - these two things will sweep away mighty barriers, and will surmount the greatest obstacles. And yet they must be used together. En-ergy without determination will go to waste. Lots of men have plenty of energy - they are full to overflowing with it; and yet they lack concentration - they lack the concentrated force that enables them to bring their power to bear upon the right spot. Energy is not nearly so rare a thing as many imagine it to be. I can look around me at any lime, and pick out a number of people I know who are full of energy - many of them are energy plus - and yet, somehow, they do not seem to make any headway. They are wasting their energy all the time. Now they are fooling with this thing - now meddling with that. They will take up some trifling thing of no real in-terest or importance, and waste enough energy and nervous force to carry them through a hard day's work, and yet when they are through, nothing has been accomplished.

Others who have plenty of energy, fail to direct it by the

power of the Will toward the desired end. "Invincible determination" - those are the words. Do they not thrill you with
their power? If you have something to do, get to work and do
it. Marshal your energy, and then guide and direct it by your
Will - bestow upon it that "invincible determination" and you
will do the thing.

Everyone has within him a giant will, but the majority
of us are too lazy to use it. We cannot get ourselves nerved
up to the point at which we can say, truthfully: "I Will. If
we can but pluck up our courage to that point, and will then
pin it in place so that it will not slip back, we will be able to
call into play that wonderful power - the Human Will. Man,
as a rule, has but the faintest conception of the power of the
Will, but those who have studied along the occult teachings,
know that the Will is one of the great dynamic forces of the
universe, and if harnessed and directed properly it is capable
of accomplishing almost miraculous things.

"Energy and Invincible Determination: -- aren't they
magnificent words? Commit them to memory - press them
like a die into the wax of your mind, and they will be a constant inspiration to you in hours of need. If you can get these
words to vibrating in your being, you will be a giant among
pygmies. Say these words over and over again, and see how
you are filled with new life - see how your blood will circu-
late - how your nerves will tingle. Make these words a part of
yourself, and then go forth anew to the battle of life, encouraged and strengthened. Put them into practice. "Energy and
Invincible Determination" - let that be your motto in your
work-a-day life, and you will be one of those rare men who
are able to "do things."

Many persons are deterred from doing their best by the
fact that they underrate themselves by comparison with the
successful ones of life, or rather, overrate the successful ones
by comparison with themselves.

One of the curious things noticed by those who are brought
in contact with the people who have "arrived" is the fact that
these successful people are not extraordinary after all. You

meet with some great writer, and you are disappointed to find him very ordinary indeed. He does not converse brilliantly, and, in fact, you know a score of everyday people who seem far more brilliant than this man who dazzles you by his brightness in his books. You meet some great statesman, and he does not seem nearly so wise as lots of old fellows in your own village, who waste their wisdom upon the desert air. You meet some great captain of industry, and he does not give you the impression of the shrewdness so marked in some little bargain-driving trader in your own town. How is this, anyway? Are the reputations of these people fictitious, or what is the trouble

The trouble is this: you have imagined these people to be made of superior metal, and are disappointed to find them made of the same stuff as yourself and those about you. But, you ask, wherein does their greatness of achievement lie? Chiefly in this: Belief in themselves and in their inherent power, in their faculty to concentrate on the work in hand, when they are working, and in their ability to prevent leaks of power when they are not working. They believe in themselves, and make every effort count. Your village wise man spills his wisdom on every corner, and talks to a lot of fools; when if he really were wise he would save up his wisdom and place it where it would do some work. The brilliant writer does not waste his wit upon every corner; in fact, he shuts the drawer in which he contains his wit, and opens it only when he is ready to concentrate and get down to business. The captain of industry has no desire to impress you with his shrewdness and "smartness. He never did, even when he was young. While his companions were talking and boasting, and "blowing," this future successful financier was "sawin' wood and sayin' nuthin'."

The great people of the world - that is, those who have "arrived" - are not very different from you, or me, or the rest of us - all of us are about the same at the base. You have only to meet them to see how very "ordinary" they are, after all. But, don't forget the fact that they know how to use the material that is in them; while the rest of the crowd does not, and, in fact, even doubts whether the true stuff is there. The man or woman who "gets there", usually starts out by realizing that he or she is not so very different, after all, from the successful people that they hear so much about. This gives them confidence, and the result is they find out that they are able to "do things." Then they learn to keep their mouths closed, and to avoid wasting and dissipating their energy. They store up energy, and concentrate it upon the task at hand; while their companions are scattering their energies in every direction, trying to show off and let people know how smart they are. The man or woman who "gets there," prefers to wait for the applause that follows deed accomplished, and cares very little for the praise that attends promises of what we expect to do "some day," or an exhibition of "smartness" without works.

One of the reasons that people who are thrown in with successful men often manifest success themselves, is that they are able to watch the successful man and sort of "catch the trick" of his greatness. They see that he is an everyday sort of man, but that he thoroughly believes in himself, and also that he does not waste energy, but reserves all his force for the actual tasks before him. And, profiting by example, they start to work and put the lesson into practice in their own lives.

Now what is the moral of this talk? Simply this: Don't undervalue yourself, or overvalue others. Realize that you are made of good stuff, and that locked within your mind are many good things. Then get to work and unfold those good things, and make something out of that good stuff. Do this by attention to the things before you, and by giving to each the best that is in you, knowing that plenty of more good things are in you ready for the fresh tasks that will come. Put the best of yourself into the undertaking on hand, and do not cheat the present task in favor of some future one. Your supply is inexhaustible. And don't waste your good stuff on the crowd of gapers, watchers and critics who are standing around watching you work. Save your good stuff for your job, and don't be in too much of a hurry for applause. Save up your good thoughts for "copy" if you are a writer; save up your bright schemes for actual practice, if you are a business man; save up your wisdom for occasion, if you are a statesman; and, in each case, avoid the desire to scatter your pears before - well, before the gaping crowd that wants to be entertained by a "free show."

Nothing very "high" about this teaching, perhaps, but it is what many of you need very much. Stop fooling, and get down to business. Stop wasting good raw material, and start to work making something worthwhile.

Claiming Your Own

IN a recent conversation, I was telling a woman to pluck up courage and to reach out for a certain good thing for which she had been longing for many years, and which, at last, appeared to be in sight. I told her that it looked as if her desire was about to be gratified - that the Law of Attraction was bringing it to her. She lacked faith, and kept on repeating, "Oh! It's too good to be true - it's too good for me! She had not emerged from the worm-of-the-dust stage, and although she was in sight of the Promised Land she refused to enter it because it "was too good for her." l think I succeeded in putting sufficient "ginger" into her to enable her to claim her own, for the last reports indicate that she is taking possession.

But that is not what I wish to tell you. I want to call your attention to the fact that nothing is too good for YOU - no matter how great the thing may be - no matter how undeserving you may seem to be. You are entitled to the best there is, for it is your direct inheritance. So don't be afraid to ask - demand - and take. The good things of the world are not the portion of any favored sons. They belong to all, but they come only to those who are wise enough to recognize that the good things are theirs by right, and who are sufficiently courageous to reach out for them. Many good things are lost for want of the asking. Many splendid things are lost to you because of your feeling that you are unworthy of them. Many great things are lost to you because you lack the confidence and courage to demand and take possession of them.

"None but the brave deserves the fair," says the old adage, and the rule is true in all lines of human effort. If you keep on repeating that you are unworthy of the good thing - that it is too good for you - the Law will be apt to take you at your word and believe what you say. That's a peculiar thing about the Law - it believes - what you say - it takes you in earnest. So beware what you say to it, for it will be apt to give credence. Say to it that you are worthy of the best there is, and that there is nothing too good for you, and you will be

likely to have the Law take you in earnest, and say, "I guess
he is right; I'm going to give him the whole bakeshop if he
wants it - he knows his rights, and what's the use of trying
to deny it to him?" But if you say, "Oh, it's too good for me!
The Law will probably say, "Well, I wouldn't wonder but that
that is so. Surely he ought to know, and it isn't for me to contradict him." And so it goes.

Why should anything be too good for you? Did you ever
stop to think just what you are? You are a manifestation of
the Whole Thing, and have a perfect right to all there is. Or,
if you prefer it this way, you are a child of the Infinite, and
are heir to it all. You are telling the truth in either statement, or both. At any rate, no matter for what you ask, you
are merely demanding your own. And the more in earnest
you are about demanding it - the more confident you are of
receiving it - the more will you use in reaching out for it - the
surer you will be to obtain it.

Strong desire - confident expectation - courage in action -
these things bring to you your own. But before you put these
forces into effect, you must awaken to a realization that you
are merely asking for your own, and not for something to
which you have no right or claim. So long as there exists
in your mind the last sneaking bit of doubt as to your right
to the things you want, you will be setting up a resistance
to the operation of the Law. You may demand as vigorously
as you please, but you will lack the courage to act, if you
have a lingering doubt of your right to the thing you want.
If you persist in regarding the desired thing as if it belonged
to another, instead of to yourself, you will be placing yourself in the position of the covetous or envious man, or even
in the position of a tempted thief. In such a case your mind
will revolt at proceeding with the work, for it instinctively
will recoil from the idea of taking what is not your own - the
mind is honest. But when your realize that the best the Universe holds belongs to you as a Divine Heir, and that there
is enough for all without your robbing anyone else; then the
friction is removed, and the barrier broken down, and the
Law proceeds to do its work.

I do not believe in this "humble" business. This meek and lowly attitude does not appeal to me - there is no sense in it, at all. The idea of making a virtue of such things, when Man is the heir of the Universe, and is entitled to whatever he needs for his growth, happiness and satisfaction! I do not mean that one should assume a blustering and domineering attitude of mind - that is also absurd, for true strength does not so exhibit itself. The blusterer is a self-confessed weakling - he blusters to disguise his weakness. The truly strong man is calm, self-contained, and carries with him a consciousness of strength which renders unnecessary the bluster and fuss of assumed strength. But get away from this hypnotism of "humility" - this "meek and lowly" attitude of mind. Remember the horrible example of Uriah Heep, and beware of imitating him. Throw back you head, and look the world square in the face. There's nothing to be afraid of - the world is apt to be as much afraid of you, as yell are of it, anyway. Be a man, or woman, and not a crawling thing. And this applies to your mental attitude, as well as to your outward demeanor. Stop this crawling in your mind. See yourself as standing erect and facing life without fear, and you will gradually grow into your ideal.

There is nothing that is too good for you - not a thing. The best there is, is not beginning to be good enough for you; for there are still better things ahead. The best gift that the world has to offer is a mere bauble compared to the great things in the Cosmos that await your coming of age. So don't be afraid to reach out for these playthings of life - these baubles of this plane of consciousness. Reach out for them - grab a whole fistful - play with them until you are tired; that's what they are made for, anyway. They are made for our express use - not to look at, but to be played with, if you desire. Help yourself - there's a whole shopful of these toys awaiting your desire, demand and taking. Don't be bashful! Don't let me hear any more of this silly talk about things being too good for you. Pshaw! You have been like the Emperor's little son thinking that the tin soldiers and toy drum were far too good for him, and refusing to reach out for them. But you don't find this trouble with children as a rule. They instinctively recognize that nothing is too good for them. They want all that is in sight to play with, and they seem to feel that the things are theirs by right. And that is the condition of mind that we seekers after the Divine Adventure must cultivate. Unless we become as little children we cannot enter the Kingdom of Heaven.

The things we see around us are the playthings of the Kindergarten of God, playthings which we use in our game-tasks. Help yourself to them - ask for them without bashfulness demand as many as you can make use of - they are yours. And if you don't see just what you want, ask for it - there's a big reserve stock on the shelves, and in the closets. Play, play, play, to your heart's content. Learn to weave mats - to build houses with the blocks - to stitch outlines on the squares - play the game through, and play it well. And demand all the proper materials for the play - don't be bashful - there's enough to go round.

But - remember this! While all this be true, the best things are still only game-things - toys, blocks, mats, cubes, and all the rest. Useful, most useful for the learning of the lessons - pleasant, most pleasant with which to play - and desirable, most desirable, for these purposes. Get all the fun and profit out of the use of things that is possible. Throw yourself heartily into the game, and play it out - it is Good. But, here's the thing to remember - never lose sight of the fact that these good things are but playthings - part of the game - and you must be perfectly willing to lay them aside when the time comes to pass into the next class, and not cry and mourn because you must leave your playthings behind you. Do not allow yourself to become unduly attached to them - they are for your use and pleasure, but are not a part of you - not essential to your happiness in the next stage. Despise them not because of their lack of Reality - they are great things relatively, and you may as well have all the fun out of them that you can - don't be a spiritual prig, standing aside and refusing to join in the game. But do not tie yourself to them - they are good to use and play with, but not good enough to use you and to make you a plaything. Don't let the toys turn the tables on you.

This is the difference between the master of Circumstances and the Slave of Circumstances. The Slave thinks that these playthings are real, and that he is not good enough to have them. He gets only a few toys, because he is afraid to ask for more, and he misses most of the fun. And then, considering the toys to be real, and not realizing that there are plenty more where these came from, he attaches himself to the little trinkets that have come his way, and allows himself to be made a slave of them. He is afraid that they may be taken away from him and he is afraid to toddle across the floor and help himself to the others. The Master knows that all are his for the asking. He demands that which he needs from day to day, and does not worry about over-loading himself; for he knows that there are "lots more," and that he cannot be cheated out of them. He plays, and plays well, and has a good time in the play - and he learns his Kindergarten lessons in the playing. But he does not become too much attached to his toys. He is willing to fling away the worn-out toys, and reach out for a new one. And when he is called into the next room for promotion, he drops on the floor the worn-out toys of the day, and with glistening eyes and confident attitude of mind, marches into the next room - into the Great Unknown - with a smile on his face. He is not afraid, for he hears the voice of the Teacher, and knows that she is there waiting for him - in that Great Next Room.

Law, Not Chance

SOME time ago I was talking to a man about the Attractive Power of Thought. He said that he did not believe that Thought could attract anything to him, and that it was all a matter of luck. He had found, he said, that ill luck relentlessly pursued him, and that everything he touched went wrong. It always had, and always would, and he had grown to expect it. When he undertook a new thing he knew beforehand that it would go wrong and that no good would come of it. Oh, no! There wasn't anything in the theory of Attractive Thought, so far as he could see; it was all a matter of luck!

This man failed to see that by his own confession he was giving a most convincing argument in favor of the Law of Attraction. He was testifying that he was always expecting things to go wrong, and that they always came about as he expected. He was a magnificent illustration of the Law of Attraction - but he didn't know it, and no argument seemed to make the matter clear to him. He was "up against it," and there was no way out of it - he always expected the ill luck. and every occurrence proved that he was right, and that the Mental Science position was all nonsense.

There are many people who seem to think that the only way in which the Law of Attraction operates is when one wishes hard, strong and steady. They do not seem to realize that a strong belief is as efficacious as a strong wish. The successful man believes in himself and his ultimate success, and, paying no attention to little setbacks, stumbles, tumbles and slips, presses on eagerly to the goal, believing all the time that he will get there. His views and aims may alter as he progresses, and he may change his plans or have them changed for him, but all the time he knows in his heart that he will eventually "get there." He is not steadily wishing he may get there - he simply feels and believes it, and thereby sets to operation the strongest forces known in the world of thought.

The man who just as steadily believes he is going to fail will invariably fail. How could he help it? There is no special miracle about it. Everything he does, thinks and says is tinctured with the thought of failure. Other people catch his spirit, and fail to trust him or his ability, which occurrences he in turn sets down as but other exhibitions of his ill luck, instead of ascribing them to his belief and expectation of failure. He is suggesting failure to himself all the time, and he invariably takes on the effect of the autosuggestion. Then, again, he by his negative thoughts shuts up that portion of his mind from which should come the ideas and plans conducive to success and which do come to the man who is expecting success because he believes in it. A state of discouragement is not the one in which bright ideas come to us. It is only when we are enthused and hopeful that our minds work out the bright ideas which we may turn to account.

Men instinctively feel the atmosphere of failure hovering around certain of their fellows, and on the other hand recognize something about others which leads them to say, when they hear of a temporary mishap befalling such a one: "Oh, he'll come out all right somehow - you can't down him." It is the atmosphere caused by the prevailing Mental Attitude. Clear up your Mental Atmosphere!

There is no such thing as chance. Law maintains everywhere, and all that happens because of the operation of Law. You cannot name the simplest thing that ever occurred by chance - try it, and then run the thing down to a final analysis, and you will see it as the result of law. It is as plain as mathematics. Plan and purpose; cause and effect. From the movements of worlds to the growth of the grain of mustard seed - all the result of Law. The fall of the stone down the mountainside is not chance - forces which had been in operation for centuries caused it. And back of that cause were other causes, and so on until the Causeless Cause is reached.

And Life is not the result of chance - the Law is here, too. The Law is in full operation whether you know it or not - whether you believe in it or not. You may be the ignorant object upon which the Law operates, and bring yourself all sorts of trouble because of your ignorance of or opposition to the Law. Or you may fall in with the operations to the Law - get into its current,   as it were - and Life will seem a far different thing to you. You cannot get outside of the Law, by refusing to have anything to do with it. You are at liberty to oppose it and produce all the   friction you wish to - it doesn't' hurt the Law, and you may keep it up until you learn your lesson.

The Law of Thought Attraction is one name for the law, or rather for one manifestation of it. Again I say, your thoughts are real things. They go forth from you in all directions, combining with thoughts of like kind - opposing thoughts of a different character - forming combinations - going where they are attracted - flying away from thought centers opposing them. And your mind attracts the thought of others, which have been sent out by them conscious or unconsciously. But it attracts only those thoughts which are in harmony with its own. Like attracts like, and opposites repel opposites, in the world of thought.

If you set your mind to the keynote of courage, confidence, strength and success, you attract to yourself thoughts of like nature; people of like nature; things that fit in the mental tune. Your prevailing thought or mood determines that which is to be drawn toward you - picks out your mental bedfellow. You are today setting into motion thought currents which will in time attract toward you thoughts, people and conditions in harmony with the predominant note of your thought. Your thought will mingle with that of others of like nature and mind, and you will be attracted toward each other, and will surely come together with a common purpose sooner or later, unless one or the other of you should change the current of his thoughts.

Fall in with the operations of the law. Make it a part of yourself. Get into its currents. Maintain your poise. Set your mind to the keynote of Courage, Confidence and Success. Get in touch with all the thoughts of that kind that are emanating every hour from hundreds of minds. Get the best that is to be had in the thought world. The best is there, so be satisfied with nothing less. Get into partnership with good minds. Get into the right vibrations. You must be tired of being tossed about by the operations of the Law - get into harmony with it.

Made in United States
North Haven, CT
27 April 2023

35966089R00178